THE
1940s

Other books in this series:

The 1900s

The 1910s

The 1920s

The 1930s

The 1950s

The 1960s

The 1970s

The 1980s

The 1990s

THE
1940s

Louise I. Gerdes, *Book Editor*

David L. Bender, *Publisher*
Bruno Leone, *Executive Editor*
Bonnie Szumski, *Series Editor*
David Haugen, *Managing Editor*

Greenhaven Press, Inc., San Diego, California

AMERICA'S DECADES

Library of Congress Cataloging-in-Publication Data

The 1940s / Louise I. Gerdes, book editor.
    p.   cm. — (America's decades)
    Includes bibliographical references and index.
    ISBN 0-7377-0302-4 (alk. paper) —
    ISBN 0-7377-0301-6 (pbk. : alk. paper)
    1. Nineteen forties. 2. World War, 1939–1945—United States.
3. Cold War. 4. United States—Politics and government—
1945–1953. I. Gerdes, Louise I. II. Series

E169.1 .A1135 2000
973.917—dc21   99-056323
                                                          CIP

Cover photo: (top) Stock Montage, Inc., (bottom) Corbis-Bettmann
National Archives, 45, 75, 165, 180, 187, 235

©2000 by Greenhaven Press, Inc.
P.O. Box 289009, San Diego, CA 92198-9009

Printed in the U.S.A.

Contents

Foreword   11

Introduction: Facing a New World in the 1940s   13

Chapter 1: The Road to War

1. 1940: Calm Before the Storm *by Donald I. Rogers*   34
During 1940, Americans were optimistic about the
economy and were spending their growing income on
luxuries and leisure activities. Although most Americans wanted to focus on the home front, they also
began to share President Franklin D. Roosevelt's concern over the wars raging in Europe and Asia and supported the preparation of a strong national defense.

2. From Isolation to Intervention *by Gerald D. Nash*   50
Appeals from British Prime Minister Winston Churchill
and continued Nazi aggression persuaded President
Franklin D. Roosevelt to offer aid and support to the
Allies despite the disapproval of isolationists and inter-
ventionists. However, the surprise Japanese attack on
Pearl Harbor and German attacks on U.S. naval vessels
in the Atlantic made entry into World War II inevitable.

3. December 7, 1941: A Day of Infamy
by Cabell Phillips   62
While people in Pearl Harbor, Hawaii, slept, an off-
shore U.S. naval vessel spotted a suspicious submarine
and cryptanalysts in Washington, D.C., intercepted a
message from Tokyo. However, the meaning of these
events came too late, and the Japanese attacked Pearl
Harbor at 7:55 A.M. killing thousands and destroying
much of the Pacific fleet.

Chapter 2: World War II

1. World War II: An Overview *by John Patrick Diggins*   80
Once the United States entered World War II, military
leaders focused on driving back Nazi aggression by tak-

ing the Atlantic, driving through North Africa, marching across Europe, and liberating the concentration camps. The Japanese vigorously defended the Pacific at the cost of many American lives, but after the United States dropped two atomic bombs on Japan, the Japanese surrendered.

2. The Policy of Unconditional Surrender
by Robert James Maddox   94
President Roosevelt demanded the unconditional surrender of Germany, Italy, and Japan not only to eliminate the future threat of militarism but to give the Allies a unified purpose. Some argued that this policy only fueled Axis resistance and, even if appropriate for Germany, the policy should not be applied to Japan because its culture and religion were closely tied to the emperor.

3. Women Warriors, Spies, and Angels of Mercy
by William B. Breuer   108
Although during World War II women could not actively participate in combat, many served by providing intelligence as spies, ministering to wounded soldiers as nurses, and serving crucial roles at home and overseas as WACs, WAVES, SPARS, and marines. Many of these courageous women lost their lives in the service of their country.

4. African Americans in Combat
by A. Russell Buchanan   120
Many African American men wanted to serve in World War II, but the military questioned not only the quality of these units but where they should employ them. The Negro press argued that African American troops were not as well trained, suggesting that segregation was part of the problem; however, many African American troops received recognition for their performance.

5. The Voice of America: Propaganda as Warfare
by Holly Cowan Shulman   133
American propagandists recognized the power of radio as a tool for psychological warfare and convinced Pres-

ident Franklin D. Roosevelt to approve the Voice of America broadcasts. The symbols and styles used by the Voice of America changed throughout the war not only because of Allied victories but because America's position in world politics was changing.

6. The Atom Bomb *by Alan J. Levine*   141
After Japan rejected the Potsdam Declaration, President Harry S. Truman decided to approve the use of atomic weapons to end the war against Japan, and on August 6, 1945, a B-29 dropped a uranium bomb on Hiroshima, and three days later another was dropped on Nagasaki. The decision was not only a result of U.S. policies and strategies but political problems within Japan.

Chapter 3: The Home Front

1. The Politics of Truth: The Office of War Information *by John Morton Blum*   152
The Office of War Information (OWI) was created during World War II to keep Americans informed about the war and government policies. Political problems both within the OWI and with other departments made it difficult for the OWI to provide the public with accurate information, and many left the department when advertisers began to distort public information.

2. Shortages, Conservation, and Rationing
by Richard R. Lingeman   163
The war in the Pacific had depleted America's rubber resources, and when conservation efforts failed, the government was forced to ration gasoline to keep citizens from driving. Americans also received rationing coupons for sugar and coffee, but what was difficult for many was being chastised for hoarding, when it was considered a virtue during the depression.

3. The Third Force: Women Go to Work
by Nancy Baker Wise and Christy Wise   177
Many women took over jobs abandoned by men who went to fight the war, and not only did these women perform well, they gained self-confidence and forever

changed the roles of women. Some gladly stepped aside when the men returned home, but many were reluctant to give up well-paying and gratifying jobs.

4. The Internment of Japanese Americans
by Diane Yancey　　　　　　　　　　　　　　　　183
The fear and paranoia that led to Executive Order 9066, ordering the evacuation of all Japanese or Japanese American citizens, represent a dark stain in the history of the United States. These people were forced to abandon their homes and businesses to be imprisoned in cramped and humiliating assembly centers.

Chapter 4: The Rise and Fall of the Motion Picture Industry

1. Hollywood Goes to War *by Allen L. Woll*　　　213
When isolationists accused Hollywood of producing films that supported America's entering the war, Hollywood argued that it was speaking for the American people who opposed the Nazi regime of Adolf Hitler. The battle against the isolationists ended when the United States entered the war, but Hollywood faced a new battle against government censorship.

2. Doing Our Part: Celebrities Support the War Effort *by Otto Friedrich*　　　　　　　　　　226
While some celebrities joined the military, others supported the war effort by selling bonds and entertaining the troops. Although film makers had to deal with the same shortages faced by all Americans, Hollywood managed to produce films that both entertained and informed.

3. Postwar Hollywood: From All-American to Un-American *by Robert Sklar*　　　　　　　239
Once World War II ended, the government renewed its attack on Hollywood, demanding a blacklist of everyone who was or had been a member of the Communist Party. When the House Un-American Activities Committee cited and imprisoned those in Hollywood who

refused to testify, the industry turned against itself, creating an atmosphere of fear that stifled creativity.

Chapter 5: Emerging Trends in Popular Culture

1. Television Takes Off

by Harry Castleman and Walter J. Podrazik   255
Although the number of television sets increased exponentially in 1947, the networks still made program decisions based on formats that had been successful in radio broadcasting. In 1948, however, the networks began to develop new programming, including the popular children's program *Howdy Doody* and variety shows like *Texaco Star Theater* that led the ratings for decades.

2. The Belles of Baseball *by Jack Fincher*   270
Worried that World War II would put an end to major league baseball, Chicago Cubs owner Philip K. Wrigley selected the best players from the women's amateur softball leagues and formed women's baseball teams that traveled the country. The women were not only skilled ballplayers, but attended charm school so that they could exemplify the all-American ideal of womanhood.

3. The Politics of Popular Music *by Lewis A. Erenberg* 281
After World War II, the public came to view musicians and popular music as a subversive and corrupting influence on American youth and culture. Because musicians often supported liberal ideals, they were suspected of Communist leanings.

Chapter 6: The Cold War

1. The Soviet-American Rift: An Overview

by Armin Rappaport   296
A rift developed between the United States and the Soviet Union as a result of disagreements on many issues from the occupation of Germany to the use of atomic weapons. To contain Soviet aggression, the Truman administration implemented the Marshall Plan and signed

the North Atlantic Treaty, which offered monetary and
military aid to the democratic nations of Europe.

**2. Drawing the Line for Freedom: The Truman
Doctrine** *by Mark Willen*   314
Persuaded by Secretary of State George C. Marshall
and under secretary Dean Acheson of the threat of
Communist expansion in Europe and Asia, congressional leaders encouraged Truman to speak before
Congress. Truman's speech, which encouraged aid to
democratic nations resisting Soviet aggression, became
known as the Truman Doctrine.

Chronology   322

For Further Reading   326

Index   329

Foreword

In his book *The American Century*, historian Harold Evans maintains that the history of the twentieth century has been dominated by the rise of the United States as a global power: "The British dominated the nineteenth century, and the Chinese may cast a long shadow on the twenty-first, but the twentieth century belongs to the United States." In a 1998 interview he summarized his sweeping hypothesis this way: "At the beginning of the century the number of free democratic nations in the world was very limited. Now, at the end of the century, democracy is ascendant around the globe, and America has played the major part in making that happen."

As the new century dawns, historians are eager to appraise the past one hundred years. Evans's book is just one of many attempts to assess the historical impact that the United States has had in the past century. Although not all historians agree with Evans's characterization of the twentieth century as "America's century," no one disputes his basic observation that "in only the second century of its existence the United States became the world's leading economic, military and cultural power." For most of the twentieth century the United States has played an increasingly larger role in shaping world events. The Greenhaven Press America's Decades series is designed to help readers develop a better understanding of America and Americans during this important time.

Each volume in the ten-volume series provides an in-depth examination of the time period. In compiling each volume, editors have striven to cover not only the defining events of the decade—in both the domestic and international arenas—but also the cultural, intellectual, and technological trends that affected people's everyday lives.

Essays in the America's Decades series have been chosen for their concise, accessible, and engaging presentation of the facts. Each selection is preceded by a summary of the article's content. A comprehensive index and an annotated table of contents also aid readers in quickly locating material of interest. Each volume begins with an introductory essay that presents the broader themes of each decade. Several research aids are also present, including an extensive bibliography and a timeline that provides an at-a-glance overview of each decade.

Each volume in the Greenhaven Press America's Decades series serves as an informative introduction to a specific period in U.S. history. Together, the volumes comprise a detailed overview of twentieth century American history and serve as a valuable resource for students conducting research on this fascinating time period.

Introduction: Facing a New World in the 1940s

World War II is often described as the defining event of the 1940s. Although America participated in the war for only four years—from 1941–1945—these years shaped the entire decade. Americans who lived through the 1940s recall events such as the invasion of Normandy, the battle for Iwo Jima, Japanese internment, and rationing. Likewise, America continues to remember and honor heroic World War II generals such as Dwight D. Eisenhower, George S. Patton, and Douglas R. MacArthur. Americans mention war movies such as *Wake Island* (1942) and *Thirty Seconds over Tokyo* (1944) as well as wartime thrillers such as *Casablanca* (1942) and *Passage to Marseilles* (1944). Americans also think of a time when Hollywood star Betty Grable was a GI pinup girl and "Rosie the Riveter" did her part.

Although the war certainly shaped the decade, after the war was over, Americans faced many of the same issues they had before the war: the fear of communism, the role of the federal government in American life, and racism. World War II, however, had changed the way that Americans approached these issues. The shape of the world had shifted politically, economically, and socially. New alliances had developed, and it was no longer clear who America's enemies were. The Soviet Union, although Communist, had been an ally and was now vying for world power; Hollywood, seen by many as a symbol of decadence and social decay, had helped win the war. Furthermore, more women than ever before had left the home to go to work, and African and Asian Americans had served their country heroically. World War II had reshaped American life, and the latter half of the 1940s reflects the way Americans responded to their new roles.

A Decade of Depression

As the decade of the 1940s began, Americans were still suffering under the economic depression that had begun in the 1930s. Before what became known as the Great Depression, Americans had believed in rugged individualism and self-determination. When the stock market crashed in 1929 and the country slipped deeper into the depression, Americans began to realize that self-determination was insufficient to restore the economy, and people began to look to the government for help. Unfortunately, they looked to a government unfamiliar with the role of restoring an economy. Mostly involved in foreign affairs, the government had acted only as an umpire in business disputes. Now it was expected to create jobs, support farmers, protect investments, and ensure its citizens' security.

Herbert Hoover, who assumed the presidency in 1929, was himself a self-made man who believed that when business leaders were asked to help the economy recover by maintaining price and wage levels, they would do so on their own without government interference. But the nation soon came to believe that only the heavy hand of a strong government could battle a foe as insidious as the Great Depression. Although Hoover was well versed in foreign affairs and was an excellent bureaucrat, Americans were looking for a strong leader to guide them out of the depression. They found him in Franklin Delano Roosevelt, a president who stretched the role of the executive branch to its limits. As Roosevelt himself suggested in his inaugural address on March 4, 1933,

> In the event that the national emergency is still critical, I shall not evade the clear course of duty that will then confront me. I shall ask the Congress for the one remaining instrument to meet the crisis—broad Executive power to wage a war against the emergency, as great as the power that would be given me if we were in fact invaded by a foreign foe.[1]

Roosevelt's New Deal

Roosevelt attacked the problem immediately. He closed the banks and would not let them reopen until examiners deemed them sound. In legislation that become known as the first One Hundred Days, Roosevelt began a program of relief, recovery, and reform, and initiated the New Deal he had promised the American people. Roosevelt worked to pass recovery legislation that set up agencies to support farm prices, employ young men, help business and labor, insure bank deposits, regulate the stock market, subsidize home and farm mortgage payments, and aid the unemployed. The National Recovery Act (NRA) encouraged business leaders to work together to create codes that would control wages and prices. These measures revived confidence in the economy.

Additional New Deal legislation followed in 1935, including the establishment of the Works Projects Administration (WPA), which put 3.5 million jobless Americans to work on roads, parks, and buildings. Moreover, the WPA provided jobs not only for laborers but also artists, writers, and musicians. Also enacted in 1935, the Social Security Act provided unemployment compensation and a program of old-age and survivors' benefits that continues today.

Although Americans recognized the need for government intervention to alleviate domestic affairs, most Americans remained isolationists, believing that the U.S. government should not intervene in foreign affairs. Despite Roosevelt's pleas, the majority of Americans maintained their noninterventionist philosophy. As history professor John Patrick Diggins writes,

> Roosevelt felt the urgency to challenge all noninterventionist traditions when he called upon America to help the world realize the four vital freedoms—freedom of speech, freedom of worship, freedom from want, and freedom from fear. But his eloquent appeal failed to change the sentiments of the numerous and disparate but adamant noninterventionists.[2]

Nonintervention, or isolationist, philosophy took many forms. The America First movement, led by Charles A. Lindbergh, the famous aviator who also admired the Luftwaffe (Germany's air force), believed that Adolf Hitler posed no threat to the United States. Some isolationists were intellectuals who distrusted the British, hated Roosevelt, and remembered President Wilson's failed promise to make the world safe for democracy. Right-wing conservatives led by Father Charles Coughlin supported the Fascist regime and Hitler's anti-Semitism; meanwhile, left-wing Communist sympathizers argued that the United States should follow the Soviet Union's lead and remain neutral.

From Isolation to Intervention

However, when Hitler attacked Poland in September 1939, Roosevelt believed that the United States should remain neutral but not inactive in the face of Nazi aggression. Accordingly, he tried to make American aid available to Britain, France, and China by obtaining an amendment of the Neutrality Acts that would make providing such aid less difficult. He also took measures to build up the armed forces despite isolationist opposition. Moreover, Roosevelt recognized that his New Deal was at an impasse. Although Americans were optimistic and were earning more and spending more, only with increased production would the economy return to its pre–Great Depression levels, so Roosevelt began to encourage bills to increase defense production.

Although most Americans began the decade hoping to keep the government focused on problems at home, they also recognized that without help from the United States, Hitler's Fascist regime might succeed in dominating all of the democratic nations of Europe. During the early 1940s, Americans who went to the movies could see newsreels of Hitler shouting inspiring speeches to the German people, parades of marching Nazi soldiers and tanks, and English cities battered by round-the-clock bombing while air-raid sirens wailed. On the radio and in newspapers, Americans witnessed the blitzkrieg in Europe as tanks and paratroopers invaded France, Holland, Belgium, Denmark, and Norway. Americans had learned from the depression that under some circumstances individuals and communities could not help themselves without intervention and assistance from the federal government. Many began to believe that if the United States did not help Europe in its battle against Nazi aggression, the United States, too, could become vulnerable.

Having easily defeated Wendell Wilkie on November 5, 1940, Roosevelt began to prepare the country for war. As the American mood began to shift, Congress began to implement Roosevelt's policies. Congress enacted a draft for military service, and Roosevelt signed a lend-lease bill in March 1941 to furnish aid to nations at war with Germany and Italy. Although neutral in the war and still at peace, America was becoming "the arsenal of democracy" as its factories began producing as they had in the years before the Great Depression. Meanwhile, Germany and Italy were not the only nations the United States had to worry about.

A Day of Infamy

The Japanese had begun aggression in Asia by invading China in 1937 and moving toward Indochina. In response, Roosevelt had been building defenses in the Pacific, creating a command in the Philippines under General Douglas R. MacArthur. Roosevelt also froze Japanese assets in the United States, and in July 1941 he imposed an embargo on crude oil. Whether Roosevelt was hoping to seek time to build defenses or was actually hoping to negotiate with the Japanese, the president did encourage the idea of a fall summit meeting. In September Roosevelt closed the Panama Canal to Japanese shipping and rejected the summit meeting unless Japanese troops were withdrawn from China. The Japanese premier, Prince Fumimaro Konoye, tried to negotiate an agreement, but General Hideki Tojo refused to withdraw from China. In late October any possibility of negotiation appeared to crumble. On November 26 Admiral Nagumo's First Air Fleet left the Kurile Islands in the North Pacific with 6 carriers, 423 planes, 2 battle-ships, 28 submarines, 2 cruisers, and 11 destroyers.

Whether the Pearl Harbor attack came as a surprise to government leaders is the subject of debate. Yet the events of that Sunday morning on December 7 remain undisputed. At 11 A.M. (EST) in Washington, D.C., Roosevelt read an intercepted message from Japan that was to be delivered to Secretary of State Cordell Hull by Japanese diplomats at exactly 1:00 P.M. Suspicious of an imminent Japanese attack, General George C. Marshall ordered that a "be on the alert" warning be sent to all Pacific bases. This warning was received at the Western Union office in Honolulu, Hawaii, at 7:33 A.M. (HST). Unfortunately, the first wave of Japanese planes attacked the naval base at Pearl Harbor at 7:55 A.M., and the second wave attacked at 9:00 A.M., sinking ships, destroying aircraft, and killing 2,403 U.S. military personnel (1,102 on the *Arizona*).

After Pearl Harbor, America's isolationist sentiments vanished. America was in shock, and on December 8, 1941, Roosevelt asked Congress to declare war against the imperial government of Japan in a speech that began, "Yesterday, December 7, 1941—a date which will live in infamy—the United States of America was suddenly and deliberately attacked by naval and air forces of the Empire of Japan." Roosevelt concluded his address with the following threat:

> Always will we remember the character of the onslaught against us. No matter how long it may take us to overcome this premeditated invasion, the American people in their righteous might will win through to absolute victory. I believe I interpret the will of the Congress and of the people when I assert that we will not only defend ourselves to the uttermost but will make very certain that this form of treachery shall never endanger us again. . . .With confidence in our armed forces—with the unbounded determi-

nation of our people—we will gain the inevitable triumph—so help us God.[3]

The United States had entered World War II.

Fear and Racism

Shock soon turned to fear and paranoia for many Americans. Suspicion especially fell on America's Japanese American population. Although advisers suggested that Japanese Americans were not a threat, General John DeWitt, who was in charge of West Coast security, disagreed and advised Roosevelt that internment was a "military necessity." On February 19, 1942, Roosevelt signed Executive Order 9066, and 110,000 mainland Japanese Americans and 15,000 Hawaiian Japanese Americans were evacuated to relocation camps. The internees were told to pack a few bags and were forced to sell their land, belongings, and businesses for a fraction of their actual value.

Although both the internees and the American people were told that the Japanese Americans were being evacuated for their own protection, the camps were like prisons—with barbed wire and machine gun towers—and were located in the most barren regions of the western states. Conditions were often cramped, unhealthy, and humiliating for the Japanese Americans sent there, and some internees died from disease or were killed for supposed escape attempts. The Japanese Americans in Hawaii fared a little better than those on the mainland. General Delos Emmans recognized that Japanese Americans made up a large part of the Hawaiian workforce, and these workers were needed to maintain the sugar industry. Emmans determined that massive internment was not only economically unwise but dangerous. It was not until the 1980s that the U.S. government recognized its mistake, giving Japanese Americans who survived internment an apology and a check for twenty thousand dollars.

Racism during the decade was not limited to fear and distrust of Japanese Americans. In 1941, President Roosevelt signed Executive Order 8802, which outlawed segregationist hiring policies by defense-related industries that held federal contracts. Roosevelt's signing of this order was a direct result of efforts by black trade union leader A. Philip Randolph, who threatened to march one hundred thousand blacks to Washington in 1941. As a result, African Americans began to seek work in war production industries.

However, tensions began to rise as African Americans and whites competed for jobs, limited housing, and ration stamps. In 1942 African Americans and whites clashed in Detroit when white workers tried to prevent African Americans from moving into the war production housing projects. In the summer of 1943 African American and white teenagers taunted one another, which led to a fight. Rumors spread, and the clash turned into a three-day riot that killed thirty-four and caused $2 million in property damage. Roosevelt finally dispatched federal troops to the city. To minorities, racism appeared to be as formidable an enemy as those America faced abroad.

Control over the Atlantic

To Roosevelt, the immediate threat was overseas, however. Although the United States declared war against Japan on December 8, 1941, Roosevelt and his advisers had been preparing for war in Europe long before the first bomb fell over Pearl Harbor. In August 1941, Roosevelt met with Prime Minister Winston Churchill of Great Britain to form the Atlantic Charter, which essentially affirmed the defense of British possessions. Problems in the Atlantic had been escalating with the destruction of U.S. merchant ships, and U.S. destroyers had been conducting "security patrols." Once war had been declared against the Axis nations—Germany, Italy, and Japan—Allied leaders decided that Germany posed the most immediate threat.

In order to ensure that supplies arrived in Great Britain and Russia, taking back the North Atlantic from marauding U-boats (German submarines) that had been sinking American merchant ships was given the highest priority. As a result of increased defense production, huge convoys of destroyers and bombers accompanied freighters and tankers that traveled the North Atlantic, eventually ending Germany's U-boat campaign.

While recovering control over the Atlantic, the Allies began planning their strategy for the liberation of Europe at the end of 1942. The Allies planned to take North Africa, then move toward Europe from the south. After having defeated Marshal Erwin Rommel's German panzer army in North Africa, the Allies, led by Field Marshal Sir Bernard L. Montgomery and General George S. Patton, invaded Sicily and moved north through Italy toward Germany.

Taking Back the Pacific

Although the war in Europe had brought some early successes, as John Patrick Diggins suggests, "in the Pacific events proceeded like one continuous catastrophe."[4] In the days following the bombing of Pearl Harbor, Japan continued its assault on the Pacific, effectively closing off both shipping and communications to Asia and the central and south Pacific Islands. While Admiral Chester W. Nimitz awaited the arrival of additional troops and ships, American aircraft carriers conducted nuisance attacks on Japanese-held islands, and General James H. Doolittle led an air attack of Tokyo. When reinforcements finally arrived from the United States, several important battles turned the tide against Japan, including the Battle of the Coral Sea, the first battle fought entirely by carrier-launched aircraft; the Battle of Midway, during which the U.S. carriers *Yorktown* and *Enterprise* sank four Japanese carriers; and the battle for the Japanese airfield on Guadalcanal, which was held by the First Marine Division under Archie Vandergrift.

Once the tide had turned, the Joint Strategic Plan for the Pacific created three commands: MacArthur was to command the South Pacific to the Philippines, Nimitz was to command the central Pacific to Formosa, and General Joseph Stilwell was to command from China to Burma. With the aid of the new multicarrier task force, the three commands slowly began to take control in the Pacific.

New Technology and Strategies

The war in Europe and the Pacific involved the introduction of new strategies and technology that changed the nature of warfare. The battle for the Pacific was just that, a battle for control over the seas and the islands that dotted the Pacific Ocean. For the first time, entire battles were being fought by carrier-launched aircraft. By May 1943 the United States had produced the first of the "fast carriers." Not only could they move faster, these carriers could also carry more planes and crewmen and were equipped with more firepower with greater range. More importantly, these carriers were equipped with advanced communications equipment that was capable of tracking ships and aircraft and could prevent the enemy from listening in. The concept of a multicarrier task force, each having three carriers, two battleships, six cruisers, and eighteen destroyers, was a new one in naval history. So successful was the task force concept that once the war was over, businesses and organizations adopted the strategic concept.

The saturation bombing of strategic cities during World War II was also a first in the history of warfare. The Luftwaffe began strategic bombing to destroy industry and wear down the morale of the enemy. After Germany had taken northern Europe, it began almost daily bombing raids on cities in England. From the end of 1943 through 1945, however, the American and Royal Air Force began the saturation bombing of industrial cities in Germany, such as Hamburg, Bremen, and later Dresden. The United States also utilized strategic bombing over Tokyo and Okinawa, a strategy the U.S. military would develop in future armed conflicts.

Minorities at War

The military was faced with another challenge during World War II. African Americans who had enlisted in the military at the outset of the war were segregated from other troops, denied training as officers or pilots, and often limited to menial positions. Although African American troops were eager to join the battle against the Axis powers during World War II, the military restricted their use because of racism within and outside of the military. Keeping these units behind in the United States adversely affected their morale. Receiving pressure from the government, however, some of the racial barriers began to come down in 1943, and the efforts of African American troops began to be recognized. For example, the air squadrons trained at the Tuskegee Institute in Alabama, who came to be known as Tuskegee airmen, engaged in combat during the invasion of Italy and the liberation of France. The 99th Fighter Squadron was successful in the air fighting over Anzio, and the 969th Battalion did well in the Ardennes campaign. Despite attitudes within the military establishment, African American troops maintained a good record, and many units had outstanding performances.

Women were another minority that the armed services had to adapt to during World War II. On May 15, 1942, Roosevelt signed Representative Edith Roger's bill, creating the Women's Army Corp (WAC), and the Navy's Women Accepted for Volunteer Emergency Service (WAVES) and the U.S. Coast Guard Women's Reserves (SPARS) soon followed. According to combat veteran and author William B. Breuer, the women who served in the U.S. Army Nurse Corps were the unsung heroes of Anzio. These nurses worked to save lives and relieve suffering of men wounded while invading Allied troops battled in Italy. Breuer describes the peril these women faced:

> Even though the hospital tents were clearly marked with red crosses on fields of white, artillery shells exploded regularly along the shoreline. While performing surgery and other duties, the nurses and doctors often heard the frightening rush of a 700-pound shell from what the GIs called the Anzio Express, an enormous 280-millimeter railroad gun, just before it rocked the terrain around the hospital with a ground-shaking blast. At night, the Luftwaffe flew over, dropped parachute flares, then unloaded bombs along the shore. . . . The presence of female nurses served as a

great morale booster for the fighting men at a time morale badly needed uplifting. So inspiring was the valor displayed by the women that an attitude developed among combat troops on the beachhead: "If they can do it, so can I."[5]

Doing Our Part

This spirit also inspired those Americans who remained on the homefront. World War II was an all-out attempt to save the American way of life, and Americans at home wanted to do their part. Historian Diggins summarizes: "High school seniors looked forward to graduation day, after which they could enlist in one of the armed services. [Female students] received instruction in first aid to help the Red Cross. Citizens undertook scrap drives, collecting tin cans, paper, metal junk, and used shoes."[6] However, once the initial war production had eaten up the nation's raw materials and the scrap that citizens could recycle, shortages began to occur, and one by one, commodities that Americans had grown to consider necessities began to evaporate.

In 1942 the government gave the Office of Price Administration the responsibility of rationing, which began with automobile tires. For most Americans, giving extra tires to their local filling station was not a problem, but asking Americans to part with the symbol of their freedom, the automobile, was too much for most. Ultimately, in order to limit use of automobiles and therefore use of rubber in the tires, the rationing of gas came shortly thereafter.

The next items to be rationed were food items such as butter, coffee, and sugar. In May 1942 war ration books were submitted to those who remained at home. When given their books, Americans were asked to declare how much sugar they had, and these stamps would be torn from their books. Although most depression-era Americans were used to doing without, behaviors that had been considered admirable during the Great Depression, such as hoarding, now became the subject of scorn, which created rumors, accusations, and guilt.

Women Go to Work

War production created a shortage of workers since so many men were needed at the battlefront. Between 1941 and 1945, 6.5 million women entered the labor force. They manned defense plants; drove buses, trucks, and tractors; and became heavy-machinery operators, mechanics, welders, and riveters.

Women who had previously worked as waitresses and hotel maids found better pay and more challenging work. However, the educated middle-class woman found military service and factory work frustrating. Moreover, women often received less pay for the same work, and labor unions were not supportive because they saw women as a threat to traditional male occupations. On the other hand, in private nonunionized fields, women enjoyed meaningful work with opportunities for advancement. When the war came to an end, those women who believed that a woman's place was in the home gladly returned to their previous way of life, but those who had enjoyed a new sense of independence or had families that depended on their income, were forced to give up their jobs, creating significant frustration.

Hollywood Does Its Part

Hollywood also did its part during the war. The studios produced films that recreated the war effort abroad, dramatizing the heroic deeds of American and Allied soldiers in combat films such as *Wake Island* (1942), *Bataan* (1943), *Thirty Seconds over Tokyo* (1944), and *The Story of GI Joe* (1945). Other films demonstrated the importance of commitment to the war effort. In movies like *Casablanca* (1942), *Passage to Marseilles* (1944), and *To Have and Have Not* (1944), Humphrey Bogart plays characters that resolve inner conflicts by making just such a commitment. Hollywood also produced training films like *Safeguarding Military Information*, which cost the movie studio $39,000, although it only billed the government $19,600. Support for the war effort can also be seen in Hollywood's documentary filmmaking: propaganda films like the Why We

Fight series produced by Frank Capra and John Huston's *The Battle of San Pietro.*

The stars themselves also joined the war effort. Actors such as Jimmy Stewart, Tyrone Power, and Clark Gable joined the service. Darryl F. Zanuck, who headed Twentieth-Century Fox, became a colonel. As historian Robert Sklar notes, Zanuck "would have required four stars to equal his Hollywood rank."[7] The famed colonel appeared in the documentary *At the Front in North Africa* (1943). Pinup girl Betty Grable and jokes from Bob Hope, who made appearances wherever the troops were stationed, improved GI morale. Hedy Lamarr and Carole Lombard sold war bonds for a kiss, and Bette Davis headed the Hollywood Canteen, where servicemen met and mingled with the stars.

The Longest Day

While Hollywood made movies that rallied America and women filled the jobs of American soldiers who fought overseas, German troops began to retreat as the Allies moved north from Italy. It became clear from Allied intelligence, however, that not only was Germany increasing its traditional production, it was also developing new technology, perhaps even an atom bomb. The Allies decided that an amphibious assault of the continent was essential to defeat Germany.

The invasion of Normandy, located on the coast of France, was the largest amphibious assault ever planned. Although named Operation Overload by Allied strategists, the invasion has come to be known as D day or the Longest Day. On May 30, 1944, over 2 million men, supported by millions of tons of equipment, airplanes, battleships, cruisers, and troop transports, assembled in England for the amphibious assault. On June 5 General Eisenhower wished the paratroopers of the 101st Screaming Eagles luck before they left to parachute into Normandy prior to the amphibious landing. Covered by naval gunfire and air bombardment, American and Canadian divisions landed on the beaches of Normandy—Utah, Omaha, Gold, Juno, and

Sword—while American and British divisions landed on the east and west flank and Ranger gunfire destroyed the German guns on the cliffs of Pointe du Hoc. Finally, after eight hours of fighting, the cliffs were overtaken and the Allies marched through France, reclaiming occupied cities until they liberated Paris on August 25, 1944.

Germany countered with one final offensive: the famous Battle of the Bulge, referred to as the largest land battle ever waged, involving more than a million men. Hitler hoped to retake Antwerp with two German panzer armies, despite objections from his commanders. However, Field Marshal Montgomery attacked from the north and General Patton came from the south, defeating the Germans on January 28, 1945. The end came swiftly as General Patton crossed the Rhine River in Germany on March 22, entered Czechoslovakia on April 22, and U.S. and Soviet troops met at the Elbe River on April 25. Adolf Hitler committed suicide on April 30, and by May 7 Germany had surrendered.

The struggle was not yet over in the Pacific, however. Despite tremendous losses, Japan continued to resist. In February 1945, sixty thousand troops landed for a thirty-six-day battle in Iwo Jima, and in April troops landed in Okinawa. Japan nonetheless rejected the terms of the Potsdam Declaration of July 26, 1945, and President Truman was faced with a difficult decision.

In 1941 Roosevelt had given permission for several projects to investigate atomic weapons, including the Manhattan Project. Since that time, the United States had developed the atom bomb. Truman approved the use of the atom bomb on Japan for several reasons: Japan refused to agree to unconditional surrender, military advisers feared the significant loss of American lives in an attack of the Japanese mainland, and the United States hoped to keep the Soviet Union from moving into China and Japanese territories in the North Pacific Ocean. On the morning of August 6, 1945, a B-29 dropped a uranium bomb on Hiroshima, and three days later, when Japan failed to surrender immediately, another bomb was released over Nagasaki. On August 15, 1945, Emperor Hirohito surrendered, and the war in the Pacific had ended.

As the war in Europe was drawing to a close and Allied troops moved through Germany, Poland, and Hungary, American troops encountered the horror of Hitler's death camps. In a letter home, Lieutenant William Cowling of the Forty-second Infantry Division, the first to enter the camp at Dachau, writes of what he and two reporters encountered as they toured the camp:

> Then we went through a building where fifty men were guarded in a room the size of your kitchen. There were hundreds of typhus cases and all through the Camp men cheered us and tried to touch us. Incidentally many of the dead and living showed signs of horrible beatings and torture. It is unbelievable how any human can treat others as they were treated. One wasted little man came up and touched my sleeve and kissed my hand. He spoke perfect English and I asked him if he was American. He said no, Jewish and that he was one of the very few left that thousands had been killed. He had been there six years. He was twenty-eight years old and looked to be sixty years old. The Germans I took prisoner are very fortunate they were taken before I saw the Camp.[8]

Similar stories came from the other concentration camps. Six million Jews lost their lives, along with 3 million Russians, Poles, Slavs, and Gypsies. When World War II came to an end, the United States, Great Britain, France, and the Soviet Union took an unprecedented step by prosecuting leaders of Germany and Japan as war criminals in Nuremberg, Germany, and Tokyo, Japan, rejecting the argument that "following orders" was a defense for war crimes.

Coming Home

Life had been forever changed by the war. Although women relinquished their jobs to the men who returned home from the war, they looked at their place in the world in a whole new way. Minorities who had served faithfully and heroically could not return to the same roles they had played in society before they left for war. Furthermore, many men who would have otherwise gone to the factory or the field, went to school when the war ended. On June 22, 1944, Roosevelt had signed the Serviceman's Readjustment Act, better known as the GI bill, which helped military members and veterans improve the quality of their lives. Some 2.25 million war veterans attended college, and millions of others received job training as well as home, business, and farm loans that cost $14.5 billion.

After the war, both the soldiers overseas and the women left behind longed for a return to their normal lives. Many eagerly started families, which resulted in the postwar baby boom—75.9 million births between 1946 and 1964. This boom put a strain on school districts, which had difficulty keeping up with the growing school-age populations. Although new schools were built, they were soon filled to capacity and portable classrooms were being installed on the playgrounds.

The Cold War

Not only had life at home changed when the war ended, but relationships among the Allies changed as well. In February 1945 the major Allied powers—Great Britain, Russia, and the United States—met at Yalta to discuss the occupation and division of Europe and the creation of the United Nations. Problems among the major powers had begun to develop. When Roosevelt died on April 12 and Truman assumed the presidency, relations between the United States and the Soviet Union became even more strained. At the Potsdam Conference in July and August, it became evident that the Soviet Union had plans for control over Europe and Asia that were at odds with those of the United States. Although the United States and the Soviet Union had been allies during World War II, a rift began to develop during postwar negotiations, and the ill will created by the disagreements between these two powers created what has become known as the Cold War.

In February 1947 Truman gathered congressional leaders together, and Secretary of State George C. Marshall and his undersecretary, Dean Acheson, described the threat of Communist expansion in Europe and Asia, suggesting that the United States provide aid to Greece and Turkey so that these countries would not fall to communism. Truman then spoke to Congress, drawing an ideological line between the democratic West and the Communist East that Churchill referred to as an "iron curtain" across Europe. Truman argued, "I believe that it must be the policy of the United States to support free peoples who are resisting attempted subjugation by armed minorities or by outside pressures."[9] This philosophy came to be known as the Truman Doctrine. Americans could no longer remain isolated in the new world that had emerged at the end of World War II.

Congress overwhelmingly approved a bill granting $400 million in aid to Greece and Turkey. In April 1948 Congress approved $5 billion for Marshall's plan to hasten European recovery and prevent Soviet expansion. Marshall called on European nations to draft a plan for economic recovery, claiming that his plan was not directed against any particular country but against hunger, poverty, desperation, and chaos.

In June 1948 the Soviet Union tested the resolve of the democratic Western powers with a blockade of Berlin. Soviet troops blocked access by road, rail, and river routes. The blockade lasted for eleven months, and Lucius Clay, who had been appointed director of the Allied Control Council of Germany at the Potsdam Conference in 1945, ordered an airlift of 1.5 million tons of supplies flown into the city, and on May 12, 1949, Soviet leader Joseph Stalin called off the blockade.

The democratic powers also recognized a need for a Western military alliance, which culminated in the creation of the North Atlantic Treaty Organization (NATO). Signing nations debated over what nations would be included, the scope, and the duration of the treaty. However, the U.S. Congress ultimately ratified the treaty on July 25, 1949, and agreed to a Mutual Defense Assistance Program.

Facing the Future

Few would question that World War II was the defining event of the 1940s. Americans who had suffered through years of economic depression pulled together, serving at home and overseas to promote and protect democracy. New forms of warfare emerged, including carrier-launched aircraft battles, strategic bombings, and task forces like the one used during the invasion of Normandy. New technology created faster carriers and more efficient antisubmarine equipment, and the fight for Guadalcanal made heroes of a new branch of the armed services—the U.S. Marine Corps. Americans also rediscovered the reality of war: the sacrifice of almost 300,000 American soldiers in battle, the extermination of 6 million Jews in concentration camps, and the obliteration of 150,000 Japanese citizens from atom bombs.

As with World War I, the end of World War II did not put an end to fear. The development and use of the atom bomb drastically altered the nature of war, and the fear of atomic and nuclear devastation would be reflected in American politics and culture for decades to come. Once the war was over, America had a new enemy. When a rift developed between the Soviet Union and the United States, America became involved in a Cold War to defend the world from Communist aggression that waged into the 1990s. The fear of communism within America's own borders led to investigations by those who sought to purge the nation of Communists, reaching from Hollywood to the nation's capital. The "Red Scare" continued into the 1950s, creating political careers, inspiring betrayal, and devastating many lives.

America had new battles to face in the decades ahead from seeds of discontent that had been planted in the 1940s. Minorities who had served their country heroically were no longer content to remain separate but equal. Although many working women returned home when the war came to an end, they had discovered the rewards of employment. Their numbers would grow in the decades that followed. These issues created new challenges for the

American people. In an address to Congress, President Harry S. Truman said, "Great responsibilities have been placed upon us by the swift movement of events."[10] The world had dramatically changed as the 1940s drew to a close, but after facing and conquering the challenges posed by World War II, Americans were well-prepared for an uncertain future.

1. Franklin D. Roosevelt, "First Inaugural Address of Franklin D. Roosevelt: Saturday, March 4, 1933," Avalon Project, Yale Law School. www.yale.edu/lawweb/avalon/presiden/inaug/froos1.htm.

2. John Patrick Diggins, *The Proud Decades: America in War and in Peace, 1941–1960.* New York: W.W. Norton, 1988, p. 14.

3. Franklin D. Roosevelt, "Franklin D. Roosevelt's Infamy Speech: December 8, 1941," University of Oklahoma Law Center. www.law.ou.edu/hist/infamy.html.

4. Diggins, *The Proud Decades*, p. 36.

5. William B. Breuer, *War and American Women: Heroism, Deeds, and Controversy.* Westport, CT: Praeger, 1997, pp. 37–38.

6. Diggins, *The Proud Decades*, pp. 14–15.

7. Robert Sklar, *Movie-Made America: A Cultural History of American Movies.* New York: Vintage Books, 1975, p. 252.

8. William Cowling, "The Letter," Library of the Holocaust. http://remember.org/witness/cowling.html.

9. Harry S. Truman, "President Harry S. Truman's Address Before a Joint Session of Congress, March 12, 1947," Avalon Project, Yale Law School. www.yale.edu/lawweb/avalon/trudoc.htm.

10. Truman, "Address Before a Joint Session of Congress."

CHAPTER 1

The Road to War

1940: Calm Before the Storm

Donald I. Rogers

In the following excerpt from his book *Since You Went Away*, journalist Donald I. Rogers reviews the economic, political, and cultural climate during 1940. Although German troops marched across Europe and into Scandinavia, Rogers writes, most Americans wanted to focus on problems at home. Americans felt optimistic over their improved economy. According to Rogers, Americans were busy enjoying their growing discretionary income: They bought new cars, fixed their teeth, and spent their money on leisure activities. At the same time, Americans began to share President Franklin D. Roosevelt's concern over the escalating wars in Europe and Asia, supporting Roosevelt's preparation of a strong national defense.

I s there *always* a calm before the storm? Americans asked themselves that question in later years as they looked back on the beginning of the fifth decade of the twentieth century. The sunshine of promise shone brightly over America in 1940 as millions began to emerge from the hopeless winter of a ten-year depression, the gravest and longest economic illness in recorded history.

There were terrible problems in Europe, of course. The headlines of American newspapers screamed them in out-size bold type. German troops invaded Denmark and Nor-

---

Excerpted from *Since You Went Away*, by Donald I. Rogers (New York: Arlington House, 1973). Copyright ©1973 by Donald I. Rogers. Reprinted by permission of Evelyn Singer Literary Agency, Inc.

way simultaneously, aided by the softening political activity of Vidkun Quisling who was to become later the Nazis' minister president in Norway. Borrowing a phrase that came from the Spanish Civil War, Hitler said the invasion was accomplished with a "Fifth Column," four from without and one from within—the traitors around Quisling.

A Time of Economic Optimism

These were serious headlines, disturbing headlines. But beside them on page one there were other headlines. They revealed that auto manufacturing was turning in one of its best years, that steel production was on the increase, that the armed services were growing—up to about 1 million men—and that employment was increasing and unemployment was dropping.

Economists predicted that the Gross National Product, the total value of the output of all goods and services, would reach $125.3 billion by the beginning of 1941, and since this was more than twice the figure recorded in the depths of the depression, many people were prone to feel twice as good about things. America had had its own problems, only now beginning to end.

There were 56 million in the American labor force, not all of them employed, of course, but most of them optimistic about their chances—unless one looked beneath the surface in the cities, where poverty-level wages were paid in many jobs not covered by the New Deal's new laws, [enacted in the 1930s during the economic depression], or in the potholes of poverty occupied by sharecroppers, pieceworkers, fishermen, farmers and even many retail employees. Earnings of $2,000 gave a worker the average median income, and many of the aforementioned earned well below that.

But such a large proportion of Americans were earning $3,500 to $5,000 or more, that it was as easy to overlook the darker side of the domestic economy as it was to ignore the idiotic antics of the madman [Adolf Hitler], in Berlin and that strutting bag of wind [Benito Mussolini], in Rome who called himself the Duce.

Casting aside the shroud of economic despair, the grocery stores and the very few newfangled supermarkets were taking on new life and color, broadening and upgrading their offerings to the public. A person could buy a loaf of bread for 8 cents; a pound of choice hot dogs in natural skins for 13 cents; a bakery pie for 12 cents; a pound of good-quality hamburger for 25 cents; a pound of coffee for about 39 cents; excellent steaks at 23 cents a pound; a leg of lamb at 19 cents a pound; a one-pound roll of fresh creamery butter for less than 40 cents. Vegetables were sold by the bunch, the pint, the quart, the peck, and not by weight. Carrots were 5 cents a bunch; radishes two bunches for 5 cents; fresh peas, 30 cents a peck.

Enjoying the New Prosperity

Magnificent new cars were rolling out of Detroit in 1940, with prices to attract customers who had been riding makeshift cars since 1930. A total of $1,200 would buy an outstanding new motorcar with all optional equipment, and $1,400 would get a luxury vehicle. A year-old Dodge sold for about $950, equipped with radio, heater and hydraulic brakes, plus many other "extras."

Gasoline to power the new cars ranged in price from 14 cents to 19 cents a gallon, depending on the octane rating and local marketing conditions. High-grade motor oil, in quantity, was less than 25 cents a quart.

The movies, in a majority of cities, cost 15 cents in the afternoon and 25 cents at night, except for weekends, when the matinee price was 25 cents and the evenings ranged up to 50 or 60 cents. Moving picture tickets cost more, of course, in the downtown theatres of the big cities like New York, Chicago and Los Angeles.

And there was radio. The 1916 prediction of RCA's president, David Sarnoff had come true and by 1940 nearly every home in America had a radio set of some kind, except in isolated ultra-rural areas. Most of them were much smaller than their predecessors and were, by now, all electric. The frequencies were not overcrowded and it was possible, after local and nearby stations signed off, to get the big 50,000-watt stations from many miles away. . . .

Radio still had a bit of growing to do. It would mature quite a bit in the following year and reach full growth after Pearl Harbor. In 1940 it was clomping into adulthood, bursting the seams of its adolescent attire and sizing up a conquerable world. The names of serious commentators were becoming familiar to millions, names like Boake Carter, Lowell Thomas, Fulton Lewis, Jr., Edward Morgan, Edward R. Murrow and the scholarly-sounding H.V. Kaltenborn, whose crispy-dry diction, replete with rolling r's, set a fashion in news delivery.

A Year of Memorable Movies and Theater

In looking back at the year on the silver screen, most Americans would say that *Gone with the Wind* was the big movie of 1940. Its star-studded cast did, indeed, carve a place in motion picture history—Vivien Leigh as Scarlett, Clark Gable as Rhett Butler, Thomas Mitchell, Olivia de Haviland and Leslie Howard. The names of the characters endured—O'Hara, Melanie, Ashley, as did the name of the plantation, Tara. The haunting theme song lingered like jasmine.

Margaret Mitchell's great story of the fall of Atlanta was not alone, however, for it was a year jammed with brilliant screen performances and memorable scripts. Hollywood, too, was emerging from the doldrums, and its moguls figured they had a lot of catching-up to do. *The Grapes of Wrath* brought Okies to the screen, victimized by corporate farming and the employers of migrant workers, and brought worldwide stardom to Henry Fonda and Jane Darwell. *The Philadelphia Story* set a new mark in sophisticated, brittle comedy, with Katharine Hepburn, Cary Grant and James Stewart. . . .

Walt Disney packed theatres with a cartoon story of what was to become one of his most lovable and unforgettable characters, *Pinocchio.* Later in the year he backed up his success with the spectacular *Fantasia,* with musical accompaniment by Leopold Stokowski and an enormous symphony orchestra. But Pinocchio and his father, Gepetto, and his pal, Jimminy Cricket, stayed around a long while.

It was a good time for musicals. On Broadway, tuneful productions included *Boys and Girls Together, Louisiana Purchase, Pal Joey, Panama Hattie* and *It Happens on Ice.*

The Great White Way, [a nickname for Broadway], still great and still bright with millions of lights in 1940, attracted throngs to see such theatre as *Separate Rooms, The Male Animal,* Robert E. Sherwood's *There Shall Be No Night, George Washington Slept Here, Johnny Belinda, The Corn Is Green, Charley's Aunt* and *My Sister Eileen.* In the fall, for serious theatre-goers, Helen Hayes revived *Twelfth Night. Life With Father,* which opened in 1939, was, of course, playing on Broadway, where it set records until 1947.

Making Music

It seemed that no part of America was very far from a juke-box as the fifth decade began. In towns and cities there were many on each block. In the most remote hamlets, they were found in the diners, the tearooms, the taverns, the variety stores and even in the gas stations and barbershops.

Big and gaudy, with flickering multicolored lights, with a visible storage file of dozens of records and a complex of selection buttons, the jukes operated for a nickel. Many of them had remote-control boxes that were strategically located at tables or at the corners of bars or on the marble-top counters of diners. For a quarter one music lover could get six plays, for a half-dollar, sixteen selections.

Throughout the land, they blared from early morning until late at night, playing popular music, selections from Broadway shows and movies, country music, even devotional music. Instrumentalists vied for popularity with trumpet, clarinet, saxophone, piano and guitar. Vocalists ran the gamut from operatic performers to crooners, to such sweet harmonizers as Ginny Sims and Harry Babbitt, and on to the nasal twangers of the country set, some of whom in later years were to enjoy much greater nationwide popularity. Large choral groups were becoming popular, epitomized by Fred Waring and his Pennsylvanians. And for a nickel, on some machines, you could buy three minutes of silence.

Voices of a New Decade

Americans did a lot of humming, singing and dancing in 1940.

From the film *Pinocchio*, they vocalized the sweet lyrics of "When You Wish upon a Star," but were likely to follow it with one of the first hoedown country tunes to gain nationwide popularity, "You Are My Sunshine."

The kooky 1939 smash hit, "Three Little Fishies" remained in many jukes throughout 1940, as did several other hits from the previous year, including, of course, Irving Berlin's timely "God Bless America," "The Beer Barrel Polka," "Frenesi" and Andre Kostclanetz' rendition of "Moon Love," adapted from Tchaikovsky's Fifth Symphony. . . .

Shortly after France fell and sued for armistice on June 17, Oscar Hammerstein II and Jerome Kern hit the music stalls and stores with the Academy Award-winning "The Last Time I Saw Paris," and box-office record-breaker Judy Garland, who at that time had never been to Paris, vocalized it from every jukebox in the land. Later, the incomparable Hildegarde pulled huge crowds to hear her sing it at the Savoy Room. Americans who had been to Paris only vicariously in the movies or in *Life* magazine, stood and wept as Miss Garland's tribute to the city on the Seine echoed from beery barrooms, crowded dancehalls and steamy diners.

For lovers and romantics there were "Fools Rush In," "How High the Moon," "Only Forever" and the instrumental rendition of "A Love Story—Intermezzo," from the movie *Intermezzo*.

The civil war in Spain, which had been slipping from the consciousness of most Americans, was brought home suddenly and dramatically by Ernest Hemingway's powerful *For*

Whom the Bell Tolls, which became an overnight best seller.

Hardly had avid readers become accustomed to the lilting Spanish names in Hemingway's novel than they were obliged to try their prowess on the furry, lispy names of the Welsh when Richard Llewellyn brought out his evocative *How Green Was My Valley*. Many an American lady, upon encountering the name of the principal female character, Angharyd, simply called her Anna. John O'Hara wrote *Pal Joey* that year (not to be confused with the play) and William Saroyan came out with *My Name Is Aram*. Thomas Wolfe's *You Can't Go Home Again* caused a stir in literary circles. James Truslow Adams published the sixth volume of his *Dictionary of American History*.

The War in Europe

The war rolled across the flatlands and rivers of Europe, through Belgium, Luxembourg and the Netherlands. The Dutch and Belgian armies capitulated and surrendered to the German armies after suffering fantastic casualties.

The Maginot line, behind which the French armies huddled, stretched for 100 miles and was said by the experts at l'Ecole du Militaire at St. Cyr to be absolutely impregnable, the finest fortification in the world. It had its own air-conditioning, its own kitchens and hospitals and supply rooms and power plants. It bristled with the full range of the French Field Artillery's modern weaponry, pointing across the border into Germany.

Hitler laughed, and his armies swept around the "impregnable" Maginot into the low countries, while the Luftwaffe roared overhead. Never mind the French fortifications, Hitler said. "We will make a fortress of all of Europe—Festung Europa.". . .

It bothered Americans to read of these events, but Europe was many miles from America, even though the Pan American Airways "Yankee Clipper" had flown from New York to Lisbon, Portugal, in the record time of eighteen hours and thirty-five minutes, with a stiff tailwind most of the way. Pan American was becoming known worldwide, and it was becoming clear that Lisbon would be the open gateway to "Fortress Europe," a gate that opened either way.

Focusing on the Home Front

There were other things to think about on the home front. Steel scrap, for instance. American junk-dealers were still selling it to Japan—almost 200 million tons in the last five years—and it was said in Pittsburgh that there was an insufficient amount of scrap on hand to operate the open-hearth furnaces for more than a few weeks.

And then there was the economy—an intriguing thing to watch.

It kept perking up, and was actually beginning to show signs of prosperity. The government was pouring the first of billions into defense spending (it was to total $8.3 billion in the next year) and the money was starting to trickle down to the man on the street. National income was reaching up to $90 billion, the newspapers reported.

A war? Sure a war in *Europe*. But no war for Americans. Europe was far away and was embroiled and ensnared in ancient problems. We had been suckered into their affairs once before, but not again. Let them fight their own battles. The United States of America was uncommitted and it seemed certain that a majority intended that it would stay that way.

It was too bad about the Jews in Germany, but Germany was a sovereign state and there was little one could do to interfere except *condemn* what the Germans were doing. Besides, there were several speakers touring America who said that the Jews had taken advantage of Germany's devastating poverty after World War I and had gobbled up all of the wealth. Thus, they implied, this military seizure of private property from the Jews might, in some circumstances, be justified. That this was being said by Americans who supposedly placed supreme value on individual life and on the sanctity of the right to own private property, wasn't challenged in many places.

We had just recovered from a serious ten-year illness. We

were still convalescing. We really couldn't do much about the rest of the world. We owed it to ourselves to get our own health fully restored. So went the basic thinking.

Spending Money and Having Fun

And the money filtered down.

Nightclubs, which had burst open in the bigger cities the week after Prohibition was repealed, suggesting to some skeptics that they might have been operating right along, now began to spring up in all of the smaller cities and towns and in the villages and on the highways leading to town. Most were just drinking spots, often boasting a dance floor and a loud jukebox, with perhaps a live band on Friday and Saturday nights. But in or near any town of any size there was a genuine "nightclub" patterned after famous ones in New York. To supply them with talent (singers, dancers, stand-up comedians and magicians), booking "circuits" came into existence throughout the country, sharply reminiscent of the old vaudeville circuits, which had died a decade earlier with the advent of the talking picture.

People were beginning to spend the money they earned. It was the first time they had been so free with cash since 1930, when they tightened up through necessity in the aftermath of the great stock market crash of October 24, 1929 and Wall Street's deathblow to prosperity on October 29, 1929.

For the first time in ten years they bought such things as jewelry, watches, radios, kitchen appliances and prime steaks. They drank scotch and bourbon and rye and gin instead of beer. Kids got their teeth straightened; adults had old and bothersome teeth extracted and ordered bridgework. Those who had delayed having children, started families. Those who had put off marriage, bought rings and licenses and set up housekeeping.

Prices began to rise, but only a little. Only the elderly and the retired grumbled about the diminishing purchasing power of their fixed incomes.

The war? That was far away. Here there were vacations to be had, the first ones in ten years, and there were new things to buy. The larder was being restocked. Wardrobes were being outfitted. You realized, of course, that mother hadn't had a new coat in five years. The priorities were *here*. . . .

Preparing Reluctant Americans for War

In the White House a troubled Franklin Delano Roosevelt read the alarming dispatches from Europe, and now, suddenly, from Asia and the Far East, and pondered on the isolationism and pacifism that seemed lodged in the land. Americans were peace-lovers. Also, they were disenchanted with war. World War I, despite the promises, had failed to make the world safe for democracy; it had failed to bring everlasting peace. If you won a war, the average fellow asked, what did you win? And then he answered his question: Nothing. You won nothing.

There was no way, Roosevelt realized, that Americans, in 1940, could have been persuaded to enter the war. Instead, he resolved, we would make America the "Arsenal for Democracy." The British, pleased, of course, but not as happy as they would have been if Americans had come to their aid with men as well as machines and weapons, cracked that Americans were willing to fight Hitler until there wasn't an Englishman left.

Roosevelt swapped fifty old destroyers to Britain for some naval and air bases in Western Hemisphere waters and quietly negotiated a deal with Iceland to allow the building of an American base there when, as and if needed. On paper, the SeaBees (naval construction battalions) came into existence.

Then, without warning or build-up, the President announced that he wanted to build a peacetime army so that if America had to go to war, she would, for the first time in history, do so *fully prepared*. He called up the National Guard and all other auxiliary services—Naval Reserve and Marine Corps Reserve, (the Coast Guard had already been absorbed into the Navy)—in a general mobilization, and asked Congress to authorize a national selective service act so that the nation could embark on its first peacetime draft in history.

It was a daring move for the President, but Hitler's hordes were marching on, and Americans, finding the President's concern to be infectious, were losing much of their isolationism, except, perhaps, in the Midwest, where British-hating Roosevelt-loathing Robert McCormick, publisher of the powerful *Chicago Tribune,* one of the most respected newspapers in the nation, garnered many followers who agreed with him that America should keep its nose out of foreign affairs.

The Selective Service Act

Congress, weighted in the Democrat column, responded to Roosevelt's command and on August 27 enacted the Selective Service and Training Act. The same measure also required that all alien residents register with the government. The President signed the draft into law on September 16, a hot, bright, sunshiny day in Washington.

He set one month from the day of signing—October 16, 1940—as the day of registration for all male citizens from ages eighteen through thirty-five.

The first American peacetime draft was underway.

In all, 16,313,240 men received their registration cards. In Washington, Secretary of War Henry L. Stimson, having been blindfolded by the selective service director, plunged his hand into a giant glass bowl and drew the card of the first selectee, and the draft machinery was set in inexorable motion. Selectees, in short order, became inductees—into the armed forces.

The day that Roosevelt signed the Selective Service Act into law, was four days after the forty-seventh birthday of a general staff colonel, a former schoolteacher and high school principal from Indiana, Lewis B. Hershey. Just before the day of the drawing, on October 15, Hershey was appointed a brigadier general and named director of selective service, a post he was to occupy until his retirement in 1971, probably the most thankless job in government. . . .

The Presidential Election

There were some people, Republicans and defecting Democrats, who said that Roosevelt was pushing the country nearer to wartime footing to scare the voters into supporting him for the third term for which he had been nominated in July at a tumultuous, rifting Democratic National Convention in Chicago. The chief executive ignored such gibes and implied that he was going to limit his campaigning because of the increasing pressures of office. Those who wished to could infer from that that he was already a wartime president, too busy for the trivia of politics.

Unlimited in his campaign efforts or his campaign spending was Wendell Willkie, an Indiana utilityman turned Wall Street lawyer, the Republican nominee, who made whistle-stop tours throughout the country, attracting large, exuberant crowds. For a candidate of the "outs," he was very well financed. He was backed by an ultra-rich fac-

President Franklin D. Roosevelt and First Lady Eleanor Roosevelt celebrate his victory in the 1940 presidential election.

tion of the eastern Establishment, which had, for sundry reasons, broken with Roosevelt. Perhaps reflecting the sympathies of his strongest and richest supporters, Willkie differed from Roosevelt mainly in domestic matters and policies, which he claimed had been neglected, and spoke eloquently of "One World," maintaining that the earth had become too small to endure isolationism on the part of any leading nation.

Before November, however FDR and his wife Eleanor managed to do a considerable amount of campaigning to cheering crowds in the most politically sensitive or politically significant parts of the nation.

And on Tuesday, November 4, Roosevelt won by another landslide (440 electoral votes), the first President to be elected for more than two terms of office in the history of the country.

It was, he said, a mandate to forge ahead with his plans for defense. Other, more ambitious plans were to be revealed after the first of the year.

A couple of weeks after the election, New Yorkers and Long Islanders celebrated the opening of the Queens Midtown Tunnel (cost $58 million) with festivities on both sides of the East River. It was just a bit too late for the 1939 World's Fair at Flushing Meadows, for which the Bronx Whitestone Bridge had been completed to handle traffic from the north and east. The Fair had run through the summer and autumn of 1940, and had closed before the tunnel was opened.

Variety noted that trumpeter Harry James had left the Benny Goodman orchestra to form his own band, and had brought along with him from the Goodman group an unknown young vocalist named Francis Albert Sinatra. Some of the old hands in the dance band business said they thought the kid didn't sing too well. And he was awfully skinny.

Preparing America's Defense

"Defense" was becoming a more important word as the year waned. "Defense plants" seemed, suddenly, to be everywhere, with new buildings springing up where there had been farmland a year before. In New England, in upstate New York, in New Jersey, in Pennsylvania and in the Midwest, old factories that had been abandoned or only partially used, were spruced up, cleaned out and reactivated.

Throughout the country, defense plants geared up to work around the clock, seven days a week. Long freight trains hooted and clattered and snaked their cars along the railroads all night long, every night in the week. Extra passenger trains were seen streaking along the rights-of-way during the daytime with white flags on the engines denoting they were "specials." If they slowed down, uniformed men could be seen inside.

Small inconveniences began to occur. Fold-down paper matchbooks began to disappear from the stores, and smokers had to switch back to the old-fashioned wooden "kitchen matches," which came in a big rectangular box and cost a nickel. Zippers, only recently introduced, disappeared from the flies of new trousers. Silk stockings fell into short supply because the material was needed for parachutes, so women painted makeup on their legs to give them that taupe tone, and some even painted stripes on the backs of their calves with eyebrow pencils. The telephone companies, which had converted the biggest cities to dial phones, as well as some of the smaller rural communities, postponed the dial conversions in hundreds of medium- and small-sized cities because copper and other materials were in shortening supply.

As winter approached, it was announced by various experts that there might be a shortage of both coal and oil because of the diversion of transportation equipment, including barges and tankers.

In many parts of the country, people who looked smugly at the gas cooking stoves in their kitchens were disappointed to learn that companies that manufactured their own "illuminating gas" would also likely be short of coking coal.

Stores reported a run on sugar and retail spokesmen cautioned against hoarding, but housewives, who either remembered the sugar shortages of World War I or had heard the older folks discuss them, paid little heed.

Emerging from the Depression

But the money kept coming faster and faster. There was not much consumer credit around in those days, so the wage-earners worked and spent—and spent.

Automobile production set a record. New cars filled the highways, despite warnings from Interior Secretary Harold L. Ickes that motorists were going to use up all the gasoline we had. Huge quantities, he cautioned, were being diverted to military needs.

At Christmastime, most of the boys who had been drafted or mobilized were sent home on furlough, and it turned into one of the merriest Christmases in the memory of most.

Retail sales smashed through and set a record.

The Depression was forgotten. Erased from memory was the fact that only two years before, in the spring of 1938, the economic slump had hit bottom and 12 million Americans had been out of work. Now everybody was working—everybody, that is, who really *wanted* to work. Or so it seemed.

The figures didn't bear that out. Poverty persisted in a great many parts of the country, notably in the South and the Middle South, where, as yet, there weren't many factories to get defense orders. But if you weren't in those sections, you didn't notice it.

In the service, a buck private got $21 a month, plus all his clothes, supplies, meals, lodging and medical and dental care. That was $21 free and clear, to spend as he wished.

America was gearing up for war, and by and large the people were enjoying it—or the results of it. It was exhilarating and it brought prosperity.

It was called "defense," not "war," and it was easy to think that the whole thing would roll along as it was going for many years to come. It was easy to think this because most Americans were simply not ready for war. Not in any way were they ready.

Especially unready for war were the military. The new draftees were sent to training camps in World War I gear, hand-me-downs from 1918. In the Carolinas and Georgia and Tennessee, woodworking factories were pressed into service to turn out wooden rifles for the trainees so they could get the "feel" of them. At Fort McClellan, soldiers used broomsticks to learn the manual of arms. At the Springfield Armory and Arsenal in Massachusetts, the blueprints for the Garand semiautomatic, recoilless, gas-ejection rifle were being studied. It was called the M-1. . . .

Booming, bustling, even bristling, America ended the first year of the fifth decade of the twentieth century in feverish activity, with most people *saying* that the nation would never again go to war, but growing numbers of them fearing that sooner or later it was bound to come.

New Year's Eve of 1940 was certainly the gayest, noisiest, costliest, celebratingest night since 1928, before the market crashed.

The lights were on all over America, and they glowed 'til dawn had brought the first daylight of 1941 from coast to coast.

From Isolation to Intervention

Gerald D. Nash

Although Americans were still reluctant to become involved in the war raging in Europe, appeals from British Prime Minister Winston Churchill and continued Nazi aggression persuaded President Franklin D. Roosevelt to encourage the use of America's resources not only to aid the Allied forces at war with Hitler's Germany in Europe, but to develop the nation's defense, writes historian Gerald D. Nash in this excerpt from his book *The Great Depression and World War II: Organizing America, 1933–1945*. To allay fears that aid to the Allies used money needed to improve America's depression economy, Roosevelt created the Lend-Lease Program, which traded European goods for American military aid, Nash explains. According to Nash, although not officially involved in world conflict, actions such as these made America a nonbelligerent, but partisan nation. Although both strict isolationists and advocates of stronger intervention disapproved of Roosevelt's decisions, when German submarines attacked U.S. naval vessels in the North Atlantic and the Japanese bombed Pearl Harbor in 1941, entry into the war was inevitable.

The fall of France brought World War II closer to America. Any illusions which Americans might have cher-

---

ished concerning Nazi intentions about world conquest or about the strength of the Allies were rudely shattered by the spectacular German victories. England alone stood between the United States and the Nazi juggernaut—and the British showed obvious signs of weakening. Americans were now forced to confront the realities of the war as it affected their own national interest.

A Presidential Appeal

The reversal in the United States' position was publicized by the president in his commencement speech at the University of Virginia on June 10, 1940, as France fell, when he said:

> Some indeed still hold to the now somewhat obvious delusion that we of the United States can safely permit the United States to become a lone island, a lone island in a world dominated by the philosophy of force.
>
> Such an island may be the dream of those who still talk and vote as isolationists. Such an island represents to me and to the overwhelming majority of the Americans today a helpless nightmare of a people without freedom. Yes, the nightmare of a people lodged in prison, handcuffed, hungry, and fed through the bars from day to day by the contemptuous, unpitying masters of other continents.
>
> Let us not hesitate—all of us—to proclaim certain truths. Overwhelmingly, we as a nation . . . we are convinced that military and naval victory of the gods of force and hate would endanger the institutions of democracy in the Western world—and that, equally, therefore, the whole of our sympathies lie with those nations that are giving the lifeblood of combat against those forces.
>
> In our unity . . . we will pursue two obvious and simultaneous courses; we will extend to the opponents of force the material resources of this nation, and at the same time we will harness and speed up the use of those resources in order that we ourselves in the Americas may have equipment and training equal to the task of any emergency and every defense.

Americans could no longer be absolutely impartial but must extend all aid to the Allies short of war, Roosevelt felt. The collapse of France had created a threat to American security in the Caribbean too. The French possessions of Martinique and Guadeloupe were in strategic locations and might possibly be occupied by Germans. To counter this danger, the Roosevelt Administration called for a meeting of Pan-American foreign ministers to meet in Havana in late July 1940. This conference displayed surprising unanimity, for large numbers of German settlers and their descendants in Argentina, Brazil, and Chile had cultivated considerable pro-German sentiment in South America. In a Declaration of Havana the participating nations declared that they would consider an attack on any one American country an attack on all. A commission was established to take temporary control of any European possessions in the Western Hemisphere to guard against possible incursions by the Axis.

During spring and summer of 1940, British Prime Minister Winston Churchill was importuning Roosevelt to transfer some U.S. naval vessels to desperately needed convoy duty in the North Atlantic. When Churchill first broached the question, Roosevelt was decidedly negative, although Churchill argued that England had lost one-third of its fleet or one hundred destroyers, and that those remaining were needed to repel the expected German invasion from the east. "We must ask therefore, as a matter of life or death," wrote Churchill, "to be reinforced with these destroyers." Roosevelt hesitated to act without congressional approval. In July the British ambassador to the United States, Lord Lothian, offered the United States the rights to military bases in Newfoundland, Bermuda, and Trinidad in return for aid. The idea of a trade had greater appeal to Roosevelt. Through his journalist friend William Allen White, he sounded out the Republican challenger Wendell Willkie on his attitude toward the proposal. Willkie agreed not to make it an issue. Meanwhile, a group of distinguished lawyers advised the president that he did not require congressional approval for a destroyer transfer, and in early fall Roosevelt transferred fifty antiquated World War I destroyers to Great Britain in return for eight American military bases in the New World. Public reaction to the transaction was mostly favorable, in part because Roosevelt had cultivated it carefully during the preceding months.

The Lend-Lease Program

While Americans were going to the polls in the fall of 1940, the English were huddling in bomb shelters and wondering about the impending bankruptcy of their government. Great Britain had spent $4.5 billion of its $6.5 billion in dollar reserves, and lacked funds to pay for further large-scale purchases of military supplies in the United States. British Prime Minister Churchill chose to present his case dramatically. As Roosevelt was vacationing in the Caribbean on a navy cruiser in early December, a seaplane approached the vessel, bearing an urgent message from Churchill. "My dear Mr. President," he wrote, "As we reach the end of this year, I feel you will expect me to lay before you the prospects for 1941. I do so with candor and confidence, because it seems to me that the vast majority of American citizens have recorded their conviction that the safety of the United States, as well as the future of our two Democracies and the kind of civilization for which they stand, is bound up with the survival and independence of the British Commonwealth of Nations. . . . [But] the moment approaches when we shall no longer be able to pay cash for shipping and other supplies. . . . Regard this letter not as an appeal for aid but as a statement of minimum action to achieve our common purpose." Churchill urged Roosevelt to provide supplies the British so desperately needed but for which they could no longer pay.

Roosevelt considered the appeal and then formulated a plan of action. After he returned to Washington and consulted with his aides, he revealed his scheme for what became known as the Lend-Lease Program. At a press conference he told reporters: "What I'm trying to do is to eliminate the dollar sign . . . get rid of the silly, foolish old dollar sign. Well, let me give you an illustration: Suppose my neighbor's home catches on fire, and I have a length of garden hose four or five hundred feet away. If he can take my garden hose and connect it with his hydrant, I may help him to put out his fire. Now what do I do? I don't say to him before that operation, 'Neighbor, my garden hose cost me $15; you have to pay me $15 for it.' What is the transaction that goes on? I don't want $15—I want my garden hose back after the fire is over. All right, if it goes through the fire all right, intact . . . he gives it back to me and thanks me very much for the use of it."

On December 29, 1940, Roosevelt spoke to Americans directly in a fireside chat. "The United States," he said, "must be the great arsenal of democracy." He asked Congress for authority to send war supplies to England in return for goods and services rather than for dollars. His pleas fell on sympathetic ears, and within two months Congress appropriated $7 billion for operation of the Lend-Lease Program. In return for supplies the British also made additional air and naval bases available to the United States off the Canadian coast and in the British West Indies.

The Road from Neutrality to Alliance

The Havana Declaration, together with Roosevelt's commencement address at the University of Virginia and the adoption of Lend-Lease, transformed the United States from a neutral into a partisan, albeit nonbelligerent, nation. This new diplomatic status was developed further by Roosevelt's authorization of limited American naval action in the first half of 1941. By then an increasing number of Americans began to realize that England was America's first line of defense. If England were defeated, no doubt the United States would be left to face Nazi Germany alone. American public opinion was shifting in favor of intervention. Since Roosevelt kept a close watch on opinions expressed in the popular press, he felt more assured in modifying the nation's neutral stance. In view of the great shipping losses the British suffered in the Atlantic at the hands of German submarines, in March 1941 Roosevelt authorized American shipyards to repair British vessels. In addition he ordered the transfer of ten Coast Guard cutters to the Royal Navy for convoy duty. And he extended the American Neutrality Patrol almost 2,000 miles into the Atlantic. The U.S. Navy was ordered to locate German submarines but not to attack them.

By the middle of 1941 Roosevelt extended American non-belligerency further. Fleets of Nazi submarines were roaming in the North Atlantic, sinking British vessels at an alarming rate of two ships daily and endangering the American supply route to England. With the United States now committed to the defense of Great Britain, the president felt compelled to take additional steps to ensure the continued flow of aid to the embattled English. That lifeline seemed threatened by a German declaration in March 1941 extending the Atlantic war zone to include Iceland as well as the Denmark Strait between Greenland and Iceland. The practical effect of this measure was that German submarines and surface vessels would roam Atlantic waters less than a thousand miles from American shores. Roosevelt considered the German action for several months before making retaliatory moves. In July 1941 he announced that U.S. Marines would occupy Iceland to prevent its possible seizure by Germany, and to ensure the defense of the Western Hemisphere. These measures made the United States a *de facto* ally of the British.

Although Roosevelt and Churchill were in almost daily contact in 1940 and 1941, the two leaders had not met personally. Roosevelt recalled having seen Churchill briefly during World War I, but the British leader could not remember the occasion. Consequently, in July 1941 Harry Hopkins went to London to arrange a secret meeting. Within a few weeks Churchill embarked on one of the Royal Navy's finest battleships bound for Argentia, off Newfoundland. Roosevelt was steaming to the rendezvous on the U.S. Navy cruiser *Augusta*. The two men met aboard the American ship on August 9, 1941. Churchill hoped to secure some kind of commitment from the United States to participate in the war, but Roosevelt refused to bind his nation in this way. The military advisors who accompanied the two men did discuss loose plans for Anglo-American cooperation at some future time, if circumstances warranted.

The outcome of this meeting was the Atlantic Charter, a joint declaration concerning common aims. This document embodied an Anglo-American vision for organization of the post-war world. That world was to be ordered according to principles based on self-determination of nations. The charter also reiterated Anglo-American adherence to the Four Freedoms which Roosevelt had enunciated in his annual message to Congress earlier that year—freedom from want, freedom from fear, freedom of speech, and freedom of religion. When the contents of the Atlantic Charter were made public a week after the meeting, Americans responded positively. In the context of growing support for his diplomacy, the president extended Lend-Lease aid to Russia a few months later.

By fall 1941 the United States was involved in an undeclared naval war. On September 4, 1941, a German submarine had attacked the U.S. destroyer *Greer* off Iceland. President Roosevelt reacted by ordering U.S. naval vessels to shoot on sight any German or Italian vessels they encountered in the North Atlantic. A few weeks later Congress approved the arming of American merchant ships.

Roosevelt's Opposition

Throughout 1940 and 1941 Roosevelt's shift to a diplomacy tending to intervention came under fire from various groups and individuals. Staunch isolationists such as Senator Burton Wheeler of Montana belittled the supposed threat from the Axis powers and castigated Roosevelt as a warmonger. Some Americans, such as Charles Lindbergh, also did not regard fascism as a threat to the United States and opposed Roosevelt's policies of aiding the Allies. There were also ethnic isolationists such as Americans of German or Irish descent, antimilitarists, left-wingers, and Communists. Early in 1941 the opponents of intervention organized the America First Committee. Through an active public relations campaign and lobbying in Congress, the committee brought its views before the American public, although international events increasingly weakened its influence.

On the other hand, the advocates of intervention felt that Roosevelt was too slow and cautious in extending aid to the Allies. Led by William Allen White, a well-known newspaper editor from Kansas, they organized the Committee to Defend America by Aiding the Allies to counter the influence of isolationists and to prod the Administration into closer collaboration with France and Britain. Despite these organizations neither the isolationists nor the interventionists swayed large numbers of Americans as effectively as the rapidly changing military situation in Europe and the Far East. The majority of Americans, however, were still holding out hope that direct participation in the war by the United States might not be necessary.

Japanese Alliances and Conquests

While Roosevelt had his hands full in dealing with the European crisis after 1939, American relations with Japan were also deteriorating. Despite protests by the United States, the Japanese continued their invasion of China, begun in 1937. One of the Japanese government's major objectives during this period was an alliance with Nazi Germany, which promised to facilitate further expansion in Asia. After tortuous negotiations Japan concluded the Tri-Partite Agreement with Germany and Italy in 1940. Japan recognized German and Italian dominance in Europe, and the European powers agreed to recognize Japanese influence in East Asia. They also promised to aid the Japanese if they were attacked by a neutral power. Such an alliance was clearly a challenge to the United States, since American insistence on Japanese recognition of the Open Door Policy and the independence of China was a cloak for allowing the

United States to maintain a dominant position in East Asia and to limit Japanese expansion there. The goals of the United States and Japan were now on a collision course.

On hearing of British recognition of Japanese conquests in China, in July 1939, Roosevelt warned Japan that he might impose embargoes on the export of raw materials such as steel, iron, and petroleum. Initially, the response of the Japanese government was restrained; but in the spring of 1940, Nazi victories in Europe emboldened the Japanese. A more militant government headed by Prime Minister Konoye came to power in July. Its military leaders decided the time was ripe to seize French Indo-China and the Dutch East Indies, now that Japan had become an Axis partner. That such moves would further antagonize the United States was clear. When the Japanese made incursions into Indo-China in July and December, Roosevelt reacted by placing embargoes on the export of aviation gasoline, scrap metals, and other vital materials to Japan. Furious, the Japanese were willing to bide their time in order to bolster their military prowess.

Within the framework of their respective aspirations, neither the leaders of the United States nor of Japan felt in 1941 that they could make significant concessions. During April and May the Konoye government offered various proposals to Washington, including the suggestion that the United States and Japan enter into a neutrality pact. Among other things, such a pact would allow the Japanese to seize British, French, and Dutch possessions in Asia. They also suggested a personal meeting between President Roosevelt and Prime Minister Konoye to attempt to settle their differences.

After the German invasion of Russia in June 1941, the Japanese became bolder and occupied the southern portion of French Indo-China. Roosevelt was furious. In July 1941 he closed the Panama Canal to Japanese shipping, impounded Japanese funds in the United States, and extended the embargo to include additional raw materials. Both sides were now taking firmer and more intransigent positions from which retreat was increasingly difficult. Konoye invited Roosevelt to a conference to discuss mutual problems, but the president, heeding the advice of his Secretary of State, declined to attend unless the Japanese first recognized China's independence. This unwillingness to compromise strengthened the position of militarists in Japan, and in September 1941 they began to make secret war preparations. In October the aggressive militarist Admiral Hideki Tojo became the new prime minister. Although negotiations continued throughout October and November, rigid and opposing positions of Admiral Tojo and Secretary of State Cordell Hull doomed them to failure.

Japan's Bold Attack

During the last week of November 1941, American intelligence sources surmised that Japanese military leaders were preparing for an attack on either American or Allied possessions. The departments of army and navy sent warnings to commanders in the Pacific indicating that Japanese troop and naval movements suggested possible attacks on Guam or the Philippines. No one knew precisely where the Japanese might strike, especially since American intelligence operations were still uncoordinated and frequently channeled confused information to various agencies in Washington. Since many American military men expected an attack on British territories in Singapore or Malaya, they were not overly concerned about other areas. In Hawaii Admiral Husband E. Kimmel concentrated the Pacific fleet at Pearl Harbor largely to minimize sabotage. General Walter C. Short rather casually dispersed his forces in the Hawaiian Islands. Thus, the United States was caught off-guard when a Japanese carrier task force loosed the first wave of 189 planes on American naval vessels and on air fields at Pearl Harbor, Hawaii. Neither this nor a second wave of 171 planes met significant opposition as they attacked the American fleet. All eight U.S. battleships in Oahu harbor were disabled; three cruisers and three destroyers were blown out of the water; and virtually all American planes on the ground were destroyed. Other Japanese forces simultaneously were attacking the Philippines, Hong Kong, Siam, Malaya, and Wake and Midway Islands. Only after the attack did the world receive the news that Japan had declared war on the United States and Great Britain.

On December 8, 1941, President Roosevelt appeared before a tense Congress to ask for a declaration of war against Japan:

> Yesterday, December 7, 1941—a date which will live in infamy—the United States of America was suddenly and deliberately attacked by naval and air forces of the empire of Japan.
>
> As Commander-in-Chief of the Army and Navy, I have directed that all measures be taken for our defense, that always will our whole nation remember the character of the onslaught against us.
>
> No matter how long it may take us to overcome this premeditated invasion, the American people in their righteous might, will win through to absolute victory.
>
> With confidence in our armed forces, with the unbounding determination of our people, we will gain the inevitable triumph, so help us God.

Within a few days Germany and Italy also declared war on the United States. Americans were now engaged in another worldwide conflict.

Despite the desire of an overwhelming majority of the American people to remain aloof from the war in Europe, by 1941 the United States was once again embroiled in a major conflict. Between 1939 and 1941 circumstances narrowed the alternatives open to American policymakers. Keeping a close pulse on public opinion, President Roosevelt had followed a restrained neutrality until June of 1940. The fall of France, however, shocked Americans into an acute awareness of what a Nazi victory in Western Europe would mean and led them to support a policy of extensive aid. But at the time of Pearl Harbor the reasons for United States entry into the war were clear to most Americans. Nazi and Japanese policies were restricting American commercial expansion in Europe and the Far East. The proliferation of Nazi and other totalitarian governments constituted an increasing threat to democracy in the United States and elsewhere. Ultimately the ideals of freedom and of the Christian-Judeo ethic were being challenged by Nazi doctrines of racial superiority and barbarism. World War II was not fought primarily because of disputes over territories, economic concessions, or political rivalries, although these played a role. From the American point of view the conflict was generated by the clash of two radically differing ideologies and lifestyles. This became a war for survival.

December 7, 1941: A Day of Infamy

Cabell Phillips

In the following excerpt from his book *The 1940s: Decade of Triumph and Trouble*, journalist Cabell Phillips provides an account of what happened on the day of the Japanese attack on Pearl Harbor—December 7, 1941. Based on the 1946 congressional report of the *Joint Committee on the Pearl Harbor Attack*, Phillips recreates the activities of the U.S. naval vessels that patrolled the waters of the Pacific; the diplomats, cabinet members, generals, and President Roosevelt, who negotiated in Washington, D.C.; the Japanese fleet that rendezvoused off Oahu; and the personnel on duty at the military base in Pearl Harbor. For example, Phillips tracks, minute by minute, the warning message to army and navy commanders in the Pacific sent from General George C. Marshall in Washington, D.C., that was interrupted by the first wave of Japanese bombs while a motorcycle messenger carried it from Honolulu. The author also describes the attack itself, the devastation, and the response. Phillips was a staff writer for the *New York Times* and the author of the first volume of "The New York Times Chronicle of American Life" and other historical works.

I n the predawn hours of Sunday, December 7, 1941, the U.S.S. *Condor,* a stubby little minesweeper, was on routine patrol through the choppy and faintly luminescent waters of the Pacific a mile and a half off the mouth of Pearl Harbor in the Hawaiians. The waning moon hung low on the western horizon, obscured most of the time by a broken overcast. Ensign R.C. McCloy, who was the officer of the deck for the midwatch, took one casual glance at the ship's clock on the bridge and made a mental note that his relief was due up in 10 minutes—at four o'clock.

Spotting a Submarine

As the *Condor* plowed along at an unworried seven knots, Ensign McCloy spotted a faint splash of white on the dark sea about 50 yards ahead off the port bow. At first he thought it was a bit of foam riding the crest of a wave. But it seemed to have a purposefulness and direction about it, and it didn't disappear as foam should have done. He swung his binoculars to his eyes and studied it a minute. Then he passed them over to his helmsman, Quartermaster 2/C. R.C. Uttrick, and asked him what he made of it.

"That's a periscope, sir, and there aren't supposed to be any subs in this area," Uttrick said.

Ensign McCloy seized the glasses and took another look. The white shadow had crossed the water toward the harbor entrance. There was no doubt in his mind about it now. It was the wake of a periscope, and even if it were one of his own—as he thought it probably was at the moment—it had no business being where it was.

Two miles away at that moment, cruising at 15 knots on routine channel entrance patrol, was the destroyer *Ward*. At 4:05 A.M. the *Ward*'s deck officer observed a blinker signal from the *Condor*, "Have sighted submerged submarine on westerly course."

General quarters rang through the whole ship and the sleepy crew of the *Ward* stumbled to battle stations. On the bridge, the order was given for full speed to the *Condor*'s side. Additional data on course and speed of the strange submarine were procured and the *Ward* began to maneuver through elaborate search patterns. Although the search continued, the general quarters alert was relaxed at 4:58 A.M.

One hour later, as sunrise lighted the skies overhead, the *Ward* spotted "a strange object" in the water two miles off the starboard bow. Closing the distance under full steam, Commander William Outerbridge, the skipper, who had again been routed out of his bunk by an excited watch officer, identified it as the conning tower of a "baby" submarine—not an American type.

At 100 yards the *Ward* fired two salvos from her forward gun. The second scored a direct hit on the conning tower, which immediately plunged from view. As she passed over the spot, the *Ward* dropped a depth charge and a moment later saw a huge, black oil bubble break the surface.

At 6:54 A.M., Honolulu time, the *Ward* radioed the commandant of the Fourteenth Naval District, Pearl Harbor: "We have attacked, fired upon, and dropped depth charges on a submarine operating in defensive sea areas."

The United States had won the first preliminary skirmish— but only that—in the as yet unrevealed war with Japan.

Radio Message from Japan

There is a five-and-a-half-hour time differential between Washington and Honolulu. At almost the precise moment that the *Condor* spotted the Japanese baby sub, cryptanalysts 5,000 miles away in the Navy Department in Washington finished deciphering an intercepted radio message from the Foreign Office in Tokyo to its Ambassador in the United States, Admiral Kichisaburo Nomura.

This was the fourteenth—and critical—part of a long diplomatic dispatch in which the Imperial Government was to turn down the urgent request of the United States for peaceful mediation between the two countries in the Pacific. The first 13 parts (decipherable because the United States had long since broken Japan's most secret code) had been intercepted the day before. These had been the subject of troubled study by President Roosevelt; Secretary of State William Franklin Cordell Hull; Secretary of the Navy Knox; General George C. Marshall, the Chief of Staff; Harry Hopkins; and a handful of others late into Saturday night. It was obvious that the Japanese were on the brink of a massive breach of peace; but precisely where and when the blow would fall none of our officials could tell. The fourteenth part, which had not been transmitted from Tokyo until after midnight, was believed to contain the key to the ominous puzzle, and was therefore awaited with trepidation.

At 9:30 on Sunday morning a courier left the Navy Department with a transcript of the fourteenth part. He delivered one copy at the office of Secretary of State Hull, who had already come down from his apartment at the Wardman Park Hotel, and took another across the street to the White House. Captain John R. Beardall, a naval aide, delivered it to the President in his bedroom at 10 o'clock.

As the President read the concluding sentence, "The Japanese Government regrets to have to notify hereby the American Government . . . it cannot but consider that it is impossible to reach an agreement," he shook his head and said, "It looks as though the Japs are going to break off negotiations."

Meanwhile, Secretaries Hull, Knox, and Secretary of War Henry L. Stimson were threshing over the implications of the message in Mr. Hull's office at the State Department. All available evidence pointed to a Japanese thrust at Indochina, and they were considering the steps to be taken by this country in that event. While they were talking, two other intercepts arrived from the Navy Department. They were in "purple" code and marked "Urgent—Very Important."

They instructed Ambassador Nomura to deliver the 14-part message to the Secretary of State precisely at one o'clock that day and, after deciphering Part 14, "to destroy at once the remaining cipher machine and all machine codes. Dispose in like manner also secret documents."

This added a sinister and portentous imminence to whatever it was that was about to happen. After satisfying themselves that the President had also received copies of the two latest messages, the conferees separated at 11:15 A.M. Mr. Knox went to his office in the Navy Building and

Mr. Stimson to his home on Woodley Road, a couple of miles away, for lunch.

The Japanese Strike Force

Bright sunlight streamed through the windows of the old State Department Building as the three Secretaries broke up their conference. But at Latitude 26 degrees North, Longitude 158 degrees West, 275 miles north of the island of Oahu, six carriers of the Pearl Harbor Striking Force under the command of Admiral Chuichi Nagumo rendezvoused just as the first gray hints of dawn touched the horizon.

This was the terminus of a 4,000-mile voyage that had begun from an obscure anchorage in the Kurile Islands [north of Japan currently part of Russia] on November 16, and which had been completed in total invisibility to the eyes of the rest of the world. The Japanese force was made up, in addition to the six carriers, of two battleships, two cruisers, and two destroyers, with a compliment of more than 15,000 men.

On board the flagship *Agaki*, the "Z" flag, which had flown at the Battle of Tsushima in 1905, was flown beneath the scarlet emblem of the Rising Sun. All hands who could be spared were called to the flight decks for a final, fanatical dedication to the task that was about to begin. In each pilot's hand was placed a mimeographed chart of Pearl Harbor, with ship positions and other target data corrected up to the last 24 hours.

"Zero" was set for six o'clock, and the first wave of planes roared in the air amid frenzied shouts of "Banzai! Banzai!" from those on deck. Ninety "Kates" loaded with bombs and torpedoes, 50 "Val" dive bombers, and 50 "Zeke" fighters circled into formation, climbed over the cloud cover to 9,000 feet, and in the sparkling early-morning sunlight streaked southward toward Hawaii.

A lowly seaman, Kuramoto, tried to preserve for posterity the rapture of the moment by writing down these words:

> . . . and now our Eagles were moving into a great formation. Our 10 years and more of intensive training would

now bear fruit. At this thought a thousand emotions filled our hearts as, close to tears, we watched this magnificent sight. One and all, in our hearts, we sent our pleas to the gods, and putting our hands together, we prayed.

Preparing a Warning Message

While Kuramoto and his friends were praying for the safe return of their "Eagles," General Marshall in Washington hurried to the War Department from his quarters across the Potomac at Fort Myer. He had been out for his usual horseback ride that morning. In response to an urgent message he reached his office at precisely 11:15.

Impassively, he read the full text of the 14-part Japanese message—he was not among those who had seen it the night before. But when he came to the two supplements, the "one o'clock" and the code-destruction messages, his granite features showed unaccustomed alarm.

"This certainly means that something is going to happen at one o'clock today," he said to the aides grouped about him. "When they specify the day, that's significant enough, but when they specify the hour. . . . Get Admiral [Harold R.] Stark [Chief of Naval Operations] on the phone for me right away."

In a tensely brief conversation, Marshall and Stark agreed on a warning message to be sent immediately to all Army and Navy commanders throughout the Pacific. Other general warnings had been sent before, the latest on November 27. But this was to have a superseding note of urgency. The general scribbled it out in longhand:

The Japanese are presenting at 1 P.M., E.S.T., today, what amounts to an ultimatum. Also, they are under orders to destroy their code machines immediately. Just what significance the hour set may have we do not know, but be on the alert accordingly.

At 11:50 General Marshall handed the message to his communications officer, Colonel Edward F. French, who put it in code and hurried it in person to the Army's Communications center. There he found that radio contact with Honolulu was temporarily suspended. On a hasty decision he turned it over to Western Union. The hour was 12:02 P.M.

 ## President Roosevelt's Call to War

On December 8, 1941, the day after Japan's infamous attack on Pearl Harbor, President Franklin D. Roosevelt made the following address to Congress, which by joint resolution formally declared war against the Imperial Government of Japan that same day at 4:10 P.M. EST.

Yesterday, December 7, 1941—a date which will live in infamy—the United States of America was suddenly and deliberately attacked by naval and air forces of the Empire of Japan.

The United States was at peace with that nation and, at the solicitation of Japan, was still in conversation with its Government and its Emperor looking toward the maintenance of peace in the Pacific. Indeed, one hour after Japanese air squadrons had commenced bombing in Oahu, the Japanese Ambassador to the United States and his colleague delivered to the Secretary of State a form reply to a recent American message. While this reply stated that it seemed useless to continue the existing diplomatic negotiations, it contained no threat or hint of war or armed attack.

It will be recorded that the distance of Hawaii from Japan makes it obvious that the attack was deliberately planned many days or even weeks ago. During the intervening time the Japanese Government has deliberately sought to deceive the United States by false statements and expressions of hope for continued peace.

The attack yesterday on the Hawaiian Islands has caused severe damage to American naval and military forces. Very many American lives have been lost. In addition American ships have been reported torpedoed on the high seas between San Francisco and Honolulu.

Yesterday the Japanese Government also launched an attack

Western Union received it in San Francisco 15 minutes later and gave it to RCA for radio transmission. RCA-Honolulu stamped the message "In" at 1:03 P.M. (7:33 A.M., their time).

---

against Malaya. Last night Japanese forces attacked Hong Kong. Last night Japanese forces attacked Guam. Last night Japanese forces attacked the Philippine Islands. Last night the Japanese attacked Wake Island. This morning the Japanese attacked Midway Island.

Japan has, therefore, undertaken a surprise offensive extending throughout the Pacific area. The facts of yesterday speak for themselves. The people of the United States have already formed their opinions and well understand the implications to the very life and safety of our nation.

As Commander-in-Chief of the Army and Navy I have directed that all measures be taken for our defense.

Always will we remember the character of the onslaught against us.

No matter how long it may take us to overcome this premeditated invasion, the American people in their righteous might will win through to absolute victory.

I believe I interpret the will of the Congress and of the people when I assert that we will not only defend ourselves to the uttermost but will make very certain that this form of treachery shall never endanger us again.

Hostilities exist. There is no blinking at the fact that our people, our territory, and our interests are in grave danger.

With confidence in our armed forces—with the unbounded determination of our people—we will gain the inevitable triumph—so help us God.

I ask that the Congress declare that since the unprovoked and dastardly attack by Japan on Sunday, December seventh, a state of war has existed between the United States and the Japanese Empire.

Presidential Address to Congress, December 8, 1941.

There was no teletype connection with Fort Shafter, headquarters of Lieutenant General Walter C. Short, the commanding general in Hawaii, so RCA handed the Washington message to one of its motorcycle messengers for delivery.

In an exploit that should surely compete for fame with the "Message to Garcia" of an earlier decade, [where Lieutenant Andrew Summers Rowan, without questioning his task, overcame obstacles to deliver President McKinley's message to General Garcia during the Spanish-American War], RCA's swift courier was interrupted on his rounds by the first wave of Japanese bombs and strafing fire to rake Pearl Harbor that morning.

General Marshall and Admiral Stark, feeling they had done all they could in view of the remaining uncertainties of the emergency, reported their action to Secretary Knox at his office in the Navy Department. He advised them, in turn, that he had learned from Secretary Hull only a moment before that the Japanese Ambassadors, Nomura and Kurusu, had telephoned the State Department at noon asking for an appointment with the Secretary for the fateful hour of one o'clock.

An Unsuspecting Military Base

Noon in Washington was 6:30 in Honolulu, the hour of sunrise. Sunday, December 7, for the few who were abroad at that hour, promised to be an uncommonly lovely day. The sky was a brilliant blue. Here and there a fleecy bit of cloud drifted in the gentle trade wind. The verdant slopes of Mount Tantalus and Mount Olympus glistened with dew.

At their berths in Pearl Harbor, tied up two-by-two, lay 94 combat and auxiliary ships of the Pacific Fleet, including 8 battleships, 29 destroyers, and 5 submarines.

Many of their crews were on weekend shore leave, for the Navy was operating under the relaxed strictures of a peacetime "Condition 3." None of the main batteries was manned. The plotting rooms were shut down, ammunition for the few machine and antiaircraft guns, which had skeleton crews that morning, was stored in locked compartments for which only the deck officers had the keys.

At Wheeler, Hickam, and Ewa Airfields the 192 usable combat planes of the Army and Marine Air arms were tied down wing-to-wing in precise, tidy rows on the aprons. Air reconnaissance at dawn was confined to three Navy Catalinas covering a narrow sector extending only 200 miles northwesterly. The Army's primitive radar equipment was being used on a training basis only and none of its antiaircraft emplacements had ammunition on hand.

No premonitions troubled the waning slumbers of Pearl Harbor at sun-up on that Sunday in 1941. Such pertinent activity as there was at that hour was centered largely in only two widely separated spots.

At a remote radar station two Army privates trying to learn the intricacies of this new long-range detection gadget picked up a large and unexpected "blip" on their scope at 7:02 A.M. They calculated its bearing at almost due north and its distance at 132 miles. They tracked it in fascinated and growing apprehension for 18 minutes. At 7:20 they called the Information Center at Hickam Field on their field telephones to report their puzzling discovery. A passing flight lieutenant who happened to receive the call told the men, "Forget it." It probably was a flight of our own planes, he said.

Almost simultaneously, Navy Lieutenant Harold Kaminsky, watch officer at the Pearl Harbor Submarine Base, was handed the radio message from the destroyer *Ward* announcing her successful attack on the strange submarine. The *Ward* had filed her message at 6:54 A.M., but for some reason it did not get to Lieutenant Kaminsky's hands until 18 minutes later, at 7:12. This was the first intimation ashore of the submarine hunt that the *Condor* had initiated three hours earlier.

The Bombing

At that improbable hour, telephone switchboards on the base were manned by 10-thumbed yeomen. It was 7:20 before Lieutenant Kaminsky was able to get through to the staff duty officer, Commander Vincent R. Murphy, who had just risen and was shaving in his quarters. Excitedly, Commander Murphy gave Lieutenant Kaminsky a list of key officers to call and told him to order the ready destroyer, *Monaghan,* to pursue the search. He finished dressing and went to his office on the double.

When he got there he found that Lieutenant Kaminsky had been unable to get a call through to the base commander, Admiral Husband E. Kimmel. Commander Murphy took over the switchboard himself. As the admiral uttered a sleepy "Hello," there was a shattering blast as the first Japanese bomb exploded on the seaplane ramp 200 yards away. It was 7:55 and the "Day of Infamy" had begun.

Now there was bedlam outside: the deep-throated whine of planes roaring past at tree-top level, the irregular thunder of bursting bombs and torpedoes, the chatter of strafing machine guns. One could glimpse the scarlet "meatball" insignia, [the Japanese red ball], on the wing-tips as the planes whipped past.

Commander Murphy ran down the hall to the communications room and dictated a top-priority radio message to the Commander in Chief of the Asiatic Fleet and to the Chief of Naval Operations in Washington:

JAPANESE ATTACKING PEARL HARBOR—THIS IS NO DRILL.

Surprise and Anger in Washington, D.C.

Washington at that moment was as calm and untroubled, outside the tight little periphery of the White House, as Honolulu had been two or three minutes earlier. Here, too, it was a clear, bright day with a touch of winter crispness in the air.

Readers of the *Washington Post* were apprised over their morning coffee that the Japanese were ominously massing their forces in the Far East, that King Leopold III of the Belgians had been married, that Soviet Ambassador Maxim Litvinov was due to arrive at National Airport at 9:40 A.M. The society columns noted that Mrs. Evalyn Walsh Maclean would entertain at Friendship that evening for her daughter and new son-in-law, Senator Robert R. Reynolds of North Carolina. And sports fans were notified that the kickoff in the Redskins-Philadelphia Eagles game was set for 2:00 P.M. at Griffith Stadium.

As one o'clock approached, Secretary Hull was sitting in his office with Green Hackworth and Joseph W. Ballantine, two of his closest aides, discussing just what he should say to the two Japanese emissaries when they arrived. They were interrupted by a telephone call from Admiral Nomura asking that the appointment be postponed 45 minutes because of difficulties they were having in decoding their instructions from Tokyo. This was agreed to.

Across the street at the White House, President Roosevelt and Harry Hopkins were lunching together in the Oval Room, discussing, as Mr. Hopkins recalled later, "things far removed from war." At the Navy Department, a few blocks away on Constitution Avenue, Secretary Knox and Admiral Stark were together in the latter's office discussing things not far removed from war.

At 1:50 a communications officer burst unceremoniously into the room and thrust into Admiral Stark's hand Commander Murphy's startling message from Hawaii: "Japanese attacking Pearl Harbor—this is no drill."

Secretary Knox exclaimed: "My God, this can't be true! They must mean the Philippines."

A moment's reflection convinced him that so wide an error was highly improbable. He hurried to his own office, picked up his White House telephone and read the message to the President. With shock and anger in his voice, President Roosevelt, too, conceded the probable accuracy of the message; he asked the Navy to rush whatever confirmation it could.

That was just the unexpected kind of thing the Japanese were capable of doing, he said turning to Harry Hopkins; at the very moment they were discussing peace in the Pacific they were plotting to undermine it. Mr. Roosevelt dialed the code number for the State Department on his private phone.

Mr. Hull had just been informed of the arrival of Ambassadors Nomura and Kurusu in the diplomatic waiting room outside his office when the call from the President came through at 2:05. After the first stunning impact of the news, Mr. Hull recalled later, he thought he would dismiss the Japanese envoys without a hearing. On second thought, he decided to see them on the remote possibility that the report was inaccurate.

His famed Tennessee anger was at white heat but under rigid control when the two smiling, morning-coated Ambassadors bowed stiffly before his desk at 2:20 P.M. He greeted them coldly and did not ask them to be seated. He flipped perfunctorily through the first couple of pages of the document—the now-familiar 14-part message—that they handed him.

Then in a voice vibrant with restraint and indignation he said:

> In all my conversations with you during the last nine months, I have never uttered one word of untruth. This is borne out absolutely by the record.
>
> In all my 50 years of public service I have never seen a document that was more crowded with infamous falsehoods and distortions—infamous falsehoods and distortions on a scale so huge that I never imagined until today that any government on this planet was capable of uttering them.

Nomura sucked in his breath as if he were about to speak. With a peremptory gesture of his hand, Mr. Hull waved him and Ambassador Kurusu out of his offices.

The Aftermath

By the time this tableau was completed a few minutes before 2:30 Washington time, Pearl Harbor was already a shambles. The first phase of the attack, which had swept in at 7:55 and lasted for about 30 minutes, had wrought 90 percent of all the damage and casualties to be inflicted that day.

Twice the attackers withdrew briefly to regroup and then roared back over the flaming, panic-stricken target.

At 9:45, just two hours after the first bomb had been dropped, it was all over. Seaman Kuramoto's Eagles winged back to their nest, 29 short of their original number.

Behind them they left a scene of chaos unmatched on American soil in all history. Dense columns of black smoke boiled high into the sunlit sky. Flames from oil and gasoline tanks shot into the air, spread out over the waters, turned buildings and trees and human bodies to cinders.

Of the eight battleships in the harbor that morning—the backbone of the Pacific Fleet—four were sunk or capsized. The remaining four, as well as three destroyers, three cruisers, and four auxiliary vessels, were heavily damaged and burning.

One hundred and eighty-eight planes were destroyed on the ground, and most of the hangars and repair facilities demolished.

Human casualties were 2,403 dead and 1,178 wounded.

Seldom in all the annals of warfare had one force won so complete and devastating a victory over another in so short a time.

Smoke engulfs the sinking USS Arizona *(foreground). The attack on Pearl Harbor pushed the United States into World War II.*

The aftermath of terror did not begin to lift from the island of Oahu for another 24 hours. Governor Joseph B. Poindexter instituted a state of emergency almost as the last Japanese planes disappeared to the north. The Red Cross set up emergency medical and feeding facilities before noon. Civil defense forces were mobilized, and families living on the base were evacuated to homes, schools, and churches in outlying districts.

Rumors of new attacks, of paratroop landings, of wholesale sabotage by Japanese residents of the island spread panic in ever-recurring waves through the civilian population. The Japanese consulate in Honolulu was raided while its members were in the act of burning their papers.

On orders from President Roosevelt martial law was declared throughout the Territory of Hawaii at 4:30 that afternoon.

The American Reaction

The American public got its first news of the disaster while the attack was still in progress. A good part of that public, at least in Washington, had its mind on anything but war that inviting Sunday afternoon. It was a day to load up the family automobile for a jaunt into the country, to get in what might be the last round of golf before winter set in, or to see the Redskins play their last home game of the season, which is what 27,102 persons did.

At 2:35 P.M. Louise Hachmeister, White House switchboard superintendent, rang up the three press associations and put them on a simultaneous conference hook-up with Steve Early, the President's press secretary.

"All on?" she asked. "AP? UP? INS? Here's Mr. Early."

"This is Steve Early at the White House," came a familiar but strained voice over the wire. "At 7:55 A.M., Hawaiian time, the Japanese bombed Pearl Harbor. The attacks are continuing and . . . no, I don't know how many are dead."

"Flash" bells on news tickers all the way across the country began to jangle. Radio programs were interrupted by excited announcers who blurted out the first bulletins.

Throughout Washington telephone facilities were swamped by the curious and the alarmed and by harassed government and military officials trying to round up their staffs.

The loudspeaker at Griffith Stadium called off the names of one admiral, general, and Cabinet officer after another, instructing them: "Please get in touch with your office at once."

Within an hour a crowd of several thousand had congregated silently on the sidewalks in front of the White House. Another thousand, strangely unbelligerent, tied up traffic in front of the Japanese Embassy on Massachusetts Avenue. As they watched, two carloads of FBI men dashed up to establish a guard over the premises—a service which the Japanese had thoughtfully already provided for themselves through the Burns Detective Agency.

The Cabinet "Big Three"—the Secretaries of State, War, and Navy—were summoned to the White House at three o'clock, after which there ensued a string of emergency orders designed to protect the internal security of the country. The FBI was ordered to pick up all Japanese aliens. The Army and Navy were ordered to throw armed guards around all military installations and government buildings. The Treasury impounded $131 million of Japanese assets in this country. The Navy clamped censorship on all outgoing cables. Private planes were grounded and radio amateurs were silenced.

At 8:30 President Roosevelt met with his full Cabinet for nearly an hour.

At 9:30 he summoned the legislative leaders from both parties, making one ostentatious omission—Representative Hamilton Fish, the New York Republican, who had been the loudest in his cries of "warmonger." The President told them he would want to address a joint session of Congress the next day.

At 11:30 P.M. the Oval Room was cleared. The President said he would take no more calls nor see any other visitors. With Harry Hopkins pacing moodily behind his chair and Grace Tully sitting across the desk with open notebook and with poised pencil, he began to dictate the simple message he would deliver to Congress at 12:30 P.M. on Monday:

Yesterday, December 7, 1941—a date which will live in infamy—the United States of America was suddenly and deliberately attacked by naval and air forces of the Empire of Japan. . . .

CHAPTER 2

World War II

AMERICA'S DECADES

World War II: An Overview

John Patrick Diggins

In the following excerpt from his book *The Proud Decades: America in War and in Peace 1941–1960*, John Patrick Diggins, a distinguished professor of history at the City University of New York, summarizes the Allied offensive against Germany, Italy, and Japan during World War II. Seeing Nazi aggression in Europe as the greater threat, Diggins writes, the Allies eliminated U-boat control of the Atlantic, drove through North Africa and Italy, bombed major cities in Germany, and ultimately conducted an amphibious assault of Normandy to liberate France. According to Diggins, Americans did not realize the true horrors of the Holocaust until Allied forces began to advance through Europe liberating the concentration camps. The war against Japan, Diggins explains, began as one catastrophe after another from the bombing of Pearl Harbor to the loss of the Philippines. Japan vigorously defended the Pacific, Diggins notes, and many American soldiers lost their lives. Not wanting to risk further loss of life, President Harry S. Truman authorized dropping the atomic bomb on Hiroshima and Nagasaki.

T he shock of Pearl Harbor created an impression that Japan and Germany had been united in their military objectives. Actually Hitler wanted Japan to attack Russia

Excerpted from *The Proud Decades: America in War and in Peace, 1941–1960*, by John Patrick Diggins. Copyright ©1988 by John Patrick Diggins. Reprinted by permission of W.W. Norton & Company, Inc.

and leave America alone. Now the outcome of the Second World War depended upon two factors without which an Allied victory would not have been possible: America's entrance and Russia's resistance.

A bleak situation faced the Allies in the spring of 1942. Although Germany was now fighting a war on two fronts, having failed to win Britain's surrender before turning on Russia, Nazism was triumphant in Western Europe, from Scandinavia to the Mediterranean. Germany had access to Mideastern petroleum and Swedish iron ore on which her war effort depended. The Fascist powers of Germany, Italy, and Japan had been preparing for war since the 1930s and their armies had already had valuable combat experience in Spain and Ethiopia. Germany and Japan could also draw upon millions of conquered people in Eastern Europe and in Asia for forced labor. Both countries, moreover, could boast of their far-reaching striking power. Within months after Pearl Harbor German submarine "wolf packs" were sinking scores of American merchant ships off the coast of Florida, New York, and Cape Cod. The torpedoing of freighters and tankers continued in the Atlantic and Caribbean for nearly two years, until the United States developed a convoy escort system to feed the vital lifeline to Britain.

Allied Advantages

The Allies—Britain and her dominions, Russia, the United States, and China—had certain advantages that in the end proved decisive. The Allies had clear numerical superiority, a unified military command structure in Western Europe directed by General Dwight D. Eisenhower, almost unlimited natural resources and industrial capacity in America and Canada immune to bombardment, and the inspirational leadership of President Roosevelt and Winston Churchill, England's indomitable prime minister, who made clear his determination to fight the war until Nazism was wiped from the face of the earth. The Allies also enjoyed a distinct psychological advantage. In Western Europe and Asia they would arrive as liberators rather than as conquerors. In contrast to the Germans and Italians, who made enemies with every conquest and had to contend with an antifascist underground, and to the Japanese, whose imperialism proved even more brutal than western colonialism, the Allies did not have to face the hatred of the European, Chinese, and Indonesian people; nor did they have to worry about uprisings and sabotage raids. In several instances the Office of Strategic Services (OSS) worked with the French and Italian resistance in preparation for paratroop landings. Except for France's unreliable Vichy government, set up by Germany, and the equally undependable Italian dictator Benito Mussolini, Hitler had no one to work with. After July 1944, when Hitler barely escaped an assassination attempt, he could not even trust his own generals.

Even though America had been brought into the war by the attack on Hawaii, Roosevelt agreed with Churchill that the Axis strength in the European theater of war warranted greater urgency than the Pacific. The first great struggle was to secure the North Atlantic. America had not only to continue lend-lease shipments to England but also find a way to get supplies to a Russia now cut off from the West and in desperate need of food and munitions. There was no alternative. American ships headed into the North Sea, infested with German submarines, and along the Norwegian coast, where German destroyers and cruisers awaited them in the fjords. So great were the casualties—on one voyage, twenty-two out of thirty-three merchant ships were sunk—that sailing to Russia became known as "the suicide run to Murmansk." And German subs continued to bring down ships throughout the Atlantic from Iceland to the Bay of Biscay. For two years the war hung in balance. Until the German wolf-pack menace was overcome, America could not ship to England the men and materials needed to stage an invasion of occupied Europe. As Germany launched more and better equipped subs, England and America quadrupled the production of ships and planes designed to deal with them, as well as electronic equipment necessary to intercept German communications. Finally huge convoys with as many as one hundred freighters and tankers were organized and escorted by destroyers, Coast Guard cutters, slow-flying bombers, and blimps armed with sonar and depth-charges. By the end of 1943 the war against the U-boat had been won due to superior Allied productive capacity and coordination of sea and air power.

Problems in the Pacific

But in the Pacific events proceeded like one continuous catastrophe. Shortly after Pearl Harbor the Japanese landed on Wake Island and Guam and secured control of communications across the central Pacific. Having captured the Malay Peninsula and driven the British out of Singapore and Hong Kong, Japan launched an amphibious assault on the Philippines. After a valiant defense of the nearby island of Corregidor, President Roosevelt ordered General Douglas MacArthur to evacuate. He left behind 12,500 American and 60,000 Filipino troops who had no choice but to surrender. The press reported the infamous "death march" from Bataan to the prison camps in which thousands of Americans, Australians, and Filipinos lost their lives from wounds and disease. Japan had also taken Sumatra and Java and their vital oil deposits and rubber plantations; with the capture of Rangoon, Japan controlled the Burma Road and had China isolated. The colonial territories of the French, English, Dutch, and Americans had all fallen to Japan and her new empire, "The Rising Sun."

The strategy of the American navy, under Admiral Chester W. Nimitz, was to play a waiting game until new ships and more troops arrived. Meanwhile, American carriers conducted nuisance sorties over Wake, the Marshalls, and other Japanese-held islands; and General James H. Doolittle led an air attack over Tokyo that did little damage but much to lift American morale. Japan had no intention of engaging in a land war with the United States. But Admiral Isoroku Yamamoto wanted to engage the American navy in full battle, assuming that a few more disastrous defeats like Pearl Harbor would persuade Americans and their government to withdraw from the South Pacific, leaving Japan to her conquests. In the summer of 1942 a reinforced American navy fought off Japanese battleships at Midway and the Coral Sea and turned back attempted landing invasions on New Guinea and on several tiny atolls in the mid-Pacific. At the battle of Midway America lost the carrier *Yorktown;* Japan lost four carriers and their air squadrons. The tide had turned.

Naval combat in the Pacific was unique in the history of warfare. The battle of Coral Sea was fought entirely by carrier-launched aircraft, with neither American nor Japanese ships coming within sight of one another. Even more unique was the war carried on beneath the oceans by submarine. Two percent of America's naval personnel accounted for 55 percent of Japanese losses at sea, including numerous merchant ships as well as carriers and cruisers. But the price was high: 22 percent of American submariners lost their lives, the highest casualty rate amongst any branch of the armed services.

The battle of Leyte Gulf, fought off the Philippines in the fall of 1944 in preparation for an invasion of the Japanese-occupied mainland, was decisive. Recognizing the strategic importance of the Philippines as a stepping-stone for America's advance into Asia, the Japanese planned an attack on small-armed naval vessels guarding troopships and landing craft. Admirals Thomas C. Kinkaid and William F. "Bull" Halsey directed their fast-carrier task forces in a bloody three-day naval campaign in which the Japanese lost three battleships, four carriers, six cruisers, and more than a dozen destroyers. Off the Philippine coast seven hundred Allied troops and cargo ships stretched to the horizon awaiting the invasion. Leyte Gulf was the greatest naval engagement in world history and the final fleet battle of World War II.

In Europe an unprecedented development in modern military theory was taking place: the doctrine of strategic air offensive, which was designed to level cities as well as factories in order to weaken the morale of the civilian populations. Beginning in 1943 the American and Royal Air Forces conducted a sustained bombardment of the industrial Ruhr Valley and seaports like Hamburg and Bremen. Later, when the war was drawing to a close, the city of Dresden was targeted with incendiary bombs that killed more than 100,000 civilians. Since Hitler had deployed a similar air-bombing strategy to attack the people of London, and since the bombing of German industrial targets seemed to relieve pressure on Russia, this massive saturation bombing had popular support. But after the war, a United States Air Force study revealed that the obliteration bombing offensive, which cost the lives of 160,000 American and British airmen, had not substantially hindered German war production.

Bombing itself would not bring victory. The Allies realized that Hitler would not surrender unconditionally unless the German army, the Wehrmacht, was defeated, and this required a colossal invasion of the continent. In 1942 the American command had planned a cross-channel operation to secure a beachhead in France in preparation for a full invasion the following year. The British wanted to wait until the Allies had overwhelming ground and air forces. Churchill, aware of the sacrifices Russia was making, opposed a cross-channel invasion but favored a lesser operation that would divert enough German troops from the Russian front so that the Red Army would not have to bear the brunt of the war. The Americans and British compromised on Operation Torch, and in fall 1942 the Allies landed in North Africa. There American and British tank commanders, Generals George S. Patton Sr., and Sir Harold Alexander and Field Marshall Sir Bernard L. Montgomery, drove through mountain and desert in pursuit of the brilliant Field Marshall Erwin Rommel (the "desert fox") and his powerful Panzer divisions. With Rommel's Afrika Korps defeated, the Allies then staged an invasion of Sicily and Italy.

The campaigns in North Africa and Italy destroyed the

myth of Germany's invincibility, and with Russia's great victory at the battle of Stalingrad in spring 1943, Nazism was in retreat everywhere. Nevertheless, German soldiers fought tenaciously as they pulled back; Hitler would hardly contemplate surrender; Rommel, who had relinquished his command in North Africa, was back in Berlin regrouping his forces; and German industry was increasing not only its production of tanks, subs, and aircraft but also beginning to develop rockets, jet-propelled fighter planes, and possibly an atomic bomb. It became clearer than ever that the Continent needed to be invaded. Germany must be attacked, her army destroyed, and Berlin captured.

The Invasion of Normandy

Operation Overlord, the June 6, 1944, invasion of Normandy, was the greatest amphibious assault recorded in history. Allied forces assembled in England consisted of French, Polish, Belgian, Norwegian, and Czech troops, as well as American, British, and Canadian. Almost three million men waited to cross the English Channel, supported by millions of tons of equipment and thousands of airplanes and naval vessels ranging from battleships and cruisers to troop transports and landing barges. Although the Allied air forces had been knocking out bridges and roads in northern France weeks before the invasion, the Normandy coast remained well fortified with German artillery emplacements, underwater and land mines, pillboxes and concrete blockhouses connected by underground tunnels, and fields of wire entanglement. Some German officers thought the landing would be at Calais because of its docking facilities and closer distance to Paris. But that seaport had been made virtually impregnable. Eisenhower and his advisors, deciding that docks and oil pipelines could be constructed after the invasion, chose the Normandy coastline.

Under cover of naval gunfire and air bombardment, six American, British, and Canadian divisions landed on the beaches. The first wave of troops had to disembark from their boats in water up to their waists and sometimes deeper, then crawl through minefields while gunfire poured down from the bluffs above. "D-Day" had its share of disaster. Some parachute drops behind the lines missed their targets, several landing craft capsized in the surf, and a crack American Ranger squadron suffered heavy casualties as it worked its way up the face of cliffs to capture German strongholds. But on the whole, the invasion went well. After eight hours of fierce fighting the cliffs had been overtaken. Soon roads were cleared and tanks and heavy artillery were moving inland to support advanced troops. The outnumbered Germans fought bravely, but one by one small towns were captured in the battles of Saint-Lô, Caen, and Cherbourg. Within weeks Allied armament divisions were moving rapidly through France toward Paris. The liberation was coming! As American soldiers advanced with the Eiffel Tower in sight, Parisians rose up against the hated Nazis. On August 25, 1944, Paris was freed and General Charles de Gaulle triumphantly entered the city. Then GIs in tanks, trucks, and jeeps poured into Paris, welcomed with tears of joy, hugs, tiny American flags, flowers, wine, and cognac.

Until Allied troops entered Germany, few Americans thought of the war as an ideological struggle against the forces of fascism. Most soldiers wanted to come home as soon as possible, and to do so they knew they must kill or capture the enemy until he laid down his arms. With such sentiments members of the twenty-eighth Infantry and 101st Airborne divisions held their position valiantly in the winter of 1944-45, finally turning back a last desperate German counter offensive in the famous Battle of the Bulge, which sealed Hitler's fate.

The Horrors of the Holocaust

Then came the horror. Not until American troops crossed the Rhine and began liberating concentration camps did they understand the meaning of the dreaded Gestapo, the "final solution," the Waffen-SS and the SS-Totenkopfver-bande (Death's Head Units). With the gates of Auschwitz and Dachau opened to the eyes of the world, western civilization recoiled in anguish. So monstrous was the sight of charred skeletons in the ovens and living corpses with shaved heads staring from the barracks that some soldiers shot SS officers on the spot. The world had always known "sin," the author and political scientist Hannah Arendt would write of the camps, but "radical evil" on this ghastly scale was so new that one no longer knew how to punish or forgive. "Just as the victims in the death factories or the holes of oblivion are no longer 'human' in the eyes of their executioners, so this newest species of criminals is beyond the pale even of solidarity in human sinfulness."

In the camps in Germany, Poland, and Hungary, six million Jews lost their lives along with three million Russians, Poles, Slavs, and Gypsies. While this mass execution was taking place, Catholic and Protestant organizations in the Western world remained almost indifferent. Not until 214 Polish priests were executed did the Vatican issue a formal protest, without any effect on the Catholic hierarchy in Germany. As to America, a 1944 November Gallup poll indicated that 76 percent of the public believed that the Germans have murdered many people in the concentration camps. Only a few Americans who read a liberal or radical journal or several Jewish publications knew it was worse than murder: the mass extermination of men, women, and children who died by gassing after being ordered into rooms disguised as shower baths. The media—the popular press, radio, and newsreels—gave the story little coverage. The influential *New York Times* relegated it to the back pages, and other papers reported the deaths as due to war-time deprivations instead of anti-Semitic insanity.

A Moral Failure?

Several relief agencies, including the "Emergency Committee to Save the Jewish People of Europe" organized in the spring of 1944, made every effort to publicize the exterminations and to persuade the United States government to undertake rescue missions. Several proposals were put forth: a request that the United Nations threaten retribution to those guilty of genocide; to call upon neutral European countries to temporarily accept refugees and guarantee that food, medicine, and clothing would be sent; to ask England to revise its 1939 policy restricting Jewish immigration to Palestine; and to have the United States open its doors to Jewish war refugees and other displaced persons. Later, as the war drew to an end and the exterminations continued with diabolical efficiency, it was suggested that the Allied air forces bomb the railroads leading to the camps. Few of these proposals became policy, and the Allies continued to bomb Dresden, not Dachau.

The Holocaust torments the conscience of those willing to remember the horrors of the past in order not to see them repeated. Before the war 94 percent of the American people denounced the *Kristallnacht,* the "Night of Broken Glass" (November 9, 1938), when German storm troopers smashed the windows of Jewish shopkeepers, looted their homes, and terrorized their neighborhoods. Yet more than 60 percent of Americans desired to keep Jewish refugees, even displaced children, out of the United States, and this sentiment remained unchanged during the war. In 1942, when news filtered out of Poland about the plight of Jews, a United Nations conference convened at Bermuda to take up the refugee problem. But the White House, State Department, and Congress all feared an inundation of permanent Jewish settlers, as did some members of the Jewish community who were wary that such a massive influx could increase anti-Semitic feelings. Eleanor Roosevelt prevailed on the State Department to allow five thousand Jewish children to enter the United States, an effort eviscerated by bureaucratic red tape and deliberate stalling on the part of anti-Semitic civil servants. Roosevelt himself was at first kept insulated from the problem by advisors concerned about the political implications of the refugee issue. Finally, Treasury Secretary Henry Morgenthau, Jr., got through to the president and with the War Refugee Board, established in 1944, the United States helped save 200,000 Jews in Europe and gave sanctuary to another 100,000 who had managed to escape the death camps. Much more could have been done, as demonstrated by the heroic accomplishments of a single individual in Hungary, the Swedish diplomat Raoul Wallenberg, who risked his life rescuing thousands of Jews. That more was not done must be regarded as the great moral failure in modern history.

Roosevelt and most of the American people believed that the best way to aid European Jews was to defeat Nazi Germany as quickly as possible. In spring 1945 Germany was caught in a gigantic pincer, with a Russian offensive blitzing through Poland and Allied divisions racing across the Rhine and into the Ruhr Valley. By April the German resistance had collapsed and Italian partisans had captured and hanged dictator Benito Mussolini. On May 1 Hitler committed suicide and six days later Germany signed an unconditional surrender.

Truman's Difficult Decisions

But the good news from the western front did little to ease the grief that Americans had felt three weeks earlier. On April 12, 1945, Roosevelt died, and when the world learned the electrifying news, people everywhere mourned. To many Americans Roosevelt's passing was like a death in the family. The most inspiring figure of the depression and war years, a symbol of hope and freedom to millions, he was suddenly gone. No one knew what to expect from the new man in the White House who had been overshadowed in FDR's illustrious presence. "Is there anything I can do for you?" Vice-President Harry S. Truman asked Eleanor Roosevelt when he heard the news. "Is there anything *we* can do for *you?*" she replied. "You are the one in trouble now."

Two vexing decisions faced Truman: how to deal with the Soviet Union, truculent now in regards to postwar Eastern Europe, and how to defeat Japan. The second issue involved some unexpected developments that had tragic consequences. In the Pacific, American strategy originally aimed to advance upon Japan through Burma and with the support of China and her teeming population. But as an ally China turned out to be weaker than expected and her leader, Chiang Kai-shek (Jiang Jieshi), seemed more interested in propping up his corrupt regime than in fighting the Japanese. Thus, shortly before his death, Roosevelt accepted General MacArthur's advice to retake the Philippines as a springboard for an assault on the Japanese mainland. MacArthur returned to the Philippines as he had earlier vowed, and after ferocious battles featuring kamikaze planes, the strategic islands of Iwo Jima and Okinawa fell to the United States Navy and marines between March and June 1945. American forces had been staging light attacks on the Japanese homeland from the islands of Guam and Saipan. But the character of the attacks now changed. Assuming that Japan could be bombed into submission, military strategists ordered raids on crowded cities using incendiary and napalm bombs. The destruction was horrifying. Large parts of Kobe and Tokyo and other industrial cities were devastated by fire storms. Eight million wooden homes were destroyed and more than 300,000 people killed. Japan was in flames, yet she still refused to surrender.

The Atom Bomb

While the air force had been furiously bombing Japan, scientists at Los Alamos, New Mexico, were completing the Manhattan Project—the testing of the first atomic bomb, which was made possible by the recent discovery of fissionable plutonium and uranium-235. On July 16, 1945, the bomb was exploded at Alamogordo, New Mexico; a quiet white flash followed by the roar of a shaking desert, and then a mushroom cloud soaring seven miles high. A week later at the Potsdam Conference, Japan was presented an ultimatum: surrender or suffer "prompt and utter destruction." Although the Japanese emperor may have wanted to capitulate, as did most Japanese, some military officers thought surrender dishonorable, and government officials ignored the Potsdam ultimatum while making peace overtures to Switzerland and Russia. At the orders of President

Truman, on August 6, a single B-29 dropped an atomic bomb on Hiroshima, and three days later a second bomb fell on Nagasaki. The crew on the Hiroshima raid felt the painful flash of light and the shock wave of air turbulence, and then they saw a towering mushroom of fire and smoke that rose 10,000 feet per minute. No one wanted to imagine the inferno below. Most of the city vanished and close to 100,000 people died instantly.

Truman's decision to use the atomic bomb has been the subject of intense and endless controversy. Truman himself, noting that Japan called for a cease-fire a week after Hiroshima (an official surrender was signed in September), defended his decision on the grounds that it saved the lives of half a million American soldiers who would have been killed in the invasion of the mainland. Every GI in the Pacific was relieved to hear about the bomb, now knowing the war would end and that they had survived it. Because of the heavy resistance with which Japan defended Iwo Jima, Okinawa, and Tarawa, battles in which some 50,000 American soldiers died, it seems likely that an invasion would have meant a prolonged and bloody war in which the Japanese and Americans would have suffered far more casualties than the lives lost at Hiroshima. The kamikaze attacks had impressed upon Americans an image of Japanese soldiers as death-defying fanatics; it could not be ignored that less than five percent of Japanese fighting men had ever surrendered in any one battle. Military experts estimated that an invasion of Japan would be more risky and dangerous than the Normandy landing. . . .

But the victorious ending of the Second World War resulted more in joyous celebration than somber reflection. On V-J Day, August 14, 1945, America turned into a saturnalia. In cities across the nation traffic came to a halt as people danced in the streets. Strangers toasted one another and, to the delightful roar of crowds, sailors grabbed and kissed passing and willing young women. Americans had good reason to rejoice. In the years since Pearl Harbor the United States had overcome the greatest crisis facing the country since the Civil War. A war that most Americans originally did not want to fight turned into one of the proudest triumphs in the history of the Republic. Yet the war had no happy ending. With the forces of fascism defeated, Americans began to read and hear about "communism," and the Soviet Union, recently regarded as an old ally, emerged as a new enemy. Once again Americans felt, as they had in 1919, that they had won the war but lost the peace. This time the feeling was worse, for there could be no postwar retreat into isolationism. In 1945, America achieved victory but not security. What had eluded the country at the end of the war was precisely what FDR had promised at its beginning—"freedom from fear."

The Policy of Unconditional Surrender

Robert James Maddox

President Franklin D. Roosevelt's commitment to the unconditional surrender of Germany, Japan, and Italy was one of the most controversial policies of World War II, writes Penn State University historian Robert James Maddox in this excerpt from his book *Weapons for Victory: The Hiroshima Decision Fifty Years Later*. To Roosevelt, unconditional surrender meant the elimination of governments whose political philosophies were based on conquest and subjugation, Maddox explains. While Roosevelt believed the policy of unconditional surrender gave the Allies a unified purpose and avoided the threat of a separate peace between Germany and the Soviet Union, Maddox reveals that critics argued that Japanese and German propagandists would use the policy to bolster resistance against the Allies. "Retentionists" argued that the policy should not be applied to the Japanese government because the Japanese had cultural and religious ties to their emperor, and rearmament was unlikely because their humiliating defeat would discredit the militarists. Proponents of the abolition of the Japanese government argued that the only way to assure a lasting peace was to insist on unconditional surrender and the abolition of all militarism.

Excerpted from *Weapons for Victory: The Hiroshima Decision Fifty Years Later*, by Robert James Maddox. Copyright ©1995 by the Curators of the University of Missouri. Reprinted by permission of the University of Missouri Press.

President Franklin D. Roosevelt and British Prime Minister Winston S. Churchill met at Casablanca, French Morocco, in January 1943. They and their staffs discussed matters such as the administration of North Africa and future operations against the Axis powers. The meeting concluded on January 24 with an outdoor press conference. In his opening remarks, Roosevelt stated, "The elimination of German, Japanese and Italian war power means the unconditional surrender by Germany, Italy, and Japan." This did not imply the "destruction" of the populations of these nations, he continued, but rather of the "philosophies . . . based on conquest and the subjugation of other people." He went on to say that the conference should be called "the 'Unconditional Surrender' meeting," to which Churchill at his side responded "Hear! Hear!" Thus was launched one of the most controversial policies of the war. . . .

A Controversial Policy

Critics have denounced unconditional surrender as a colossal error; one referred to it as "perhaps the biggest political mistake of the war." German and Japanese propagandists used it to promote the belief that the Allies meant to destroy their societies, some have pointed out, thereby bolstering the will to persevere. Failure to hold out prospects of a negotiated peace also undermined those Germans who otherwise would have been encouraged to overthrow Hitler. This, in turn, might have resulted in German capitulation before Soviet armies penetrated into the heart of Europe. The formula also weakened the position of Japanese peace advocates, who might have ended the Pacific conflict months earlier had assurances been given that their emperor could be retained.

Defenders of unconditional surrender emphasize how speculative such criticisms necessarily are. Propagandists in the Axis powers controlled the media, and unconditional surrender merely provided them with additional grist for their contention that national survival was at stake. Besides, through countless radio broadcasts and other means, the Allies repeatedly declared—as FDR had in his original announcement—that the formula did *not* mean social destruction and enslavement. Potential conspirators against Hitler and the Japanese moderates most certainly were aware of these promises.

Even more important, the armies of both nations held effective power and without their support no group could have entered negotiations for peace. Not only were the militarists' own hands stained by complicity in bringing on the war and in the commission of widespread atrocities, but also the terms they would have insisted on to salvage their own status would have been unacceptable. In short, there is no way of telling whether the doctrine prolonged the war in any way.

The Symbol of a Unified Purpose

The value of the unconditional surrender formula, advocates argue, far outweighed any drawbacks. It offered an uncomplicated, inspirational slogan for popular consumption. It served as a pledge to suspicious Soviet leaders that the United States and Great Britain would make no separate peace. Most important, it provided the lowest common denominator of war aims among the Allies, thereby preventing divisive disputes before victory was attained. "Frankly, I do not like the idea of [tripartite] conversations to define the term 'unconditional surrender,'" Roosevelt wrote on one occasion. "Whatever words we might agree on would probably have to be modified or changed the first time some nation wanted to surrender."

No doubt Roosevelt did value the phrase as a slogan, by which he often set great store. Throughout the war he considered American morale a delicate commodity and often made significant concessions to it. He had agreed to the invasion of North Africa against the advice of his top military advisers in part because he believed it was imperative for public opinion that the United States go on the offensive against Germany as quickly as possible. "It is of the highest importance," he told his advisers, "that U.S. ground troops be brought into action against the enemy in 1942."

The "Darlan Deal"

Events surrounding the North African landings in November of that year provided additional reasons for promulgating the doctrine. French officials and troops in Morocco, Tunisia, and Algeria were at least nominally loyal to the so-called Vichy government, a quasi-fascist, collaborationist regime established after German victory in 1940. Resistance by some 120,000 French soldiers in North Africa might imperil operations being carried out by mostly inexperienced invasion forces. To avoid this potential catastrophe, Allied commander Dwight D. Eisenhower negotiated an armistice with a high-level Vichy official, Admiral Jean Darlan, who happened to be in Algiers at the time. Eisenhower also had Darlan installed as commander in chief of French military forces and as head of the civil government in North Africa. What became known as the "Darlan Deal" aroused great furor in the United States because it struck many as a perversion of what the war was supposed to be about.

Roosevelt, intimidated by the public outcry, for several days refused to support what Eisenhower had done. Only strong protests by FDR's personal chief of staff, Admiral William D. Leahy; Army Chief of Staff George C. Marshall; and Secretary of War Henry L. Stimson prodded him into defending Eisenhower's actions. He tried to placate critics by announcing that negotiations for an armistice had been motivated by the understandable desire to save lives, and that military and civil arrangements were temporary expedients "justified by the stress of battle." Darlan's assassination in December and the subsequent inclusion of Free French leader General Charles De Gaulle in the North African government helped to defuse the situation, but doubts remained. Unconditional surrender served notice that there would be no more such questionable "deals" in the future.

The Darlan episode also had bearing on relations with the Soviet Union. Numerous reports had reached Washington and London of Soviet-German contacts in Sweden and elsewhere. If Joseph Stalin believed that the United States and Great Britain might be willing to strike a bargain with Germany, as they had with Darlan, would this not influence him to seek his own accommodation? Anglo-American failure to meet Soviet demands for a second front in Europe made this scenario more plausible. Roosevelt rashly had led Stalin to believe that such an operation would be mounted in 1942. The decision at Casablanca to postpone an invasion yet another year could only deepen the latter's suspicions that his allies were willing to see the Soviets and Germans tear each other apart while they waited to make advantageous settlements at little cost to themselves. Words were poor substitutes for action, but Roosevelt hoped to prevent a separate Nazi-Soviet peace by committing the United States and Great Britain to total victory.

FDR's devotion to the formula went well beyond such tactical considerations, important though they were. Noted for his vacillation on many issues, he rejected numerous subsequent requests to "clarify" the doctrine, thereby rendering it less ominous to the enemy in hopes of weakening resistance. Such requests, at various times, came from the British, the Combined Chiefs of Staff, the American Joint Chiefs of Staff, and the State, Navy, and War departments. Roosevelt occasionally wavered, but in the end spurned such pleas because he believed unconditional surrender was a prerequisite for achieving a lasting peace.

Refusing to Repeat the Mistakes of WWI

His familiarity with the concept had more recent application than General Grant's nickname. Toward the end of World War I, a heated debate had arisen in the press and in Congress over the terms that should be extended to Germany. "Unconditional surrender" became a popular phrase. Several Senate resolutions employed it as the only acceptable basis on which the war should end. War hero General John J. Pershing, commander of the Allied Expeditionary Force in France, supported it, as did Theodore Roosevelt. Franklin, in his capacity as Assistant Secretary of the Navy, could not speak to the issue openly but his conduct suggests that he was closer to his cousin's point of view than to President Woodrow Wilson's "Peace Without Victory." In a debate over disposition of the German navy, FDR as acting secretary urged the president to demand surrender rather than internment of the fleet, despite protests that the Germans would balk at such harsh treatment.

Roosevelt later became well aware of the use Adolf Hitler and others had made of the "stab in the back" thesis: that Germany had not lost the war militarily but had been betrayed by Jews and Marxists at home. He was determined that there be no repetition. When asked at a press conference in July 1944 whether unconditional surrender "still stands," he replied: "Yes. Practically all Germans deny the fact that they surrendered during the last war, but this time they are going to know it. And so are the Japs." Two weeks later he told reporters that the peace he envisioned would be "nothing like last time. That is out. That was a gift from God and General Ferdinand Foch."

Reluctant to be specific about the formula, FDR often relied on a story about General Ulysses S. Grant's conduct at Appomattox Courthouse at the end of the Civil War. There, he said, Grant refused to discuss Robert E. Lee's repeated appeals for conditions. Finally, only *after* Lee agreed to unconditional surrender, Grant showed himself generous in providing food to hungry soldiers and permitting officers to keep their horses for the spring planting. No one, apparently, informed Roosevelt that his version of history was fictitious. Grant had acquired his nickname years earlier during a campaign in the western theater. No exchange such as Roosevelt imagined ever took place between the two generals.

Roosevelt's Intentions Toward Germany

FDR wrote and spoke more often about his intentions toward the Germans than the Japanese. He regarded Germany as by far the greater threat, which is why he gave the European theater highest priority. As time went on, particularly after the successful Allied invasion of France in June 1944, it became obvious that Germany would be defeated long before Japan. Finally, treatment of Germany involved issues requiring agreement with the Soviet Union, which had not yet gone to war with Japan by the time of Roosevelt's death.

He was less benign toward the German people in private than his public allusions to Grant's generosity suggested. "We have got to be tough with Germany," he told Secretary of the Treasury Henry J. Morgenthau in August 1944, "and I mean the German people not just the Nazis. We either have to castrate the German people or you have got to treat them in such manner so they can't just go on reproducing people who want to continue the way they have in the past." A few weeks later he spoke in the same vein to Secretary of War Stimson. Too many Americans and British believed that "only a few Nazi leaders" were responsible for what had happened, he said, and that "is not based on fact. The German people as a whole must have it driven home to them that the whole nation had been engaged in an unlawful conspiracy." His subsequent flirtation with Morgenthau's drastic plan to convert Germany into an agrarian nation provides another example of his attitude.

Roosevelt's Intentions Toward Japan

There is little reason to suppose that he felt much differently about how Japan should be treated, as indicated by his "And so are the Japs" statement cited above. That would have been implausible considering Japanese atrocities in China during the 1930s and their attack on Pearl Harbor. In April 1943, when he learned that the Japanese had executed several American aviators captured after an air raid on Tokyo a year earlier, he wrote Secretary of State Cordell Hull that he was "deeply stirred and horrified," and approved a note to the Japanese government stating that the United States intended to punish those officials responsible for "such uncivilized and inhuman acts." As the Americans had been sentenced at public trials held in

Tokyo, it was obvious that approval had come from the highest levels of government. Reports of the Bataan Death March reached Washington a few months later. Roosevelt withheld announcement until early 1944, at which time he told newsmen he thought the affair "gives us a pretty good slant . . . on the mentality of the Japanese."

Roosevelt had provided no intimation of relenting on unconditional surrender for Japan by the time of his death on April 12,1945. Churchill had made such a suggestion at the Yalta Conference in February. Why not invite the Soviet Union to join the United States, Great Britain, and China in issuing a declaration calling upon Japan to surrender unconditionally? Confronted with such great-power unity, Churchill went on, the Japanese might ask "what mitigation of the full rigor of unconditional surrender would be extended to her if she accepted the ultimatum." He said it would be up to the United States to decide, but "there was no doubt that some mitigation would be worthwhile if it led to the saving of a year or a year and a half of a war in which so much blood and treasures would be poured out."

FDR was unenthusiastic. He said the matter might be discussed with Stalin, but doubted an ultimatum would have much effect on the Japanese "who still seemed to think that they might get a satisfactory compromise." He told Churchill he doubted that they would "wake up" until all their islands had "felt the full weight of air attack." Instead of suggesting a four-power declaration, Roosevelt negotiated an agreement with Stalin to join in the war against Japan after the defeat of Germany in return for concessions in Manchuria and elsewhere.

The Nature of Unconditional Surrender

Roosevelt reported on the Yalta meeting before a joint session of Congress on March 1, 1943. Agreements reached with Stalin and Churchill, already published in the conference communiqué, enabled him to be more specific than before as to what would be done with Germany: occupation, destruction of Nazism and militarism, punishment of war criminals, disarmament, and the extraction of reparations. Further along in his speech he indicated that something resembling such treatment awaited the Japanese, whose unconditional surrender "is as essential as the defeat of Germany." This "is especially true if our plans for world peace are to succeed. For Japanese militarism must be wiped out as thoroughly as German militarism."

The Cairo Declaration of November 1943 already had committed the United States to severe treatment of Japan with regard to territorial possessions. At their meeting in Egypt, FDR, Churchill, and Chinese leader Chiang Kai-shek had agreed to force Japan to return Manchuria and Formosa (Taiwan) to China, evacuate Korea as a prelude to its eventual independence, relinquish all Pacific islands acquired since World War I, and "be expelled from all other territories which she has taken by violence and greed." In short, as one historian put it, the goal of the Cairo Declaration was "to squeeze the Japanese genie back into the pre-Perry bottle." To secure these objectives, the declaration concluded, the signatories would prosecute the war until "the unconditional surrender of Japan."

Four days after Roosevelt's death, new president Harry S. Truman addressed a joint session of Congress. He called upon all Americans to support him in carrying out the ideals "for which Franklin Delano Roosevelt lived and died." The first of these was unconditional surrender. "So that there can be no possible misunderstanding," Truman stated, "both Germany and Japan can be certain, beyond any shadow of a doubt, that America will continue the fight for freedom until no vestige of resistance remains!" To enthusiastic applause he declared: "Our demand has been and it *remains*—Unconditional Surrender!" (emphasis in original).

Applying the Policy to Japan

But the issue was not as simple with regard to the Japanese as Truman made it out to be. He had inherited from Roosevelt an ongoing debate within the administration over how the formula should be applied to the emperor of Japan. The question took on ever greater urgency in the following months because it appeared that its resolution would have a decisive effect on when the war would end, thereby involving many thousands of lives on both sides. FDR's unwillingness to discuss definitions of unconditional surrender left Truman with few clues as to his predecessor's intentions.

Everyone agreed that Japan had long since lost the war by the spring of 1945. B-29 bombing raids were systematically destroying its cities; the naval blockade of its home islands was progressively becoming more effective; and by April American forces had recaptured the Philippine Islands and had invaded Okinawa, which lay only three hundred miles from Japan proper. The Soviet Union served notice in April that it would not renew its neutrality pact with Japan and began transferring troops to the Manchurian border. Finally, the long-awaited German surrender in early May meant that the United States and its allies could devote their entire resources against Japan in the future.

What was equally obvious, however, was that Japan still retained the ability to exact a fearsome toll should an invasion become necessary. The bloody struggle for Okinawa, which lasted until late June, provided a grim reminder that Japanese spirit remained high. They fought virtually until the last man at the cost of more than forty-seven thousand American casualties. Their army of two million men in the home islands could be expected to resist at least as fiercely in defense of Japanese soil. The first large-scale use of kamikazes (suicide aircraft) at Okinawa provided an even more nightmarish preview of things to come. Japan had thousands of trainers and obsolete fighters that could be converted into kamikazes with relatively little pilot training because of the short distances they would be required to fly while operating near Japanese shores.

The Retentionists vs. the Abolitionists

Any alternative to invasion was desirable provided it did not compromise larger objectives. Those who might be called "retentionists" offered just such a prospect. They argued that all informed Japanese knew their situation was hopeless, and that moderates in the government were searching for a way out of the war. The unconditional surrender formula undermined the peace advocates because it guaranteed neither Hirohito's personal inviolability nor continuation of the imperial system. Because of the emperor's unique cultural/religious status within the national polity, no patriotic Japanese could advocate surrender without assurances that these minimal criteria would be met. Such assurances could be included in a public statement calling upon Japan to surrender, or given through third-party diplomatic channels.

Retentionists promised additional dividends. The only way to attain an orderly surrender was through an imperial rescript, without which Japanese troops everywhere might continue to fight regardless of what orders the government in Tokyo issued. Later, perhaps as a constitutional monarch, the emperor would provide a stabilizing influence on a society in transition. Retentionists minimized the threat of Japan rearming for revanchist purposes, claiming that the militarists and their allies would have been thoroughly discredited for having led the nation to such a humiliating defeat. Besides, they pointed out, the United States could not occupy Japan forever. Deposing the emperor instead of using him as an instrument for change would cause an embittered Japanese people to reinstall him or a successor as soon as they could. Under such circumstances Japan once again would become a threat to peace in Asia.

"Abolitionists" warned against the seductive notion of an early peace. As FDR had explained at Casablanca and repeatedly thereafter, the goal of unconditional surrender was to enable the Allies to uproot and destroy those institutions and philosophies in the Axis nations that had brought on war in the first place. The monarchy was inextricably bound up with Japanese militarism and the warrior tradition, abolitionists said, regardless of the conduct of any particular incumbent. Continuation of the imperial dynasty would provide a rallying point for the resuscitation of militarism in years to come. Japanese "moderates," in this view, provided a frail reed upon which to base hopes for lasting peace. They "do not differ materially in their national ambitions, their idea of Japanese destiny, and their ruthlessness from the so called militarists." And they had willingly cooperated with the latter when conquest appeared to produce the desired results.

Understandable though it was to want to end the fighting as quickly as possible, abolitionists believed that a premature armistice would betray both the sacrifices already made and future generations if a resurgent Japan chose the path of aggression again as Germany had done after World War I. The only way to assure lasting peace was to fight it out until unconditional surrender enabled the United States and its allies to occupy Japan for as long as it took to achieve full democratization.

A Matter of Speculation

This debate, with variations introduced according to changing circumstances, continued virtually until the end of the war. As the arguments necessarily were speculative, who could say which side was correct? Would assurances about the emperor and the throne strengthen Japanese moderates, as the retentionists predicted, or have the opposite effect? Japanese spokesmen boasted that the hideous losses sustained at Iwo Jima and Okinawa had weakened the American will to go on fighting. Abandoning unconditional surrender would appear to validate this claim, bolstering the hard-liners' argument that holding out would produce even more favorable terms. At best the United States would offer a negotiated peace rather than undergo the bloodbath an invasion was sure to produce; at worst it surely would do so after suffering the crushing defeat on Japanese beaches militarists promised to administer.

There were domestic considerations as well. FDR had pledged that those responsible for the war at the very least would be removed from positions of responsibility, if not prosecuted as war criminals. Individuals familiar with Japan's political structure could debate (as they still do) Emperor Hirohito's culpability in bringing on the war. But most Americans, who had little idea of the intricacies of the Japanese system, tended to bracket him with Hitler and Mussolini as a great deal of wartime propaganda had encouraged them to do. There were few adults who had not seen newsreels or photographs of him astride his white horse reviewing Japanese troops, some of whom no doubt later killed or wounded American boys. To advocate the sanctity of one who to whatever degree bore responsibility for Pearl Harbor and atrocities such as the Bataan Death March was to invite charges of betraying FDR's legacy and the memory of those who had died in what was regarded as a war of treachery. Racist attitudes toward "Japs" also did not encourage forbearance with regard to the emperor.

The Soviet Influence

Relations with the Soviet Union had implications for applying the unconditional surrender doctrine to Japan. Roosevelt had gone to Yalta believing that an invasion of the Japanese home islands probably would be necessary. Soviet participation in the war could save an untold number of American casualties. They could pin down Japanese forces in northern China and Manchuria, interdict shipping between Japan and the mainland, and provide air bases in Siberia for a bombing campaign against Japanese cities. Stalin as far back as October 1943 had promised Secretary of State Hull that the Soviet Union would join the conflict provided it received sufficient concessions to justify such an endeavor to the war-weary Soviet people. At the Teheran Conference a few weeks later, FDR had expressed his willingness to grant such concessions and he had them placed in writing at Yalta.

The Yalta Far Eastern agreement provided for Soviet entry into the Pacific war two or three months after the end of hostilities in Europe. In return the Soviets would receive from Japan the strategically located Kurile island chain and the southern half of Sakhalin Island. They would get from China a lease on Port Arthur for a naval base, a "preeminent" interest in the commercial port of nearby Dairen, and joint operation of the Chinese-Eastern and the South Manchurian railroads. Except for the Kuriles, all of these concessions had been seized by Japan from Imperial Russia in the war of 1904–1905. Stalin on his part expressed his "readiness" to conclude a pact of friendship and alliance with the American-backed Nationalist government of Chiang Kai-shek, an unstable coalition challenged by a vigorous Communist movement. FDR hoped such a pact would help Chiang consolidate control over all of China after Japan's defeat.

During the period after Yalta, clashes with the Soviet Union over the governance and boundaries of Poland, the amount of reparations to be taken from Germany, and a host of other issues had strained the Grand Alliance. Even Roosevelt, who had dedicated himself to bettering Soviet-American relations throughout the war, became exasperated by Soviet behavior. Less than a week before his death, he approved a telegram to Winston Churchill stating that the military situation soon "will permit us to become 'tougher' [toward the Soviet Union] than has heretofore appeared advantageous to the war effort." What appeared to American officials as systematic violations of the Yalta agreements involving Europe caused doubts about Stalin's intentions in the Far East. Such doubts naturally raised questions about the desirability of Soviet participation in the conflict, and about the role it would be in American interests for Japan to play in the postwar world.

Women Warriors, Spies, and Angels of Mercy

William B. Breuer

In the following selection from his book *War and American Women: Heroism, Deeds, and Controversy*, William B. Breuer, a decorated combat veteran and military historian, tells the stories of courageous women who aided the war effort during World War II. Breuer discusses how station chief Allen W. Dulles of the Office of Strategic Services in Switzerland recruited Mary Bancroft to obtain information on the activities of the German opposition to Adolf Hitler. Although women were not allowed to actively participate in combat, Breuer writes, army and navy nurses were subject to the same brutal conditions, placing themselves in great peril to tend to the wounded, and many lost their lives. According to Breuer, the Women's Army Corps (WACs), the navy's Women Accepted for Volunteer Emergency Service (WAVES), the U.S. Coast Guard Women's Reserves (SPARS), and women marines were assigned to crucial roles at home and overseas, including flight training, the installation and operation of sophisticated radar and navigation equipment, and cracking Nazi codes.

I n neutral Switzerland, a tiny, mountainous enclave surrounded entirely by Adolf Hitler's forces in France, Italy, Austria, and Germany, Allen W. Dulles did business in a

Excerpted from *War and American Women: Heroism, Deeds, and Controversy,* by William B. Breuer. Copyright ©1997 by William B. Breuer. Reprinted with permission of Greenwood Publishing Group, Inc., Westport, CT.

building at Herrengasse 23 in the picturesque, medieval city of Bern, a hotbed of intrigue. The lettering on a small sign next to Dulles's front door stated "Special Assistant to the American Minister." But the sign was merely part of the games that those involved in international espionage play. Dulles, as nearly all of the hundreds of German and Allied spies roaming about Switzerland knew, was actually the Office of Strategic Services (OSS) station chief.

Dulles was fond of tweed jackets and bow ties, wore rimless spectacles, and was seldom caught without his briar pipe—a stereotype of Hollywood's version of a kindly, middle-aged college professor. Despite his deceptively mild appearance, Dulles was tough-minded and cagey. A lawyer by trade, he had been posted to Bern during World War I, ostensibly as an employee of the State Department. Then he was doing the same thing he was doing a war later—collecting intelligence from inside neighboring Germany.

Dulles was fortunate to have arrived in Switzerland at all. In early November 1942 he had been in France on "legal work" when the Allies invaded North Africa and Adolf Hitler immediately sent troops to occupy all of France. Dulles managed to catch the last train to Switzerland.

Recruiting a Spy

On his arrival in Bern, Dulles's staff consisted of two other persons. But in this uneasy corner of Europe he began to weave his espionage network. With the Swiss border now sealed, he set about recruiting "talent" from among American citizens living in Switzerland. One of his early recruits was Mary Bancroft. She was the daughter of the publisher of *The Wall Street Journal,* a large, New York City-based newspaper. She was a fiery political liberal and Democrat—no doubt to the consternation of her conservative father. A comely brunette in her early forties, Mary had concrete opinions and seldom, if ever, was reluctant to express them.

Bancroft was engaged in free-lance journalism when Allen Dulles asked her to take a job in his Bern office analyzing German newspapers and magazines for the reports he telephoned almost nightly to OSS headquarters in Washington. It was the first step in plunging her into the murky yet intriguing domain of international espionage. Dulles had other things in mind to draw on her talents than digesting German publications.

Mary was a complex woman—restless, always seeking some new adventure. She lived in Zurich, where she sought out the noted Swiss psychiatrist, Carl Gustav Jung, because she was stricken by prolonged bouts of sneezing while at social affairs, mostly, Jung would discover, because she was bored.

Bancroft saw Jung on and off for several months and was thought to have developed an affection for him, although he was twenty-five years older. One of his colleagues, a woman psychiatrist, did not share Jung's high regard for the outspoken American. Dealing with Bancroft, she said, was "like wrestling with a boa constrictor."

Loquacious Mary Bancroft had never kept a secret in her life, as far as anyone was aware. But one night in his Bern quarters, Allen Dulles, puffing on his pipe, fixed Mary with a stare and said without a trace of humor, "Contrary to general belief, I think you can keep your mouth shut."

She was angered by his bluntness but kept listening. Dulles had a crucial job to be done, and there was no one else to do it, he said. He was going to assign the task to her. If she was unable to keep quiet about it, "Five thousand people will die," he added.

Bancroft was shaken—but moved. Her face turned pale. But she agreed to the assignment. No longer would her task be to thumb through German periodicals. Now she was a full-fledged OSS agent. Perhaps she had taken on the job out of patriotism, perhaps from a desire to get involved in an intriguing adventure. In his best cloak-and-dagger fashion, Dulles told her, "You will soon get a call from a Dr. Bernhard."

Mary didn't sleep well that night. Obviously she was going to take part in something big. But never did she dream that the task for which Dulles had chosen her would be of such a shocking magnitude: involvement in an undercover operation to murder Adolf Hitler.

The Plot Against Hitler

"Dr. Bernhard" was the code name for Hans Bernd Gisevius. A bear of a man, six feet four inches and 260 pounds, he was an agent of the *Abwehr*, Hitler's secret service (SS), and assigned to the Nazi consulate in Zurich. Gisevius, a lawyer, had joined the Gestapo in 1933, only to be ousted six months later because of his lack of enthusiasm for the Nazi cause. Then he became a member of the Berlin police, but he was fired for criticizing the SS, Hitler's elite army within an army.

In 1939, Gisevius joined the *Schwarze Kapelle* (Black Orchestra), a tightly knit secret group of prominent German military officers, government officials, church and civic leaders who were conspiring to "eliminate" Adolf Hitler. A short time later he became an agent for the *Abwehr* and was sent to Zurich where he became the eyes and ears of the German anti-Hitler conspiracy. He was posted at the German consulate under diplomatic cover as vice-consul.

In February 1943 Gisevius, at great peril to himself, sought out Allen Dulles. In a scenario reminiscent of a Hollywood spy thriller, the two men rendezvoused on a black night on the steps of the World Council of Churches building in Bern. The German told about the anti-Nazi group in Germany and how it hoped to throw the Fuehrer out of power and sign a separate peace treaty with the Western Allies to keep the Soviets out of Germany.

Dulles was impressed by Gisevius's sincerity and his reasons for seeking destruction of the Hitler regime. A few more covert meetings were held, and plans were worked out for Gisevius to furnish couriers for bringing secret information out of Hitler's headquarters in Berlin to Bern.

The OSS chief was eager to keep this intelligence bonanza flowing and he figured the key to pleasing Gisevius lay in a book he was writing about his role in upsetting Hitler's applecart. The German desperately wanted it translated so that the book could be published in the United States the moment the war in Europe ended. Dulles promised to provide a skilled translator—cerebral Mary Bancroft.

Spying on Spies

While working with the German on the book, Bancroft was given a second mission: In essence, she was to spy on Gisevius and report to Dulles everything that he said. She wondered how two men, who seemed to be rowing the same boat, could be so distrustful of one another. Soon she would learn that in espionage, no one takes anything for granted; participants were always on guard against treachery.

In June 1943 the telephone jangled impatiently in the Zurich apartment of Mary Bancroft. The caller identified himself as Dr. Bernhard and asked to come see her that same afternoon. When she opened the door, a hulking forty-year-old man with a stiff Prussian bearing came into view. Mary was thrilled to know that this man with whom she was to work was a leader in the nefarious plot to kill Adolf Hitler. That meant that she, too, was playing a role in the dark conspiracy.

On this first visit, Gisevius brought 1,400 pages of his manuscript. More pages were brought to her in the weeks ahead. The translation was tedious, demanding, and exhausting. Their sessions invariably triggered spats and long discussions about philosophical matters. In time, the liberal American accepted the fact that the German was a hopeless right-winger, but she also was convinced that he was a sincere, Christian man who was putting his life on the line for his beliefs.

In early May 1944 Bancroft learned from Hans Gisevius that the Schwarze Kapelle was preparing yet another bold scheme to kill Adolf Hitler. Thirty-six-year-old Lieutenant Colonel Klaus Philip Maria Count von Stauffenberg, a German aristocrat who had lost an eye, an arm, and part of the other hand while fighting in North Africa, was to fly from Berlin to the Fuehrer's headquarters behind the Russian front for a conference. Von Stauffenberg would carry a bomb in a briefcase, set the timer, and place it at Hitler's feet while the participants were gathered around a conference table. Then he would use an excuse to leave the building and fly back to Berlin after the explosion.

Bancroft doubted if the plan would work. But she didn't express that view to her friend Gisevius, who was involved in ironing out details of the plot. Yet she felt a lofty sense of power. She doubted if any other American woman had even heard of the Schwarze Kapelle, much less the conspiracy's effort to wipe out the Nazi regime in one fell swoop.

The Nurses of Anzio

Although officially recognized as noncombatants, Army and Navy nurses overseas sometimes found themselves in peril because of the shifting tides of battle. One of these instances came in January 1944 when an American and British force of 70,000 men landed far behind German lines in Italy at Anzio, a small port on the west coast. The plan was for the invaders to drive rapidly northward for thirty miles and capture the glittering prize of Rome.

However, the Germans reacted rapidly and ringed the beachhead, only twenty-five miles long and four to seven miles deep, with troops and tanks, trapping the invaders.

The Berlin Bitch, as a German female propagandist was called by the GIs, taunted the Allied troops over Radio Berlin: "Hello out there, boys and girls at Anzio. How does it feel to be cooped up in the world's largest self-containing prisoner-of-war camp?"

In the Devil's inferno of Anzio, there was no "rear area." German artillery observers looking down on the bridgehead from the mountains around the beachhead could scan every foot of ground and call in deadly salvos. So crowded was the Allied-held territory that the four evacuation hospitals, housed in clusters of tents, were located along the shorelines next to supply and ammunition depots, communications posts, various headquarters, and other prime German targets.

Nearly 200 women of the U.S. Army Nurse Corps—the

The Flygirl

In this excerpt from Life *magazine, journalist Melissa Fay Greene provides a brief glimpse of the American reaction to Women Airforce Service Pilots known as WASPs.*

They were well-kept secrets, the 1,830 female civilian pilots who reported for training during World War II. They were such well-kept secrets that when the first truckload of wavy-haired, slim-waisted, lovely young women arrived at Avenger Field outside Sweetwater, Texas, in February 1943, the base commander exploded: "What in the hell are you doing here? Get off my air base!" The gates were finally, grudgingly, opened. The young women—attired in dresses, pearls and high heels—were immediately put through 45 minutes of calisthenics. As they limped into the barracks and unpacked their suitcases, Avenger Field became America's first and only coed air base.

When news about the flygirls got out, people everywhere asked, What in the world are those women doing down in Texas? The answer was that the newly organized Women Airforce Service Pilots (WASPs) were training to aid in the war effort, if not as fighters, then as a force behind the lines. By war's end, the WASPs would pilot every model of military plane. They would ferry aircraft from factory to base; they would serve as test pilots and flight instructors; they would provide shuttle service for officers; they would tow targets for artillery practice. They would die in service, 38 of them.

Life magazine went to Sweetwater in 1943 and took pictures of pilots with bows in their hair, writing letters home, sunbathing. "Girls are very serious about their chance to fly for the Army at Avenger Field," the article read, "even when it means giving up nail polish, beauty parlors, and dates." It was a puff piece, levity amidst the war news. Back then, there didn't exist the visual or print vocabulary to convey the moral seriousness, patriotism and love of danger in these people who looked like Hollywood starlets.

Melissa Fay Greene, "The Flygirl," *Life*, June 1999.

unsung heroes of Anzio—toiled around the clock to relieve the suffering and save the lives of wounded men. These nurses performed their duties while wearing steel helmets, fatigues, and combat boots. They faced danger as great as anyone else in the bridgehead.

Women Under Fire

Even though the hospital tents were dearly marked with red crosses on fields of white, artillery shells exploded regularly along the shoreline. While performing surgery and other duties, the nurses and doctors often heard the frightening rustle of a 700-pound shell from what the GIs called the Anzio Express, an enormous 280-millimeter railroad gun, just before it rocked the terrain around the hospital with a ground-shaking blast. At night, the Luftwaffe flew over, dropped parachute flares, then unloaded bombs along the shore.

Frontline troops had a name for the evacuation hospitals: Hell's Half-Acre. It was a place to be avoided. Sometimes the GIs concealed minor wounds to keep from being sent back to the tented medical centers. On occasion, wounded soldiers on cots in the hospital were hit a second or third time by shell or bomb fragments.

The presence of female nurses served as a great morale booster for the fighting men at a time morale badly needed uplifting. So inspiring was the valor displayed by the women that an attitude developed among combat troops on the beachhead: "If they can do it, so can I."

When the Germans had collected sufficient strength from all over Italy, they launched a powerful offensive to wipe out the Allies. It appeared that the Germans were about to break through to the sea, so General Mark W. Clark, the U.S. commander in Italy, decided to evacuate the nurses to keep them from being captured. Then he had a change of mind. Pulling out the women could be a portent of disaster and spread panic among the hard-pressed troops.

At mid-afternoon on February 7, twenty-year-old Corporal Charles H. Doyle, a paratrooper, was reclining on his cot as a patient at the 95th Evacuation Hospital. His sensitive ears perked up as he heard a familiar roar in the sky. He could not see from under the canvas, but a Luftwaffe bomber was streaking over the beachhead, chased by Allied fighter planes. Perhaps seeking to escape his tormentors by gaining altitude and speed, the German pilot jettisoned his bombs. One or more of the explosives landed on the 95th Evac, killing twenty-three persons, including three women nurses, a Red Cross lady, several male medics, and a few patients. Corporal Doyle escaped unscathed.

Women of Courage

One of those killed in the bombing was Lieutenant Colonel Blanche F. Sigman, chief nurse. Altogether, six women nurses died through enemy action on the Anzio beachhead, and sixteen others were wounded. The nurses who had been killed received Purple Hearts posthumously, and the wounded women were awarded the same medal. Four nurses received Silver Stars, the first American women to earn that decoration for valor.

The all-out German drive for victory was halted, and a few weeks later, the Allied force charged out of the beachhead and raced to Rome, which was captured on June 4, 1944.

Elsewhere in Europe, Lieutenant Agnes Mangerich and thirteen other Army flight nurses, along with several male medical technicians, were on an airplane bound for Bari, Italy, when the pilot had to crash-land in German-occupied Albania, in the Balkans. Violent storms and enemy gunfire had disabled the craft.

With little food, Mangerich and the others trudged through the mountainous, rocky terrain eight hours a day, bound for an American camp on the Adriatic coast, 800 miles from the crash site. It was winter and bitterly cold; the group spent Thanksgiving, Christmas, and New Year's Day trekking through deep snow, stopping at any shelter they could find. The hikers suffered from infectious boils, body lice, and bouts with dysentery.

After sixty-two days, the exhausted marchers reached

the camp, where they were greeted by soldiers armed with chicken, fruit, and chocolate bars. "I had only one thing in mind, however," Mangerich recalled. "I curled up in a sleeping bag in a little cave. Don't know how many hours—or days—I slept. Finally, someone tugged at me and said, 'The boat's here!'"

Women Warriors at Home

Although Women's Army Corps (WACs) and Army and Navy nurses were on active duty in many parts of the world, the law prohibited the Navy's Women Accepted for Volunteer Emergency Service (WAVES), the U.S. Coast Guard Women's Reserve (SPARS), and Women Marines from serving outside the United States. Yet all contributed significantly to the war effort at home. At Cherry Point Marine Air Station in North Carolina, 80 percent of the control-tower operations were handled by women Marines. WAVES serving in naval aviation taught instrumental flying, aircraft gunnery, and celestial navigation.

WAVES officers and SPARS officers, nearly all of them university graduates, were involved in finance, chemical warfare, and aerological engineering. At Norfolk, they helped install sophisticated radar on aircraft carriers and other warships.

For the first time, top-secret projects were opened to military women. Both the Navy and the Coast Guard utilized females in Long-Range Aid to Navigation (LORAN) stations, and WAVES were involved in a night-fighter training course. At a hidden communications center in Washington, D.C., WAVES officers spent countless hours staring at electronic screens, watching for "blips." It was boring, seemingly senseless work; the women had never been told the reasons for their job. When they were finally informed that each blip represented a U.S. ship being sunk, the task took on meaning and morale soared.

WAVES Lieutenant Mary Osborne was assigned to a super-secret Naval Intelligence facility in Washington. Her job had its roots back in mid-1939, just before England went to war with Nazi Germany. British scientists had cracked the Enigma code, which was used by the German armed forces and diplomats to send wireless messages. Adolf Hitler and other leaders were convinced that the code was unbreakable.

Throughout the war, the British intercepted the German messages and gave the code name Ultra to all intelligence gathered from Enigma. British Prime Minister Winston Churchill had agreed to share the Ultra information with the United States, so Mary Osborne and her WAVES colleagues were receiving this information by wireless from England for transmittal to government and military leaders in Washington.

WACs in the Pacific

On the other side of the world from Washington, D.C., in May 1944 the first contingent of WACs arrived in Australia, 2½ years after Pearl Harbor. They would serve under General Douglas MacArthur, who, after his escape from the Philippines early in the war, had established his headquarters in Brisbane.

Despite meager manpower and resources, ninety days after MacArthur had reached Down Under, he sent his troops northward to invade Japanese-held New Guinea, the world's second largest island, a land of jungles and swamps, scarcely changed from the Stone Age. For nearly two years, the Diggers (as the Australian soldiers were known) and the GIs had been fighting what MacArthur called a "hit-'em-where-they-ain't" campaign of speed and surprise. His troops leapfrogged Japanese coastal strongholds along the northern spine of 1,300-mile-long New Guinea. Fighting was as brutal and nasty as history had known.

Soon after their arrival in Australia, the WACs were shipped to Port Moresby, on the eastern tail of New Guinea, which is shaped like a squatting turkey. There the enlisted women were quartered within a barbed-wire compound under armed guard. They were "pardoned," the WACs complained, only to go to work or to social functions that had been officially approved. If a WAC had a date with a male enlisted man, the event had to be approved in advance. And the women had to be back inside the compound no later than 11:00 P.M.

Neither the WACs nor the male soldiers detailed to guard their compound were happy with the situation. No official explanation was given for the strict security measures. Some WACs thought the high command feared that the women might be raped by GIs who hadn't seen an American woman in a year and a half.

As MacArthur's forces battled their way along the torturous jungle road to Tokyo, his women soldiers followed. Later, he stated:

> I moved my WACs forward early after occupation of captured territory because they were needed and they were soldiers the same manner that my men were soldiers. . . . They were eager to carry on as needed.

The WACs and Army nurses had to cope with the same brutal environmental conditions as did the men in the primitive southwest Pacific: 100-degree temperatures; torrential rains; suffocating humidity; knee-deep mud; billions of mosquitoes; chiggers; poisonous snakes; leeches; tall grass that slashed human flesh like a razor blade.

African Americans in Combat

A. Russell Buchanan

Although African American men were eager to join the battle against the Axis powers during World War II, the military restricted the use of African American troops because of racial attitudes within and without the military. A. Russell Buchanan, in the following excerpt from his book *Black Americans in World War II*, asserts that the quality of Negro troops came into question, although the Negro press tried to point out that the training of Negro troops was often inferior, urging the desegregation of white and black troops. Even General Dwight D. Eisenhower argued that Negro units had not been tested enough in battle to support any conclusion regarding their performance, and well-trained troops performed admirably. For example, the 99th Fighter Squadron was successful in the air fighting over Anzio and the 969th Battalion did well in the Ardennes campaign. Despite attitudes within the military establishment, Negro troops maintained a good record, and many units had outstanding performances.

Editor's Note: Although the term Negro is seldom used today, the author of the following selection employs the vocabulary used during the period he is examining to describe African Americans.

Excerpted from *Black Americans in World War II*, by A. Russell Buchanan. Copyright 1977 by A. Russell Buchanan. Reprinted with permission from ABC-CLIO.

When the United States entered World War II, sending Negro troops outside the forty-eight states became a problem. Political and military leaders gave a variety of reasons why Negroes should not be deployed to certain regions. The governors of British West Indian possessions feared the response of their populations to the arrival of well-paid and well-clothed Negro troops. Australia's "White Australia" policy excluded Negroes. The governor of Alaska, Ernest Gruening, believed that mixing Negroes with native Indians and Eskimos would be bad. The air corps opposed sending Negroes to Iceland, Greenland, and Labrador. The Mormon Church objected to Negro troops in Mormon communities. Liberia did not want American Negroes because they would enjoy preferred status in comparison to the Liberian population. These protests were referred to Secretary of War Henry L. Stimson, and he created a simple guiding rule: Negroes would not be sent to countries where they were not wanted if the United States had been asked to send troops to that country. Otherwise, the army would determine where Negroes would go. Initially, Stimson went along with the stereotyped idea that Negroes should not be sent to far northern places, but they were later used to aid in the construction of the Alcan [Alaskan-Canada] Highway.

Sending Negro Troops Overseas

The movement of Negro troops overseas was slowed despite the Stimson rule. For example, only Negro service units were initially sent to the United Kingdom. Australian officials requested that Negroes already sent to Australia be returned to the United States or deployed elsewhere. General George C. Marshall asked General Douglas MacArthur for his views, and MacArthur replied that by using the troops "in the front zones away from great centers of population" he could "minimize the difficulties involved and yet use to advantage those already dispatched."

By the end of 1942, Negro troops sent abroad were proportionately fewer than their numbers in the overall strength of the army. The inspector general, Major General Virgil L. Peterson, and his assistant, General Benjamin Oliver Davis [the first African-American to reach the rank of General], questioned whether it was advisable to continue training and equipping Negro units that could not be used in the different theaters. The Selective Service System, however, continued to pour men into the army and the question was rejected. The arguments over the deployment of Negro troops continued in staff studies and surveys. It was argued that Negro soldiers should not be sent to Caribbean bases because their standard of living was higher than that of the local population, but the counterargument noted that the standard of living of white troops was also higher. It was also argued that Negroes were better adapted to the tropics and that white soldiers could be released for duty elsewhere. The domestic friction between Negro and white soldiers in 1941 and 1942 led a few observers to contend that Negro troops should not be sent to any foreign country.

The army gave specialized training to troops assigned to areas with great extremes of weather, but many Negroes sent to work on the Alcan Highway were unaccustomed to subzero weather and found it difficult to adjust to the cold climate and isolation. The higher pay given to civilians increased the Negro's discontent with working on the road. A contingent of Negroes sent to the Belgian Congo adjusted to the weather readily but had distasteful racial restrictions imposed on them by Belgian authorities. The troop buildup in Great Britain for the invasion of Europe resulted in considerable friction between Negro and white troops. The British had never relished the immigration of Negroes from their own possessions, yet many British citizens resented the attitude of white American soldiers toward the Negro. The British objected to the imposition of white American mores on their society.

Criticism by Negroes centered on their slow rate of deployment and Jim Crow practices in overseas theaters. The National Urban League's *Opportunity* noted that a booklet distributed to American soldiers stationed in England was "another don't book." "Its contents," wrote the editor, "consist largely of admonitions in the form of don'ts, with simple explanations of the differences in the customs and character of the English and American people." The pamphlet first advised soldiers, "when you see a man in the uniform of the United States Army, no matter what his color or race, he is your comrade in arms, facing the same dangers you face, fighting for the same things you are fighting for," and then proceeded to list the don'ts:

Don't degrade him by the use of degrading epithets such as "nigger."

Don't attempt to exclude him from any place open to other American soldiers.

Don't attempt to philosophize on the race question. The Army doesn't need philosophers but fighters and you may get mixed up.

Don't defend lynching when some of our Allies question you about this uncivilized practice. It is indefensible.

The editor of *Opportunity* commented, "We think such a book with a few modifications for home consumption, is imperative."

Negroes in Combat

Relatively few Negro combat troops were sent to the front in 1942. The 24th Infantry Regiment was sent to the New Hebrides in anticipation of an advance to Guadalcanal, but it arrived after the heavy fighting was over. There was talk of deploying a Negro regiment to Hawaii as its main defense but there were several objections raised. General Davis felt that Negroes were concerned over the army's failure to give Negro soldiers a chance to fight. He formally recommended to the McCloy Advisory Committee in April 1943 that it propose sending a Negro combat unit immediately to a forward area.

The air corps' 99th Pursuit Squadron, sent to North Africa in April 1943, was the first Negro unit to see combat, and it became involved in controversy. Lieutenant General Carl Spaatz, commander of the Fifth Air Force in North Africa, refused to rush the unit into action despite the attention given it by the press. The squadron later participated in attacks on Pantelleria, and Lieutenant Colonel Benjamin O. Davis, Jr., squadron commander, was relieved of command in August and returned to the United States to command and train a new fighter group.

General Spaatz received official reports on the squadron which suggested that it was inferior to white units in combat. The group commander, for example, reported that formation flying was "very satisfactory until jumped by enemy aircraft, when the squadron seems to disintegrate." He also noted that Colonel Davis asked that his men be taken out of combat for three days because of fatigue during the campaign in Sicily and that white pilots in combat longer had kept flying. General Spaatz forwarded the reports to General H.H. Arnold, chief of army air forces, with a moderating statement that he had personally visited the squadron and that there had "been no question of their ground discipline and their general conduct." Spaatz concluded, however, that the analysis of the squadron had been fair: "I feel that no squadron has been introduced into this theatre with a better background of training than had by the 99th Fighter Squadron."

The report was particularly damaging because it seemingly indicated that Negro units were inferior even when they had been well trained. Consequently, it was recommended that Negro fighter squadrons be assigned to rear defense areas and that the training of Negroes for a proposed medium bomber group be dropped. The long period of training given Negro pursuit pilots was thus cited against them.

Reviewing Negro Units

General Marshall received the recommendations in October 1943 and ordered a complete review of Negro units in combat; questionnaires were sent to commandants in all areas. Commanders in the South Pacific reported that Negro units were kept in rear areas subject only to occasional bombings. The report indicated that Negro officers and men were not as effective as whites. Commands in the Southwest Pacific reported that no Negro units were in combat but that service troops had performed well under fire—Negro officers were rated as average.

One Negro unit in India, the 823d Engineer Aviation Battalion, had been under fire and its conduct was reported as magnificent. Reports on Negro service units in North Africa ranged from satisfactory to less than satisfactory. General Dwight D. Eisenhower praised the maligned 99th Fighter Squadron for its strafing attacks in Sicily and noted that engineer and antiaircraft ground units had performed well. Significantly, Eisenhower's report suggested that Negro units had not been tested enough in battle to support any conclusions regarding their performance.

Colonel Davis informed the advisory committee that the 99th Pursuit Squadron had made early errors and had experienced lack of confidence, but he was convinced that the situation improved later. The investigation continued and it was reported that, if there had not been enough testing of Negroes in combat on the ground, there had been in the air. The report recommended that Negro air units not be used in active areas.

The air corps then faced the problem of what to do with the Negro medium bomber unit in training for combat duty. General Arnold decided on October 27, 1943, that the group would continue training and be deployed to North Africa. Meanwhile, the 99th Fighter Squadron remained on duty in Italy. There was little combat there during this stage of the war, but the squadron was heavily engaged in flight operations. The squadron built self-confidence and eventually gained recognition within the 79th Fighter Group. Additional Negro fighter units were sent to Italy in 1944.

The use of Negro ground units in combat presented continuing problems. Negro groups insisted that Negro troops be given a fair share of action, yet commanders were reluctant to accept Negro troops. Lieutenant General Millard F. Harmon, commanding army forces in the South Pacific, argued in 1943 that his logistic problems—long distances and transportation difficulties—demanded only the most effective troops. Harmon's need for manpower was so great, however, that he agreed to use one Negro regiment in combat and to garrison forward areas if white troops were unavailable.

Questioning Military Policies and Training

The backlog of Negro units in the United States had increasingly adverse effects on morale—particularly when the army began converting combat infantry for service in engineer and artillery units. Negro leaders questioned the War Department about the conversion and Secretary Stimson's reply increased Negro discontent. Stimson asserted that the selection of units to be changed "had been based solely on the relative abilities, capabilities and status of training for the personnel in the units available for conversion." He added, "It so happens that a relatively large percentage of the Negroes inducted in the Army have fallen within the lower educational classifications, and many of the Negro units accordingly have been unable to master efficiently the techniques of modern weapons."

Truman K. Gibson, Jr., William Henry Hastie's, [who in 1943 resigned in protest against discrimination in the military], successor as civilian aide to Secretary Stimson, predicted that Stimson's letter would produce an outraged response. Gibson also objected because the letter was not referred to him or the advisory committee for comment before it was distributed. Gibson's prophecy was correct; the Negro press reacted bitterly, and an editorial in *Crisis* termed Stimson's letter "probably the most inept letter of the war" and one "which has infuriated Negro Americans as has no other single incident since Pearl Harbor."

The Stimson statement and the resulting protests focused attention on the problem of what to do about Negro combat troops. The McCloy Advisory Committee studied the problem in February 1944 and recommended in early March "that, as soon as possible, colored Infantry, Field Artillery, and other Combat units be introduced into combat . . . and that schedules if necessary be changed." The commitment of Negro units to battle thus resulted from public and political pressure rather than the requests of commanders in the field. Commanders accepted the recommendations only when it was clear that Negroes would be sent to forward areas.

The preparation and deployment of troops for combat were complicated and at times confusing. In general, the quality of preparation and training determined how troops would perform in the field. Poor training resulted in unsatisfactory performance, and large, well-trained units usually performed well. The attendant publicity and the views of critics and supporters made the task of unit commanders even more difficult. Consequently, according to African-American author Ulysses Lee [who served during WWII], the career of Negro troops was atypical.

Improvements and Setbacks

Negro units went into action in the Pacific and reacted as did other newly trained units. Assistant Secretary McCloy summarized one report: "Although they show some important limitations, on the whole I feel that the report is not so bad as to discourage us." He continued by citing the performance of the 99th Fighter Squadron: "You remember that they were not very good, but that Squadron has now taken its place in the line and has performed very well." Stimson agreed but in his opinion Negro troops would succeed only with white officers.

The 99th Fighter Squadron gradually changed its image in the European theater. The squadron performed well in the air fighting over Anzio, and Major General John K. Cannon, earlier quite critical, told the men of the 79th Fighter Group and the 99th Fighter Squadron, "It's a grand show. You're doing a magnificent job." The actions of the Negro pilots were broadly covered and strongly praised in the press. *Crisis* reported that the fliers were "no longer on trial . . . they have now assumed a position of leadership in combat and pursuit."

The 93d Division advanced from island to island in the Pacific, usually engaged in rearguard and sometimes "mopping up" actions. Ulysses Lee summarized its work: "Whether or not the Division moved to the asset side depended largely on the viewer and his interpretation of the value of doing unglamorous but necessary work."

The Negro 370th Regimental Combat Team weeded out substandard men and replaced them with volunteers during training. Its morale was high and it was deployed to Italy, where it was warmly welcomed. The team moved into action, and at first had the advantage of following a retreating enemy that offered little resistance. Observers noted that the soldiers acted as any new unit might in the limited action—they were not aggressive but seemed responsive to learning the art of war. The real test came in an attack on a vigorously held German position (the Gothic Line) in heavy rain and mud. After a month of fierce combat, the team's morale deteriorated. A few instances of individual heroism were reported, but officers noted that the troops had a tendency to panic and in some cases they refused to continue the attack. Many of the officers were killed or wounded and leadership became a real problem. The commander of the 370th wrote, "Morale went down, esprit de corps departed, determined resistance on the part of the enemy began, difficult terrain was encountered, and so the natural result was that combat efficiency was lowered."

The arrival of the rest of the 92d Division did not help the situation because there was serious disaffection between its soldiers and their officers. An investigating officer recommended that the commanding officer be removed, but the recommendation was rejected. Since both sides were on the defensive, nothing of consequence occurred for a brief period. It was thus decided to reorganize and shift some of the units from the front lines. While these changes were being made, Gibson paid a visit to the Italian front at the invitation of General Mark Clark. Gibson talked with hundreds of officers and enlisted men in an attempt to find the facts and the reasons for the team's failures.

Facing Criticism

Gibson held a press conference in Rome on March 14, 1945, arranged by the army's public relations officer at the request of war correspondents. In this conference Gibson reported what he had already told army officials. He acknowledged that "there have been many withdrawals by panic stricken Infantrymen," and stated that there were also "many acts of individual and group bravery." He noted that there was an "unsatisfactory promotion policy" for Negro officers, and that the command maintained a racist attitude. In addition, Gibson noted that there was a large percentage of Negro soldiers in Grades IV and V who had come from civilian backgrounds where there was little chance for the "inculcation of pride in self or even love of country."

Newspapers like the *New York Times* praised Gibson for his candor, but the Negro press reacted strongly against his reports. *Crisis* published a lengthy editorial entitled "Negro Soldier Betrayed" and excoriated Gibson. The editor asked,

> If the 92d Division is made of 92% illiterates and near-illiterates, whose fault is it? Certainly not the Negroes. . . . Why would the War Department, if it really wanted to give a fair test, send a division into the front lines with 92 out of every 100 men in the two lowest classifications? The 92d was licked before it started.

The editor continued,

> It must be remembered that these men were beaten up by bus drivers, shot up by military and civilian police, insulted by their white officers, denied transportation to and from the post, restricted to certain post exchanges, and jim crowed in post theatres.

The editor concluded that segregation was the root cause

and recommended that the War Department move as quickly as possible "to wipe out segregation of fighting men according to color."

The 92d Division went into the spring offensive of 1945 greatly changed in character. It included a white regiment, an American-Japanese regiment, and a virtually new Negro regiment with officers of both races. The fighting went well at the outset, but some of the original officers were killed and the situation deteriorated. A few individual units and men distinguished themselves for ability and heroism, but elsewhere in the division morale was low. Some Negroes believed the introduction of white troops implied that Negroes could not fight by themselves. Negroes in other units expressed the hope that they would not be judged by the poor showing of the 92d Division.

Quality and Quantity

Only about 2 percent of all the Negroes in the army were in the 92d Division. Most Negroes were in the service forces, which operated in small units attached to large white groups. Negroes thus performed a variety of duties throughout the world. They were involved in the major campaigns in Europe and the Pacific and in a host of other places from Alaska to Liberia. Negroes served in the quartermaster corps, as engineers, in antiaircraft batteries, and in port and amphibious truck companies. They operated smoke generators at the front and served in ambulance companies. "The sheer quantity of work performed by Negro troops," wrote Ulysses Lee, "often operating on round-the-clock schedules, was tremendous." Their performance was not perfect, but in general they maintained a good record in service and in their relations with white troops and with the people of foreign countries.

From the standpoint of Negroes and whites alike, one of the most satisfactory records was achieved by Negroes in the artillery and armored units which served in Europe. They were outstanding in the Ardennes campaign during the German counteroffensive. After the siege of Bastogne,

Major General Maxwell D. Taylor, commanding the 101st Airborne, wrote to the commander of the Negro 969th Battalion expressing appreciation for its "gallant support." He stated, "This Division is proud to have shared the Battlefield with your command." Tank battalions and tank destroyer crews also distinguished themselves in the European campaign. One tank destroyer battalion performed badly and a subsequent investigation showed that it was manned with an excessive number of soldiers from low AGCT grades.

Asking for Volunteers

A very significant breakthrough almost occurred toward the end of 1944. High army officials decided to accept Negro volunteers as individual infantry replacements due to a critical shortage of infantry riflemen replacements. Late in December the army called for volunteers:

> To this end the Commanding General, Com Z, is happy to offer to a limited number of colored troops who have had infantry training, the privilege of joining our veteran units at the front to deliver the knockout blow . . . your comrades at the front are anxious to share the glory of victory with you. Your relatives and friends everywhere have been urging that you be granted this privilege.

The notice ended by expressing confidence in Negro volunteers.

When news of the plan reached Supreme Headquarters, Allied Expeditionary Force (SHAEF), Lieutenant Walter Bedell Smith saw that calling for introduction of volunteers into units "without regard to color" might embarrass the War Department, and he protested to General Eisenhower. Eisenhower rewrote the directive deleting that reference to color, leaving the inference that Negroes would be assigned to Negro units and that if the supply was greater than the need "these men will be suitably incorporated in other organizations so that their service and their fighting spirit may be efficiently utilized."

More than 4,560 Negro troops volunteered in response to the original notice before it was replaced by Eisenhower's revision—the original plan was to accept 2,000. It is difficult to estimate what the response would have been if the volunteers had known that they would be placed in small segregated units rather than integrated individually into white units. The men went through retraining and were assigned in platoons to fight with white troops. Their motivation was high, and the men were welcomed as needed allies at the front; there was less enthusiasm in quiet sectors. General Davis later traveled through the Twelfth Army Area and received good reports on the volunteers. Volunteers not quite as well trained also did well with the 6th Army Group and the Seventh Army. Ulysses Lee summarized: "In the Negro Infantry rifle platoons, the employment of Negro troops moved farthest from traditional Army patterns."

The Voice of America:
Propaganda as Warfare

Holly Cowan Shulman

Although radio did not develop until after World War I, American propagandists soon recognized its potential to undermine Nazi propaganda. In late 1942, President Franklin D. Roosevelt authorized the Voice of America. In the following excerpt from her book *The Voice of America: Propaganda and Democracy, 1941–1945*, Holly Cowan Shulman, whose father was head of the Radio Program Bureau of the Office of War Information, describes how the style of propaganda broadcast over the radio changed during the war from John Housemann's theatrical broadcasting designed to agitate early in the war to the more calm news reporting begun after the successful Allied invasion of North Africa. Shulman describes how propaganda uses cultural myths and symbols to motivate listeners, explaining that as America's position in the world changed so did the cultural myths and symbols broadcast by the Voice of America.

T he Voice of America broadcast to Europe twenty-four hours a day throughout the Second World War from a building on West Fifty-Seventh Street, a former Chevrolet dealership with high ceilings, large rooms, and vast display windows. When not at their desks in glass cubicles, policy leaders divided their time between meetings in Washington, streams of official visitors, and endless staff sessions. In this cavernous building renowned but underpaid European writers translated propaganda policy into radio shows as they churned out stories on battles and American war production. Announcers retreated from the babble of languages into soundproof rooms where they enacted their scripts with an upbeat American sound. "This is New York," the Voice of America proclaimed, "the United States of America, calling the people of Europe." This was the Voice of America at war.

International radio propaganda developed in Europe and Asia during the 1930s, and by September 1939, when Germany invaded Poland, every major power except the United States had its own international broadcasting service. America did not officially enter the world of international propaganda over-the-air until 1942, but once launched, the Voice of America became a permanent instrument of international politics. . . .

A New Form of Political Persuasion

The art of political persuasion, or what one leading American propaganda theorist defined as "the control of opinion by significant symbols," has existed since the beginnings of recorded history. But popular democracy and the mass media transformed it from a minor activity into an instrument of total warfare. The propaganda battles waged by the belligerent powers in the First World War had been prominent and frightening. Propagandists in every nation had projected ugly atrocity campaigns through words and images: posters, leaflets, speakers, and films. This newly visible weapon survived the war, at least in people's minds, as a weapon of terrifying potential.

During the next two decades, fears of propaganda merged with concerns about the hidden powers of radio. Professional broadcasting had not begun until after the Great War ended, but once on the air, radio's potential influence was quickly understood. Words spoken into a radio microphone reached men and women sitting at home, listening to their radios. Within weeks of assuming office in 1933 President Roosevelt demonstrated how effectively he could use radio to reach ordinary citizens. His "fireside chats" became a milestone in politics and broadcasting. Until that March a single White House employee had handled all presidential mail, even during the First World War and the panic following the Wall Street crash in 1929. But following his first fireside chat unanswered letters piled up in Roosevelt's White House. Roosevelt established through radio a direct—an almost personal—relationship with the American electorate. The president had proven the political importance of radio.

When it first began, broadcasting reached a strictly local audience. Programs could be heard only by those who could pick up a long- or medium-wave signal sent from a nearby transmitter. But in the early twenties the invention of short-wave broadcasting expanded the potential influence of broadcasting, and by extension of propaganda, because use of shortwaves allowed radio signals to be heard over a longer distance. Short-, medium-, and long-wave broadcasting are all characterized by amplitude modulation (AM). The shorter waves of the radio spectrum, however, are reflected off the upper layers of the ionosphere, bouncing around the globe like stones skipping across water and striking the earth at regular intervals. This "skip distance" effect allowed short-wave broadcasting across international boundaries. As early as 1924, low-powered, high-frequency transmissions could be received thousands of miles away from their points of origin.

In the late twenties European governments seized on this new radio technology and began setting up short-wave broadcasting services. The first nation to do so was Holland, aiming to bind together the far-flung elements of the Dutch empire; it was soon followed by France, Belgium, Italy, and Great Britain. These early imperial stations were thinly disguised instruments of colonial policy, and they demonstrated the potential use of short-wave radio for international propaganda. When Adolf Hitler took over Germany, however, he converted radio into an aggressive weapon of foreign policy. By the end of the 1930s German radio was on the air over twenty-one hours a day, working to divide, confuse, and fragment the world.

Using Propaganda as a Weapon

Then, in the spring of 1940, Germany overran western Europe. The Nazis not only used armored motorized vehicles; they employed propaganda to undermine their enemy's will to fight. The fall of France persuaded U.S. government leaders such as John J. McCloy, and liberals outside the government such as Viking Press publisher Harold Guinzburg and newspaper columnist George Fielding Eliot, that a blitzkrieg of ideas was as effective as a blitzkrieg of tanks.

These events reinforced American fears of propaganda. Americans had been deeply alarmed by the excessive emotions and hatred brought to the surface by George Creel's Committee on Public Information during World War I, and most of the nation, including President Roosevelt, rejected propaganda as a formal instrument of foreign policy. Yet political leaders and intellectuals were frightened by what they believed to be the might of Nazi propaganda. Roosevelt appointed a special committee to study the problem in late 1940. Henry L. Stimson, the secretary of war, warned the committee that the Germans were undermining the American institutions of freedom of the press and freedom of discussion, and that the nation would have to fight back. Stimson's assistant secretary, John J. McCloy, told the committee that the army needed to mobilize for propaganda warfare just as much as it needed to do so for ground and air warfare. And the liberal playwright cum presidential speech writer, Robert E. Sherwood, boldly proclaimed that America had to fight Nazi propaganda with American propaganda. In July 1941, working under presidential orders, Sherwood created the Foreign Information Service (FIS), which in June 1942 became the Overseas Branch of the Office of War Information (OWI). The American government launched its war of words, and six months later the president authorized the Voice of America. . . .

In 1942 American propagandists believed they could influence the French, while they doubted that they could reach many Germans. Both the Occupied and Vichy French governments forbade their citizens from tuning in enemy stations, but the German government not only outlawed listening, it did so under penalty of death. Since 1940 the French had turned to the British Broadcasting Corporation (BBC), and American propagandists hoped the French would include the Voice of America in their listening habits. By 1944 propaganda to France had a special mission: to support the Allied liberation of western Europe.

The Changing Style of Propaganda

The propaganda broadcast by the French desk changed dramatically over the course of the war. In 1942 the first director of the Voice of America, John Houseman, created the initial broadcasting style of the Voice of America. Houseman came from the world of theater, radio drama, and film. He had, for example, produced "War of the Worlds," the radio science fiction program that in 1938 so alarmed listeners living near the supposed Martian invasion site in New Jersey that many packed their families and belongings into their cars and fled. He brought to the Voice his experience in experimental radio and his knowledge of drama-as-propaganda, or agitprop, and he used these techniques to originate a unique-sounding station whose very tones urged the French to rise up and resist the Nazis.

Following the American-led Allied invasion of North Africa in November 1942, however, the propaganda style of the Voice gradually altered. Increasingly it acquired a patina of calm and neutral news reporting, while its message shifted from encouragement of resistance to explanations of the coming Allied liberation of France. Between 1942 and 1944 the forms in which the Voice of America cast its propaganda moved from agitation to factual news reporting, a shift necessitated by the increasing American emphasis on Allied military victory.

These changes were part of a larger trend that had begun in the First World War, and that had taken place in all countries, both Allied and Axis. During the Great War, propagandists on both sides relied on the strength of moral argumentation. Themes of "our cause is right" and "the enemy's cause is wrong" predominated. World War I propaganda emphasized the brutality of the enemy, to the point of fabricating enemy actions in order to underline the moral righteousness of the propagandists' cause. During the Second World War—at least in Europe—Allied propaganda took a more sober and less emotional, moralistic, or didactic approach to the problem of persuasion, muting overt statements of ideology and dropping most allusions to enemy bestiality. Only the Nazis retained this style of propaganda. More and more, Allied propaganda relied on the presentation of facts and information. This trend was visible from the beginning of the war, but it became clearer the longer the war lasted. By 1944 the shift to an informational format of propaganda was pronounced.

Using Myths and Symbols

All propaganda operates by taking cultural myths and symbols and reworking them in the service of nationally conceived aims. Nazi propaganda, for example, used and expanded on an important German myth and employed it at home and abroad. According to this myth, Germany was a young and pure nation, a nation of Siegfrieds, fighting evil schemers out to destroy the German people. Throughout the war German propagandists drew on this myth; its power was so strong that even when, in 1944 and 1945, propagandists wanted to change course in the face of Allied victories and Axis defeats, they could not do so; they could alter much of their style, but they could not escape the mythical universe they had constructed.

American propaganda also used national images, symbols, and myths: America was an innocent giant whose

mission was to save war-tired Europe. This myth of innocence, with deep roots in American culture, prevailed
throughout the war and colored and shaped propaganda's
news and pronouncements on American foreign policy. . . .

The changes in propaganda over the course of the war
were generated by a shifting intellectual and cultural climate. American culture during the war years traveled from
the social realism and experimental modernism of the thirties to a conservative realism. The style of the propaganda
radio programs had become increasingly factual and detailed rather than imaginative and experimental. It had
moved, as it were, from the dramatic scripts of Norman
Corwin to the seemingly straightforward news broadcasts
of Edward R. Murrow, just as the poster propaganda of the
OWI had altered from the social realism of Ben Shahn and
the modernist abstractions of Jean Carlu to the conservative realism of Norman Rockwell and the photo posters
cranked out to plaster the walls of the liberated streets of
Europe. The propagandists also worked within the intellectual environment of changing social science theories on
the achievable goals and potential influence of propaganda. Before the war social scientists believed that the
thoughts and opinions of the radio listening audience could
be moved through the conscious manipulation of a whole
range of symbols and arguments. By the end of the war
they no longer believed that propaganda could transform
thought or provoke action.

A New America

The most important reasons why Voice of America propaganda changed between 1942 and 1944 lie with the war itself. The Second World War transformed America: its position in the world, its domestic politics, and its culture. By
1944 America had become a world power concerned with
maintaining postwar stability and order. At home, the war
had ended the Great Depression and with it the pressing
need for reform and social experimentation. Postwar
America would soon emerge as a more prosperous and

conservative nation than it had been in the thirties. In short, the United States of 1946 was a very different place from the United States of 1939.

In February 1942, when the Voice of America first went on the air, the Allies were losing the war. By February 1944 it had become clear that the Allies had won and that the achievement of final victory was only a matter of time. The abundant resources of the United States, combined with the strength of the Soviet Union, had defeated the Axis. Equally important, throughout most of 1942, until the Allied invasion of North Africa on November 8, the United States had no troops in Europe: America did not go to war in Europe, except at sea, until the very end of 1942. For the first nine months of broadcasting by the Voice of America, therefore, the United States was not fighting the European war with soldiers, but with industrial supplies, military buildup, promises, hopes—and propaganda. In 1943 the Allies turned the tide of the war; in 1944 they invaded Normandy, liberated Paris, and in October freed all of France. The war slogged on in Europe for another seven months, and in the Pacific for another three months after that; but the war had been won.

The Atom Bomb

Alan J. Levine

When Japan rejected the terms of the Potsdam Declaration of July 26, 1945, President Harry S. Truman was forced to make a difficult choice. On the morning of August 6, 1945, a B-29 dropped a uranium bomb on Hiroshima, and three days later, when Japan failed to surrender immediately, another bomb was released over Nagasaki. In the following excerpt from his book *The Pacific War: Japan Versus the Allies*, historian Alan J. Levine explores the development and use of the atom bomb. Levine discusses the Manhattan Project that developed an atomic weapon and the problems the project faced separating the rare uranium isotope and creating the artificial plutonium that would fuel the chain reaction. The author also discusses the political and strategic reasoning behind the decision to use the bomb as well as the political problems within Japan that made surrender so difficult.

The development of the atomic bomb was the product of the greatest research and development project in history. The development of the Apollo moon rocket was by comparison an easy affair, a short excursion into relatively well-known territory. The discovery in the 1930s that the uranium atom could be fissioned had opened the prospect of the early release of the energy of the nucleus of the

Excerpted from *The Pacific War: Japan Versus the Allies,* by Alan J. Levine. Copyright ©1995 by Alan J. Levine. Reprinted with permission of Greenwood Publishing Group, Inc., Westport, CT.

atom—previously regarded as no more than a possibility for the indefinite future. Using Albert Einstein as a channel, the nuclear scientists brought the possibility of the atomic bomb to the attention of President Roosevelt in 1939; over the next two years, preliminary research was done, which clearly indicated that there was a good chance that atomic weapons could be built in time to be used in the war. At the Washington Conference of June 1942, the Western democracies, wrongly fearing that the Germans might be ahead of them in a race to develop atomic bombs, decided to launch a major project to build the bomb in the United States. In fact, while the Germans, and even the Japanese, had small-scale work on atomic weapons underway, they lacked the interest and the resources for a decisive effort.

The Manhattan Project

The atomic bomb project, the "Manhattan Project," was an enormous task. There seemed to be two main roads to a weapon; the Americans decided to take both of them—and each had forks. A rare isotope of uranium, U-235, could fuel an explosive chain reaction in a bomb. But only one uranium atom in 140 is a U-235 atom, and separating the desired isotope was fantastically difficult to accomplish on an industrial scale. Ultimately plants using three different isotope separation processes—electromagnetic, gaseous diffusion, and thermal diffusion—were constructed.

An "artificial" element, plutonium, only recently produced by researchers, could also be used in a bomb. It, however, had to be made in a nuclear reactor and then chemically separated from the uranium and other fission products in which it was embedded. The first nuclear chain reaction was initiated in a crude experimental reactor at the University of Chicago in December 1942. The Manhattan Project built a series of reactors and separation plants to produce plutonium for a bomb at Hanford, Washington, while plants to separate the U-235 isotope were built at Oak Ridge, Tennessee—two brand-new cities that had to be built from the ground up.

142

Problems with the Project

The scientists and engineers had to solve fantastically difficult problems. The basic chemical and metallurgical properties of plutonium, at first available only in microscopic quantities, were unknown, and those of uranium proved to be little known. Both materials were hard to work with. Graphite of unprecedented purity had to be made for the moderators of nuclear reactors, and fluorocarbon plastics had to be developed for use in the uranium isotope-separation plants. The equipment used at Hanford and Oak Ridge had to be of unprecedented reliability; once the plants were started, they had to be run by remote control, for the materials being processed were radioactive, poisonous, violently corrosive, or all three. Building the pumps and isotope-separation "barriers" for the U-235 gaseous-diffusion plant at Oak Ridge and learning how to "can" the uranium fuel slugs in the Hanford reactors—they had to be cooled by water but had to be kept from direct contact with it—proved the supreme technological problems of the project.

Prickly problems cropped up at late stages. When the first Hanford reactor went into operation in September 1944, it was soon shut down by an unexpected "poisoning" effect caused by xenon-135 gas produced by the fission process. Fortunately, the reactors' design had been flexible; they had to be rebuilt to take on more uranium fuel. The gaseous-diffusion and electromagnetic separation plants at Oak Ridge failed to accomplish a sufficiently high degree of separation; a new plant using the thermal-diffusion process was hastily built to enrich the "feed" for the electromagnetic plant.

Compared to the problem of making the fissionable material, the design and assembly of the bomb, which took place at Los Alamos in New Mexico, was a straightforward business. By early 1945, it was reasonably certain that both uranium and plutonium bombs would be available during 1945 and that the former at least would have an explosion equivalent to that of 10,000 to 20,000 tons of

TNT. It was so certain that the uranium bomb would work that it did not have to be tested. The first plutonium bomb, whose power and reliability were less certain, was tested at Alamogordo, New Mexico, on July 16, 1945. It proved even more powerful than the uranium bomb.

Unknown to the democracies, the Soviets had their own atomic bomb project well underway, although they had not been able to pour major resources into it while the war with Germany raged. Although the Manhattan Project had a policy of almost obsessive secrecy and compartmentalization, perhaps to the point where work on the bomb was hindered, it was penetrated at several points by Soviet spies. Their most important agent, the German refugee physicist Klaus Fuchs, worked on both the gaseous-diffusion plant and the design of the bomb. The Western democracies had beaten the Axis in a race that the latter had not really run, but their next foes were close behind them.

Choosing the Targets

For months the Americans had considered how to use the A-bomb. General Leslie Groves, the head of the Manhattan Project, set up a target committee to select objectives that had not yet been damaged, were militarily important, and whose destruction would hurt Japan's will to fight on. The committee picked Hiroshima, Kokura, Niigata, and Kyoto as targets; at Secretary Henry L. Stimson's order, Kyoto was dropped from the list because of its special cultural significance. Later, Nagasaki was substituted. These cities were put off limits for conventional bombing so that atomic attacks would have more spectacular effects. Hiroshima was ultimately put at the top of the target list because it was wrongly thought to be the only target city where there were no American prisoners of war.

Secretary of War Stimson had a group of leading officials and scientists, the Interim Committee, which had been studying the broad issues posed by the development of nuclear energy, independently discuss the use of the bomb. They considered the possibility of a "demonstration" use of the bomb or a specific warning mentioning the bomb but rejected this and confirmed Stimson's opinion that the bomb should be used in a surprise attack on an important war installation surrounded by housing. They concluded that no safe demonstration that would convince the Japanese could be devised. If the Japanese were told of a demonstration beforehand, they might shoot down the bomb-carrying plane or bring prisoners of war to the selected site. If the bomb was a dud, a demonstration might backfire.

One member of the committee, Undersecretary of the Navy Ralph Bard, later changed his mind and recommended that a specific warning be issued before an atomic attack. Some people, such as Lewis Strauss and Edward Teller, wanted to demonstrate the bomb's power by dropping it on a forest outside Tokyo or exploding it at high altitude over the city; but they made no headway. Many scientists disliked using the A-bomb or wanted a specific warning or a demonstration before using it militarily. In the later famous Franck Report, some expressed opposition to using the bomb. But the Franck Report, although containing many valuable observations on the implications of nuclear energy, did not advance any arguments against dropping the bomb likely to convince those responsible for ending the war.

On July 25, 1945, the strategic air command in the Pacific was ordered to launch the atomic attacks as soon as weather allowed visual bombing after August 3. The order was to stand unless the president informed Secretary Stimson that Japan had accepted the Allied terms. Both available bombs were to be dropped as quickly as possible—the destruction of Hiroshima and Nagasaki was effectively ordered at the same time.

The peace faction welcomed the Potsdam Declaration although Togo wanted the terms clarified and perhaps assurances on matters other than the Emperor. He still hoped that the Soviet channel would be helpful and ignored the ultimatum that was clearly intended. He wished to remain noncommittal. But the military wanted the declaration openly rejected. They wanted better terms and indeed hoped to undo those demanded in the Cairo Declaration and to keep at least some colonies. Admiral Toyoda, the Navy Chief of Staff, later explained to American interrogators that "we looked upon that as a declaration but not as one whose terms would actually be applied to us." Such was the mentality the Americans and the Japanese moderates had to deal with. The Supreme Council for the Direction of the War at first formally agreed not to reply

A Letter from Einstein: Science vs. Politics

In the following letter to President Franklin Delano Roosevelt, Einstein speaks on behalf of his friend and colleague Dr. Leo Szilard about the lack of contact between policymakers and the scientists who were working on the atom bomb. The letter did not reach Roosevelt prior to his death on April 12, 1945.

112 Mercer Street
Princeton, New Jersey
March 25, 1945

The Honorable Franklin Delano Roosevelt
President of the United States
The White House
Washington, D.C.

Sir:

I am writing to introduce Dr. L. Szilard who proposes to submit to you certain consideration[s] and recommendation[s]. Unusual circumstances which I shall describe further below introduce me to take this action in spite of the fact that I do not know the substance of the considerations and recommendations which Dr. Szilard proposes to submit to you.

In the summer of 1939 Dr. Szilard put before me his views concerning the potential importance of uranium for national defense. He was greatly disturbed by the potentialities involved and immediately; but the military finally secured an outright rejection of the Potsdam Declaration.

The Impact of the Atom Bomb

A specially trained B-29 group, with planes modified to carry the A-bomb, was based on Tinian. On the morning of August 6, 1945, a B-29 dropped a uranium bomb on Hiroshima with a power equivalent to 14,000 tons of TNT. The tremendous flash scorched concrete, leaving the sil-

---

anxious that the United States Government be advised of them as soon as possible. Dr. Szilard, who is one of the discoverers of the neutron emission of uranium on which all present work on uranium is based, described to me a specific system which he devised and which he thought would make it possible to set up a chain reaction in un-separated uranium in the immediate future. Having known him for over twenty years both from his scientific work and personally, I have much confidence in his judgment and it was on the basis of his judgment as well as my own that I took the liberty to approach you in connection with this subject. You responded to my letter dated August 2, 1939 by the appointment of a committee under the chairmanship of Dr. Briggs and thus started the Government's activity in this field.

The terms of secrecy under which Dr. Szilard is working at present do not permit him to give me information about his work; however, I understand that he now is greatly concerned about the lack of adequate contact between scientist[s] who are doing this work and those members of your Cabinet who are responsible for formulating policy. In the circumstances I consider it my duty to give Dr. Szilard this introduction and I wish to express the hope that you will be able to give his presentation of the case your personal attention.

Very truly yours,

(A. Einstein)

William Lanouette and Bela Silard, *Genius in the Shadows: A Biography of Leo Szilard, the Man Behind the Bomb*. Chicago: University of Chicago Press, 1994, pp. 261–62.

houettes of vaporized human beings; farther away it melted the eyeballs of people looking in the direction of the blast. A huge mushroom cloud rose over the ruined city, much of which was consumed by a raging fire storm. Figures for atomic bomb deaths vary wildly, but it is fairly certain that the immediate effects of the bomb and radiation sickness killed over 70,000 people, and perhaps as many as 130,000, often in particularly horrible ways.

But the Japanese military leaders were not bowled over. A meeting of the Supreme Council on August 7 was inconclusive. In fact, Joseph Stalin seems to have found the A-bomb more impressive; he speeded his entry into the war, originally scheduled for the latter half of August. On August 8, Soviet forces invaded Manchuria and northern Korea. The Soviets had accumulated a vastly superior force. Although the Soviet troops numbered only 1,500,000 men to 1,000,000 Japanese troops, many of the latter were poorly trained, newly mobilized reservists or Manchurian Chinese. The Japanese tanks and planes were obsolete and in any case were heavily outnumbered. Many of the planes and antiaircraft guns were deployed to defend southern Manchuria against B-29 attacks. The Japanese had only light artillery. The main Soviet attack was launched by Rodion Yakovlevich Malinovsky's Trans-Baikal Front in the west. Striking from an unexpected direction, over difficult terrain, it thrust deep into southwestern Manchuria to meet up with a secondary attack from the Soviet Maritime Provinces. The Soviet forces were well equipped and their spearheads were supplied by transport planes when they outran their ground supply lines. Although the Japanese fought hard, Manchukuo proved a house of cards. On August 19, 1945, the Manchukuo Army units mutinied. But by then Japan had surrendered.

The Supreme Council for the Direction of the War met again on August 9, due to an initiative stemming from the Emperor. While it met, a B-29, unable to hit Kokura, its primary target, dropped a plutonium bomb on Nagasaki, causing at least 40,000 deaths, and perhaps as many as 70,000.

Luckily, the Nagasaki bomb, although more powerful than the Hiroshima bomb, did not touch off a fire storm. The Americans would have had a third A-bomb ready by August 15, but on August 10, President Truman ruled that no more bombs should be used until further notice.

The Surrender

But the Supreme Council was deadlocked. The Minister of War and the Army and Navy Chiefs of Staff no longer opposed a general acceptance of the Potsdam Declaration but demanded that the monarchy be preserved, that war criminals must be tried by Japan, that Japanese forces must disarm and demobilize themselves, and an occupation of Japan must be avoided. (The Army Chief of Staff, Umezu, was willing to accept a limited occupation excluding Tokyo.) The civilian members and Navy Minister Yonai agreed with the demand for an assurance on the monarchy but viewed the other demands as impractical. Only the Emperor broke the deadlock. By misleading the military, the civilians set up an Imperial Conference. Such conferences were only supposed to ratify decisions already made by the cabinet; no one, especially the military, had wanted the peaceably minded Hirohito to actually decide anything. When the deadlock became obvious at the Imperial Conference on the night of August 9–10, Prime Minister Suzuki asked Hirohito to decide between the two factions, having arranged a situation where the military could not disagree with such a move. The Emperor came down on the side of the civilians. A message was sent to the Allies offering to accept the Potsdam terms on the condition that the monarchy be preserved.

Arguments ensued in Washington. Byrnes stubbornly and stupidly fought a concession on the monarchy. Although Truman overruled him, the reply Byrnes sent to Tokyo was so vague that it provoked a new crisis there. The Japanese had to request a clarification of the terms, and the Emperor again had to intervene to enforce the decision to surrender. Even so, on August 14, Army extremists tried to overthrow the government to prevent the surrender. But the high command would not support them, and the coup was foiled. On August 15, Japan announced its surrender. But final arrangements for the surrender and occupation took weeks to arrange. The formal surrender was signed on September 2, 1945, aboard the battleship *Missouri,* in Tokyo Bay, ending the Second World War. Yet true peace seemed as far away as ever. And ever since, mankind has lived under the shadow of the weapon that brought the Second World War to an end.

CHAPTER 3

The Home Front

The Politics of Truth: The Office of War Information

John Morton Blum

In the following selection taken from his book *V Was for Victory: Politics and American Culture During World War II*, eminent political historian John Morton Blum discusses the creation and development of the Office of War Information (OWI), an agency designed to keep the American people informed about the progress of the war as well as the policies and aims of the government. Blum explains how politics, including conflicts with other agencies and the media, made it difficult for those assigned to the OWI to provide the public with information. For example, the War Department wanted to keep details of the war from the American people to avoid undermining their confidence in the military, but the OWI believed the people had a right to know the truth. The writers recruited by the OWI early in the war, Blum writes, became disenchanted when advertising men began to distort the material distributed by the OWI, believing the OWI was no longer providing information but instead selling the war to the American people. Blum is professor emeritus in history at Yale University.

The executive order of June 1942 establishing the Office of War Information (OWI) defined a seemingly broad

Excerpted from "Prescriptions for War Information," by John Morton Blum, in *V Was for Victory: Politics and American Culture During World War II*. Copyright ©1976 by John Morton Blum. Reprinted by permission of Harcourt, Inc.

mandate: "to coordinate the dissemination of war information by all federal agencies and to formulate and carry out, by means of the press, radio and motion pictures, programs designed to facilitate an understanding in the United States and abroad of the progress of the war effort and of the policies, activities, and aims of the Government." The facilitation of understanding implied much more than the mere broadcast of facts and figures, and implied, too, as it affected the policies of the government, an obligation to defend as well as to explain them. That obligation in turn, however appropriate for wartime propaganda, naturally whetted the suspicions both of the press and of political partisans who feared that the interpretation of government policies would spill over into advocacy of the Roosevelt administration. Particularly in addressing domestic rather than foreign audiences, co-ordinator Elmer Davis [a veteran newspaperman and radio newscaster], had to cut a narrow path between a neutrality toward policy that would impede understanding and an advocacy that would provoke Republican tempers. He had also to satisfy the reasonable demands of the press for war news without alienating powerful federal agencies eager to bend information to their own advantage. He had further to work through the media, which had already, as he knew, frequently perceived the war as melodrama. Yet Davis had to proceed with the authority only of a co-ordinator.

Organizing the OWI

Within a few months, Davis organized his agency along clear, functional lines. He divided domestic operations among seven desks, each responsible for providing information about a particular phase of the war effort. The deputy at each desk represented OWI in dealing with the bureaus or departments making policy in his area of concern. Each was to maintain a program "to give the public a clear and accurate picture of . . . the war," and those programs were "to be carried out" by another set of officers, "the chiefs of the media bureaus." Overseas operations, charged with reaching both friendly and enemy peoples, were organized by region, with major desks responsible for Europe and for Asia. Many domestic information programs, Davis presumed, would also serve to educate the world about American wartime policies and goals.

Every program, domestic or foreign, was subject to the explicit approval of the Board of War Information, a kind of agency cabinet that met daily. Initially it included Davis, Archibald MacLeish, Robert Sherwood, Milton Eisenhower, and Gardner Cowles, Jr. Of that able and prestigious group, MacLeish and Eisenhower, the younger brother of the commanding general of the European Theater of Operations, did not long remain with the agency. Sherwood, the renowned playwright, an intimate of Harry Hopkins and a speech writer for Roosevelt, was responsible for overseas operations. Cowles, a close friend of Wendell Willkie, was a prominent publisher whose properties included two Iowa newspapers, a radio station, and *Look* magazine. He served under Davis as the director of the media desks of the domestic bureau, a position from which he came to exercise a large influence within OWI. His cabinet, Davis hoped, would generate clear, continuous and penetrating policies, and would also have sufficient authority to permit OWI to control information programs throughout the government.

Conflicts from Within

Those hopes were circumscribed by the same conditions that had affected the Office of Facts and Figures (OFF). Almost from the outset, Davis's chief advisers disagreed about the appropriate direction of information policy. Depressed by the flaccidity of the liberal spirit in the United States, MacLeish in November 1942 urged Davis that "the American people should make up their minds now—meaning as soon as possible—meaning before the war ends—as to the things they are fighting for." Further, MacLeish believed that OWI, even at the risk of attacks upon it, should "accept responsibility for the job of putting before the people . . . the principal issues which must be decided, in a form which will excite and encourage discussion." Eisenhower and Cowles were dubious. "We know," Eisenhower wrote Davis on December 1, 1942, ". . . that in the end the people as a whole will decide . . . and we may also be certain that we will not be completely satisfied with the decision. For that decision will be a compromise between widely divergent economic and political views." OWI should therefore develop no blueprint of its own but concentrate on disseminating the relevant facts that would encourage discussion and "all shades of opinion. . . . We must maintain our policy of objectivity. . . . O.W.I. . . . should continue to be thought of primarily as an *information* agency." As Eisenhower put it directly to MacLeish, "Our job is to promote an understanding of policy, not to make policy." MacLeish replied that "the basic question is whether O.W.I. is to be a mere issuing mechanism for the government departments. I gather it is your position that it should be. On that I disagree . . . emphatically." But Davis and his colleague forced MacLeish to retreat to an unsuccessful effort to link OWI to a State Department planning group. OWI itself, as Eisenhower had understood, had no mandate from Congress or the President to undertake to define the purpose of the war or to try to sell its definition.

Conflicts with the Military

Indeed, its mandate as an "issuing mechanism" was far from clear. Officials in the War and Navy departments always contended that Davis could "advise" but not "direct." He was unable to bring the Army or the Federal Bureau of Investigation to release more than skeletal information about the Nazi saboteurs landed in the United States from German submarines, captured and then tried by a military tribunal. The Navy ordinarily issued communiqués that gave the impression of calculated reticence about American losses. Admiral Ernest J. King, the Navy's chief, so it was said within OWI, would like to have released only one statement during the entire war—the one announcing victory. Davis defended the Navy's communiqués, such as they were, rather lamely as being "much closer to the complete story than those of the enemy." It would be "most unfortunate," he continued, if "resentment of any failings" of the Navy in the subsidiary field of information were to "undermine public confidence in their capacity" to fight and to win the war. Yet Davis obviously felt some resentment himself. In contrast to the Navy, he explained, the Office of War Information followed "the guiding principle . . . that the American people have a right to know everything that is known to the enemy, or that would not give him aid if he found out. . . . We believe that the better the American people understand what the war is about, the harder they will work and fight to win it. We are not press agents for the government. We expect to set forth . . . the difficulties with which both the military and civilian branches of the government are faced, and their shortcomings as well as their successes."

That expectation clashed with the professional habits of the Army and Navy, while Davis's concern for the integrity of information contrasted with the tactical purpose of Colonel William Donovan, the head of the Office of Strategic Services (OSS). Donovan conceived of his activities abroad as an "adjunct to military strategy," a vehicle for planting stories and rumors that would cripple the enemy and enhance the reputation of the United States. His branch of psychological warfare by its very nature conflicted with the comparatively benign propaganda mission of the OWI, for psychological warfare had often to bury rather than expose the truth about American prowess and policy.

Battling Other Departments

Prodded by Donovan, the War Department moved to obtain control over both psychological warfare and foreign propaganda. "Both of these functions," Secretary of War Henry L. Stimson wrote Roosevelt in February 1943, "are definitely weapons of war." Davis and Donovan, Stimson complained, had "differed vigorously . . . as to the scope and jurisdiction of their separate duties. As the head of the War Department, I am in the position of the innocent by-stander in the case of an attempt by a procession of the Ancient and Honorable Order of Hibernians [Irish Catholics] and a procession of Orangemen [Irish Protestants] to pass each other on the same street. I only know that every Army commander . . . in a foreign theater, if the present difficulties persist, will be subjected to great embarrassment and danger to his operations." As a solution, Stimson proposed placing representatives of the OWI and the OSS on a committee which the Joint Chiefs of Staff would dominate. Donovan had agreed to that plan, but Davis had not, partly because Stimson, with magisterial disdain, had insisted upon selecting the OWI representative whom Davis was titularly to appoint. The issue was never really resolved. Roosevelt did not approve Stimson's proposal, but Davis could not establish operational jurisdiction over the information practices either of the OSS or of the armed services.

Stimson was more imperious but no more zealous than others in asserting his independence of the Office of War Information. William M. Jeffers, a brusque, tough business executive whom Roosevelt had made Rubber Director, attempted unsuccessfully in April 1943 to kill a story about the continuing shortage of automobile tires, an account based on Jeffers's own report to the President of the previous February. Perhaps in part because MacLeish had been wounded by government disingenuousness about rubber, Davis was furious with Jeffers. "Mr. William Jeffers," Davis announced on April 19, 1943, "tried to stop me from telling the American people facts about rubber which had been certified as correct by his own office. So long as I am here I propose to tell the people the truth as accurately as I can ascertain it, whether Mr. Jeffers likes it or not." Davis had done so, and Jeffers did not like it. "I can get along very well on the rubber program," he replied through the newspapers, "without Mr. Davis."

The Politics of Truth

Tougher by far than Jeffers, Secretary of the Interior Harold Ickes defied OWI late in 1943 by publishing over its objections an article in *Collier's* dealing with the United Mine Workers' strike in the bituminous coal fields. Ickes criticized the miners' demand for higher wages as inflationary, which it was, but he blamed the strike also on the "unbending posture" of the War Labor Board. The walkouts, he wrote, constituted "a black—and stupid—chapter in the history of the home front," a phrase Davis had wanted deleted. The article, Davis complained to the White House, was "one to which this office has serious objections, on the grounds that some of the statements are at variance with the Government's policy in the coal matter." Because Davis was supposed to "facilitate an understanding" of that policy, he argued that Ickes had violated appropriate jurisdictional lines. For his part, Ickes, whose pungent phrases had already made his point, explained innocently that he had not intended to ignore the opinions of the OWI, but an "unconscionable" delay in receiving them had permitted the article to go into print without the recommended deletions.

The episodes with Jeffers and Ickes revealed some of the difficulties that plagued Davis. He was seeking at once to get federal agencies to tell the truth and to persuade them to do so in a manner that would not undercut official policy, with which they at times disagreed. Yet Roosevelt had given him the authority only of a coordinator. Furthermore, the problem was not just jurisdictional. There were questions of substance at issue. Davis felt obligated to admit the persistence of shortages, which harassed administrators were endeavoring to overcome in the face of partisan but often accurate charges of ineffectuality. Davis felt equally obligated to explain, and however inadvertently thereby to support, government policies on inflation, which others besides Harold Ickes considered inequitable in various of their applications. One OWI publication on inflation advocated the Treasury's position on taxation, which struck conservative congressmen as an attack on legitimate business profits and personal income. The middle road was hard to find and harder to follow, especially where the military were involved. Confident that the American people could take bad news, Davis wanted to tell them more about casualties and losses than did the armed forces, who prevailed. Their publicity, as the Director of the Budget pointed out, continually overplayed victories and thus generated undue public optimism and complacency.

Conflicts with the Media

Conflicts over the content of information also arose, during the first year of Davis's tenure, both within the OWI and between the agency and the media. The questions of the comics and the movies exemplified the latter problem. The Bureau of Intelligence of the OWI found the content of American motion pictures continually distorting, continually frivolous in addressing the issues of the war. Living in luxury, Andy Hardy, absorbed by adolescence, was oblivious to the war. When ideological conversation occurred between good and bad Americans billeted in one of Hollywood's fictional cantonments, it tended to terminate with an "Oh, yeah" and a sock on the jaw. Hollywood's policemen and federal agents constantly followed false leads while amateur sleuths apprehended enemy spies and saboteurs. Even in *Casablanca,* the message of the Czech freedom leader was buried beneath the cynicism of Rick, so memorably conveyed by Humphrey Bogart. It was still the same old story: with few exceptions, *Wilson* and *Mission to Moscow* for two, films designed for the box office carried no message of purpose or idealism. On the contrary, producers during the war relied upon the kind of entertainment—love stories, situation comedies, adventures—that had filled theaters in peacetime. The movies, Archibald MacLeish concluded, were "escapist and delusive," a contributing factor to the failure of Americans to understand either the origins or the objectives of the war.

After surveying the comics, two psychologists reported

to the OWI that most of the heroes had donned uniforms (Superman and Lil' Abner were exceptions), but did not understand global war. In most comic strips, Americans won their battles alone, allies were nonexistent or subordinate, the enemy was a pushover. Only two popular comics satisfied the analysts. In "Terry and the Pirates" the Chinese were admirable fellows. Even better, Joe Palooka had buddies in the Army who made fluent statements against race prejudice and Anglophobia, though Joe himself was becoming rather too bloodthirsty. Comic strips conveyed especially unfortunate messages about the home front: "The effect of the war on the civilian is only a subject of humor. The home front's actions and thoughts and the demands on the civilian, have yet to receive serious and sympathetic treatment." Aside from "Gasoline Alley," the comics had neglected civilian defense, various shortages of civilian goods, and the recruitment needs of the Army. Those matters were ordinarily either the object of derision or the occasion for near hysteria, as in "Orphan Annie." Yet the comics reached millions of Americans who read almost nothing else. The OWI therefore published some comic books of its own, primarily for distribution to civilians overseas, though many copies reached American soldiers. One such, "The Life of Franklin D. Roosevelt," a Republican congressman condemned as unfair political propaganda, a waste of the taxpayers' money, and—intending no irony—an unhappy imitation of "Tarzan of the Apes." Earlier, the *Wall Street Journal* had defended the comics on the ground that the artists would lose their readers if their heroes did not triumph single-handedly. The OWI, not the comics, according to the *Journal,* was unrealistic. By that standard, Davis, like MacLeish before him, had to suffer the treatment of the war according to habits of the media that he was powerless to reform.

The Role of Advertising

There were those within the OWI who accepted just about that standard with regard to the role of advertising. Gardner

Cowles, Jr., in February 1943 told the annual advertising awards dinner that advertising was needed to win the war. If advertising was not yet fully organized for that purpose, he said, the fault lay with the OWI and "would be remedied very soon." Within two weeks, the agency had taken a long step in that direction. The OWI planned to publish a new magazine, *Victory,* for circulation in Europe and among liberated peoples there. Copies also reached American troops in England. *Victory,* OWI announced, would contain paid advertising copy, partly to defray the cost of publication, partly for other, illuminating reasons. Advertising, the agency said, "lends an appearance of authenticity to a magazine," and German, Italian, and Japanese propaganda journals therefore carried advertising. (By implication, the United States had to be as authentic commercially as were its enemies, an odd point for an American propaganda agency to make.) "Institutional advertising," moreover, told "an exceedingly powerful story of the war effort of American business." (Perhaps sometimes it did, but one senior advertising executive had complained publicly about "schoolboy pictures of zooming American bombers winning the war thanks to Filch's Bolts and Nuts . . . stomach-turning copy.") Finally, "the Office of War Information felt that American business should have the opportunity to keep alive trade names and brands throughout the entire world in anticipation of a peaceful international trade." Doubtless that noble war aim would indeed organize the energies of American advertising, as Cowles had promised.

The influence of advertising men within OWI ultimately demoralized the writers in the publications bureau. They had been laboring, many of them, since the early weeks of OFF, to prepare pamphlets and other copy about the war that would transcend, on occasion contradict, the typical output of the media and their sponsors. They admired Elmer Davis and respected Gardner Cowles, but they found their position intolerable after Cowles brought in as his senior assistant William B. Lewis, a former vice president of the Columbia Broadcasting System. With support from Cowles and ultimately Davis, Lewis curtailed the production of pamphlets and turned instead to relying upon the initiative of the press in reporting about domestic programs. That decision reflected adversely particularly on Henry F. Pringle, the head of the writers' division, a liberal and iconoclastic journalist and historian. Pringle and his associates felt they had used the press effectively. They cited the wide reporting derived from their pamphlets about American aircraft, drinking in the armed forces, the shortage of doctors, and the importance of employing Negroes in war industry. Even "creative pamphlets," such as that on the Nazi occupation of Warsaw, had received extensive publication. The real issue, they felt, arose because Lewis intended to abandon the careful provision of information about issues and substitute "advertising techniques." Cowles admitted as much. The writers, he said, "resented the fact that I brought in experienced advertising men and sought to persuade industry to use its advertising program to help war information."

That resentment, along with an accumulation of other grievances, in April 1943 provoked a spate of resignations. Among others, Henry Pringle, Harold Guinzberg, president of Viking Press, Henry Brennan, former art editor of *Fortune,* Edward Dodd, a vice president of Dodd, Mead, and Arthur Schlesinger, Jr., then a precocious but already an incisive historian, left the OWI. As Lewis had intended they should, they also left the field to the advertisers, the men and the ideas that had earlier distorted the publications and broadcasts of the Treasury's bond program and of the OFF. One development that precipitated the crisis prompted Pringle to a splendid summary of the issue at stake. Lewis had grouped a number of desks under a new Bureau of Graphics and placed in charge Lieutenant Commander Price Gilbert, formerly advertising manager for Coca-Cola. Pringle produced a mock poster to characterize the change. It displayed a Coca-Cola bottle, wrapped in the American flag, with a legend below: "Step right up and get your four delicious freedoms. It's a refreshing war."

Shortages, Conservation, and Rationing

Richard R. Lingeman

Soon after the United States entered the war, Americans began to experience shortages, and conservation efforts and ration boards were set up everywhere, writes editor and political satirist Richard R. Lingeman in the following excerpt from his book *Don't You Know There's a War On? The American Home Front, 1941–1945*. The war in the Pacific had depleted much of the nation's rubber supply, Lingeman explains, but President Franklin D. Roosevelt was reluctant to restrict the American use of the automobile. However, the author notes, when conservation efforts failed to solve the problem, the government instituted gasoline rationing. Lingeman also discusses the rationing of sugar and coffee, and the confusion faced by many Americans who had learned the virtue of hoarding during the economic depression and were now chastised for doing so.

The effort in the factories and the mines to mobilize for war at first gradually, then rapidly made itself felt on civilian shelves. The pre- and post-Pearl Harbor flush of prosperity ate up the nation's inventory of refrigerators, automobiles, stoves, irons and other durable goods. As the steel, aluminum and other mineral-processing industries strained to expand their capacities to meet the insatiable demands of war, acute metal shortages resulted. Even in 1942, as the American public dabbled its feet in war and went about consumption pretty much as usual, a series of serious shortages loomed upon the horizon, each followed by the disappearance of another amenity of civilian life that long habit had converted into near necessities.

The Office of Price Administration [OPA] began its stormy and arduous career as inflation fighter and food rationer in April, 1941, when it was created as the Office of Price Administration and Civilian Supply by executive order. Its mission was to prevent "price spiraling, rising costs of living, profiteering and inflation," but its powers were largely "jaw-bone." Leon Henderson, the veteran New Deal economist who was its first director, labored strenuously but with little effect—concentrating on raw materials rather than finished goods—as the defense-stimulated economy heated up and prices rose 10 percent during the year. With the coming of war, the government moved in vigorously, if erratically, to regulate the economy, pouncing first on groceries, clothing and other commodity prices and rents, while leaving farm prices and wages alone. The Emergency Price Control Act of January 30, 1942, gave the OPA teeth; the General Maximum Price Regulation of April 28, 1942, brought about 60 percent of all civilian food items under a form of control which froze prices at their store-by-store March levels. In January the OPA already had got itself into the rationing business by issuing, on its own initiative, a tire-rationing plan; it never relinquished the rationing territory. Ration boards were set up in every county in the forty-eight states, and more than 30,000 volunteers were recruited to handle the vast paper work involved in controlling prices on 90 percent of the goods sold in more than 600,000 retail stores and issuing a series of ration books to every man, woman and child in the United States. As the war drew on, nearly every item Americans ate, wore, used or lived in was rationed or otherwise regulated. It was the most concerted attack on wartime inflation and scarcity in the nation's history, and by and large it worked.

The Rubber Shortage

Rubber was first to go to war—a national crisis for the Japanese conquests in the Far East had gobbled up 97 percent of the nation's crude rubber supply. Only 660,000 tons had been stockpiled—versus an annual civilian consumption of 600,000 to 700,000 tons. The government quickly clamped a freeze on tires, followed by a ban on recapping tires. Only a few could get a certificate to buy a new tire or a recapped one. Anyone who owned more than five tires per car was supposed to turn in the extras to their local filling station. A nation of some 30,000,000 automobile owners reeled from the shock. Some seemed bent on driving their tires down to the rims; others paid exorbitant prices—$25, $50 each for new ones. Others put their cars away for the duration. One journalistic traveler on America's highways found tires the sole topic of conversation among travelers at wayside stops:

During World War II, the United States experienced all types of shortages, including rubber. Pictured are piles of used tires that will be reclaimed and used in the war effort.

"For one thing, [tire rationing] is giving the layman-driver a weird lingo. He now . . . talks of such things as the fabric of a tire and the carcass, of recapping and retreading, as if they were things he learned as a tiny tot, and of the potential yield of rubber plants on the great alkali deserts."

While the experts debated and the government from President Franklin D. Roosevelt (FDR) on down procrastinated about what measures to take beyond tire rationing, practically everyone had ideas on just how to solve the rubber shortage and restore every American's sacred right to drive an automobile as fast and as far as he liked. Suggestions poured into the War Production Board (WPB) and to the OPA. Many were ingenious, if offbeat; others were from the realm of science fiction and even political satire—*viz.*, the suggestion that all the government had to do was reclaim all the tires on Works Progress Administration (WPA) wheelbarrows. . . .

But until the necessary synthetic plants could be built (1941 production was only 12,000 tons) and the Brazilian plantations put into production (Far Eastern competition had beaten out the Brazilian rubber industry in the early 1900's), the nation would have to live off its stockpile supplemented by reclaimed and scrap rubber, and of course 75 percent of this would have to go to the military—and would probably be inadequate. Meantime, what of the war workers who drove to work—not to mention truckers, buses, taxis and essential drivers like doctors? Of course reclaimed rubber was relatively plentiful—a total of 85,000 tons would be produced during the time period—but it was unsuitable for many military needs, and besides, after being reclaimed three times, it lost its bounce. What was needed, simply, was $700,000,000 worth of new synthetic rubber plants capable of turning out 800,000 tons annually. The civilian faced a bleak future.

Looking for Solutions

His government did little of note for several months to impose any order on the rubber chaos. The obvious answer was a rigidly enforced conservation policy for civilian drivers, a policy that would literally save the driver from himself—in short, gas rationing, for no other limitations would be enforceable. But FDR dawdled, lacking the political courage to deprive the American citizen of his cherished freedom of the road. At one point, the President seemed to have placed his hopes on a massive scrap rubber drive to solve the nation's problems. This took place in June with Petroleum Coordinator Harold L. Ickes' enthusiastic support. Suggesting darkly that "we suspect that there are people hoarding rubber, and there may even be people in official life who are doing a little hoarding," Ickes ordered all the rubber floor mats in his Interior Department building donated to the cause. This brought a bristling reply from the Buildings Department, which pointed out that it owned the mats, so they were not Ickes' to donate; besides, they were needed to keep people from slipping on the marble floors. The next time Ickes was at the White House, he spied a rubber floor mat, rolled it up and gave it to his chauffeur with instructions to drop it off at the nearest rubber salvage depot.

Millions of Americans followed Ickes' lead and ransacked closets and attics and cellars for old overshoes, hot-water bottles and beach balls and hauled them to the nearest gas station collection point. Like Ickes' floor mat, much of this material was already made of reclaimed rubber and hence only good for making more floor mats; still, a total of 335,000 tons was collected.

But the rubber shortage was not solved, and the President continued to shilly-shally. According to Bruce Catton, who was employed by the WPB at the time, Roosevelt told a meeting of his chief production advisers, "Personally I'm not worried about the rubber shortage." At a press conference he was asked about gas rationing and allowed he could understand why a man in Texas, say, living next door to an oil well with four good tires on his car would be opposed to any limitations on his freedom to use his car as he saw fit. (Shortly before that performance, Roosevelt had said he was considering a proposal to requisition every tire in the United States.) The remark was perhaps a bow to his Southern coalition, as well as the Western states, all of whose representatives opposed gas rationing.

Rationing Gas

Gas rationing was announced for the East Coast beginning in May 1942. This was not aimed at cutting down on driving and saving tires; it was because of a real fuel shortage resulting from the large number of tankers sunk by German subs in the Atlantic. The Eastern seaboard depended on tanker shipments for 95 percent of its oil, prewar; a pipeline, known as the Big Inch, was being built to link the Texas oilfields with the Northeastern states, but this would not be completed until early 1943. The overburdened railroads would help, but not enough to alleviate the shortage. When Leon Henderson announced his plan to allocate each motorist from two and a half to five gallons a week, the oil industry and its good friend in Washington, Ickes, let out a wounded bellow, Ickes calling Henderson's program "half-baked, ill-advised, hit or miss." A propaganda barrage accused Henderson of maliciously trying to make the American people unhappy and labeled gas rationing an exercise in official sadomasochism whose only purpose was to instill in the American people a proper mood of wartime self-abnegation. The rationing in the East was seen merely as a stepping-stone to nationwide rationing. Be that as it may, Easterners took to rationing with reasonable calm and a probably normal amount of chicanery. On the May 10, 1942, weekend, the last before rationing began, traffic was below normal, contrary to predictions of a last-minute spree of madcap pleasure driving. More than 200 members of Congress asked for and were given X cards allowing unlimited gasoline, causing some raised eyebrows.

The President, under the pressure of his advisers, finally appointed a commission headed by the universally respected Bernard Baruch to look into the rubber situation. The commission reported back that the only way to save tires was to limit mileage for the entire nation, and the only way to do that was to ration gasoline, curtail nonessential driving and cut down on speeds. Armed with this holy writ from the sage of Wall Street, Roosevelt ordered nationwide gas rationing, a ban on pleasure driving and a 35-mile speed limit on all of the nation's highways. Gas rationing went into effect on December 1, 1942; it had taken Americans nearly a year to tighten their belts this mere one notch; hardly anyone, from Roosevelt on down, was blameless for this procrastination. Leon Henderson, who, as he himself predicted, had become the most unpopular man in America, resigned, and was replaced by former Senator Prentiss M. Brown, a Michigan New Dealer.

The basis of the ration system was the A, B and C sticker system. An A sticker owner received the lowest gas allocation, four (later three) gallons a week, which the government estimated, at 15 miles to the gallon, would permit 60 miles of driving. The B sticker holder had essential driving to do—such as a war worker who drove his car in a car pool—and received a supplementary allowance. The C card holder needed his car for essential activities—a doctor, for example—and was given additional allocations. Obviously, if you were an A card holder, you were a nobody— a nonessential who puttered about in his car on insignificant little errands while cars packed to the roof with joyriding war workers or large sedans driven by powerful men with mysterious connections blew carbon monoxide in your face. It is, of course, the American Way of Life to Get Ahead, and everybody who could find the flimsiest pretext of essentiality tried to convince his local OPA board that he deserved better of them. One OPA estimate had it that nearly half of all American drivers had B or C stickers (there was also a T sticker for truckers, who could get all the gas they needed) meaning an army of 15,000,000 drivers going about essential occupations, even though a Gallup Poll had shown that of the 45 percent of American workers who drove their cars to work, three-fourths said they could get to work some other way if necessary.

The Outcome of Rationing

Gas rationing and attendant regulations aimed at cutting down on driving did bring a noticeable decline in cars on the streets. In big cities one could ply the unpopulated boulevards with rarely a start or stop for traffic. Deliveries were curtailed by department stores, and the slogan was "Don't delay, buy it today, carry it away." In the East, milk deliveries were cut to every other day, while newspapers (some using horse-drawn wagons) made only one daily delivery of editions to each newsstand. The decline in driving was accurately reflected in gasoline tax revenues; in New York State revenues for the first three months of 1943 were $6,600,000 compared to $13,500,000 for the same period in 1942. Most significant of all, the auto death rate fell dramatically: on Labor Day, 1942 (before nationwide rationing), there were 169 deaths in auto accidents; in 1941, there had been 423. It was estimated that the highways were being used at only about 20 percent of capacity.

So gas rationing has its salutary results—or so a group of professional cheerer-uppers had it. One of these was Donald Culross Peattie, the naturalist, who extolled the joys of walking, presumably restored to the land by the advent of gas rationing.

I came back to my desk with blood tingling, with every stale, mundane concern washed out of my head. I had heard the titmouse calling his merry song of *peet-o, peet-o* and song sparrows tuning up on the adder branches where the catkins were hanging out all pollen-dusty and fertile. I had heard the brook gurgling.

Theoretically, if a car owner wanted to travel for pleasure, he had to use his feet—or take the train. In January, 1943, the OPA banned all pleasure driving; even the nonessential A card holder could not use his niggardly three gallons except in pursuit of "essential" business which the OPA defined as "necessary" shopping; attending church services or funerals; getting medical attention; meeting emergencies involving a "threat to life, health or property"; or trips for family or occupational necessities. The OPA ruled that a driver might sample nonessential pleasures on an essential trip (such as stopping for a soft drink) as long as he did not "add as much as one foot to the distance traveled in his car for such a purpose." This came as a shock to the A's; they had thought their sacrifice entitled them to burn up their paltry share in any way they wanted. Of course, such a ban was difficult to enforce, and OPA men took to hanging around racetracks and athletic stadiums, copying down license numbers of out-of-county cars on the theory that just getting to the athletic spectacle was per se pleasure driving. In Rochester, New York, those who had driven to a symphony concert had their books taken away by OPA sleuths; in New York City owners of cars parked in front of nightclubs and restaurants were similarly penalized. Miscreants could lose their gas ration if caught. The ban was finally revoked in September, 1943. Petroleum Coordinator Ickes said it had been necessary because of a gasoline shortage in the East; however, he added cryptically that although the crisis had passed, there was still not enough gasoline to permit any pleasure driving. (For a period during the next year enormous military demands lowered the basic gas allotment to two gallons a week.) . . .

Counterfeiting or Alternative Transportation

Gas and tire rationing inevitably gave rise to a black market. Correctly sizing up the opportunities for illegal gain in this area, professional criminals moved in, and their operations harked back to Prohibition days. The favored *modus operandi* was to counterfeit ration coupons. The forged coupons (most of which were C coupons, the most generous ration) might be sold to individual drivers by the packet at prices as high as 50 cents a coupon. More frequently, however, the mob's "salesmen" sold them to filling-station operators, who were thereby enabled to sell gasoline at prices ranging from 10- to 25-cents a gallon higher than the ceiling and account for these illegal sales, by turning in the counterfeit coupons to the OPA. Some of the filling station operators were willing accomplices, but in some areas the mobs threatened honest operators with physical violence if they did not join the scheme. There was a case in New Jersey where a woman operator, who refused to take the mob salesman's coupons, was tortured with a burning paper torch. When she fainted, the gang departed but not before they had taken her money and burned all her legitimately collected coupons. . . .

In some areas of the country, especially the East Coast, there were times when you couldn't get any gas at all. In the summer of 1942 the pumps literally went dry; most stations closed, and motorists and truckers were stranded. Some stations remained "closed" or "out of gas" to save old customers. In New York, drivers would sometimes tail a gasoline tank truck until, like a pied piper, the truck had collected a string of cars following it to its destined delivery point. Cars would line up for blocks—as many as 350 of them—when word spread that a filling station had received a gasoline shipment.

There were alternatives, of course. New York suburbanites and California war workers alike resorted to bicycles, but bicycles were rationed, too, and people had to have a certificate of necessity from their local ration boards before they could purchase a new one. Walking was possible—even enjoyable to some—but because of a shortage of hides and increased Army demands, shoe rationing for civilians was put into effect in February, 1943. Three pairs of shoes a year was not exactly hardship rations—in 1941 the average American bought 3.43 pairs of shoes. In England the wartime ration was about one pair per year. But by 1944 large military demands had squeezed the civilian supply down to two pairs per person. One of the side effects of shoe rationing was another hoarding spree—this time of clothing, which, rumor had it, was next on the list. In New York, clothing stores experienced a 53 percent jump in business during the first week of shoe rationing. Lord & Taylor finally took a full-page ad in the *New York Times* to announce: "We wager $5,000 that clothes will NOT be rationed this year." At least one bride received a Number 17 (shoe) stamp as a wedding present.

Rationing Food

Of greater impact on American life than gas rationing was the rationing of food. People coped with gasoline rationing by curtailing unnecessary trips, forming car pools and share-the-ride clubs, and eking out the life-span of their worn prewar cars and tires (after all, one did not really *need* a new car every year or two). But except for those with the money and elastic consciences for black-market patronage, food rationing hit everyone alike. The first table item to become scarce was sugar, rationing of which began in April, 1942. Scarcities presaging some kind of rationing had occurred in some areas as early as December, 1941. Everyone knew in advance that sugar was going to be rationed, however novel the idea of rationing anything in America was to many people. There was a wave of buying that began immediately after Pearl Harbor. Everyone from bootleggers to housewives who had long memories of the World War I sugar shortage rushed to buy 100-pound bags, and grocers were forced to limit purchasers to 10 pounds each. This artificial shortage quickly became a real one in early 1942, after imports from the Philippines ceased and the shortage of shipping made transportation of the Cuban and Puerto Rican crops difficult. And even though the entire yearly crops of these and other Caribbean sugar producers would be acquired by the United States, there was never enough to meet the increased demands of military and civilian needs. Sugar rationing was never eased and indeed continued without surcease through 1946. In 1945, a bad crop year, civilians consumed 70 percent of the prewar level.

So it was that on balmy nights in early May, 1942, Americans trooped to their local schools, where teachers issued War Ration Book One for each member of the family. Many submitted jovially to this first wartime sacrifice; it seemed little enough price to pay for the privilege of "doing something" for the war effort. For the hoarders it was a moment of truth; they had to make depositions of how much sugar they had on hand; stamps equivalent to this stockpile would be torn from their books. Some carried it off with aplomb: "Poor little mixed up me—only one teensy little cup of sugar in the house. I'm just too scatter-brained to think ahead, I guess." But others caved in under the stern eye of the local schoolmarm, confessed their supplies and took their loss of stamps gamely. And after all, the ration, which averaged out to 8 (later 12) ounces per person per week, was not all that catastrophic. . . .

Rationing Coffee

The subsequent rationing of coffee in November, 1942, proved among other things, that the hoarding psychology was deeply ingrained in the American character. As did sugar, coffee became scarce several months before rationing was put into effect. As early as June, railroad dining cars started serving it only at breakfast, hotels cut out refills, and coffee ads urged voluntary rationing: "Now we're all sharing coffee—by drinking three cups instead of four." Warning of rationing was officially given a month in advance; housewives responded by cleaning out most of the stocks on hand. A week before the beginning of rationing the government froze sales, announcing the freeze on a Sunday, when stores were closed—a practice that became OPA tradition.

Consumers met the shortage by an increasingly familiar pattern of behavior. Most made do on the ration of one pound per person every five weeks. Those who couldn't patronized the black market, tried stretchers like chicory or followed FDR's tongue-in-cheek advice to rebrew used grounds. The latter piece of advice got the President in hot water with the National Coffee Association, who feared that consumers might learn to like this economical practice and continue it after the war. "We respectfully suggest," it wrote him piously, "that it is harmful to imply even in a spirit of levity that the little coffee we do have should be spoiled in the brewing, and that such waste of good coffee should be practiced to help win the war . . . the American people rightly prefer to have fewer cups of pure, fresh, stimulating coffee properly brewed, rather than more cups of recooked dregs of a watery or adulterated brew." Meanwhile, out in Kansas City, librarians reported a rush on books about soybeans—somebody or other had said that you could brew a good cup of ersatz from them. The mania for substitutes contributed to a tidy little door-to-door salesmen racket in which housewives were offered a so-called powdered coffee, which was actually cracked wheat (it tasted awful).

Scarcity gave coffee an aura of luxury it had never had before. Noncoffee users started drinking it to use up their stamps or gave their ration as wedding presents. When the girls got together for luncheon, the noncoffee drinkers might trade their cup for the dessert of a coffee-starved lady.

The Evils of Hoarding?

When rationing was taken off in July, 1943 (they had, after all, a lot of coffee in Brazil; lack of cargo space had caused the shortage), a funny thing happened: Coffee sales dropped temporarily. Apparently, rationing had increased its desirability. A postscript to the coffee crisis was provided when the OPA issued War Ration Book Four in the fall of 1943. Housewives noticed there was a stamp in the book labeled "coffee" and another coffee rush began. The OPA had to undertake newspaper and radio campaign to convince the ladies that it would never, never again ration coffee.

"Hoarding" was evil but never very precisely defined. Was buying a single extra can of condensed milk hoarding? An Office of War Information radio program implied that it was. There was definitely a stigma attached to someone who acquired more than his share. The First Lady tried to capitalize on this by implanting the subtle thought that "It's wonderful what your neighbors know about you." Sometimes this community pressure degenerated into gossip compounded of a good deal of envy. In some communities rich people became the butt of rumors that they had vast stores concealed in underground vaults. One little girl got up in school to tell her classmates proudly about the old Colonial house they lived in, which had a secret room. Now, she went on, Daddy used it to keep all his extra tires!

The traditional homemaking virtues were made obsolete by the new rationing ethos. This moral shift was expressed in a contemporary book called *Consumer Problems in Wartime*:

> What was right for the consumer yesterday, even a virtue, is wrong today. The woman who rails at strikes in industry or red tape and incompetence in public officials may have closets stored with canned goods or sugar and coffee. Once that would have meant foresight and good management. Today, it means that ugly thing—*hoarding*.

There was a popular phrase which went: "I'm just stocking up before the hoarders get there."

The Third Force: Women Go to Work

Nancy Baker Wise and Christy Wise

In the brief excerpt that follows, writer Nancy Baker Wise and journalist Christy Wise discuss what they call the third force: women on the home front who successfully took up the work abandoned by the men who went off to fight the war. According to the authors, these women gained advantages beyond a paycheck, including camaraderie with male and female coworkers and increased self-confidence. Some women gladly stepped aside when the men returned from war, the authors write, but others who had proven themselves capable of challenging work became frustrated. However, the authors note, these women performed well and were accepted into what was once an all-male world, and they forever changed the role of women.

W hen the Japanese attack on Pearl Harbor in December 1941 drew the United States into World War II, increased mobilization of the armed forces was immediate and intense. Within a year, hundreds of thousands of American men from eighteen to thirty-nine years old were fighting in the Army, Navy, Marine Corps, and Coast Guard, having left their businesses, offices, and factories. Ultimately, more than sixteen million Americans served in the armed forces in World War II.

Excerpted from *A Mouthful of Rivets: Women at Work in World War II*, by Nancy Baker Wise and Christy Wise. Copyright ©1994 by Jossey-Bass Inc., publishers. Reprinted with permission from the publisher.

Women, too, joined the armed services, becoming Women's Army Corps (WACs), Women Accepted for Volunteer Emergency Service (WAVES), and the Coast Guard's SPARS, taking desk jobs, driving jeeps, and becoming instructors to free the men for active duty.

A Third Force at the Home Front

A third force emerged to maintain the wartime economy and production so vital to victory—the women at home. Wives, mothers, sisters, and girlfriends left their families, schooling, or other jobs to learn the skills required to continue the work abandoned by the men, and to perform the new work of defense production. They were quick learners. By 1943, two million women were in war industries, and American production far outpaced that of Axis countries. At a Tehran gathering of Allied leaders in 1943, Russian premier Joseph Stalin gave this toast: "To American production, without which this war would have been lost."

For professional women, the war offered a chance to break into careers or management positions that otherwise would have been off limits, such as the civilian fliers and air traffic controllers. Some women found themselves doing work they never would have imagined for themselves—and loved it. This happened to the New York office manager who gave up a good-paying job to contribute to the war effort but was employed as a secretary rather than at the plant. After her threat to join the WAVES, the management moved her to flight operations, where she became a clearance officer and flight tester.

Women's motives for working were primarily financial and patriotic. Having lost their sole wage earner to the battles overseas, many women had no choice but to go to work to supplement the small stipend they might be receiving. With the effects of the Depression still weighing heavily on many families, women and men alike were delighted with the prospect of work, often traveling thousands of miles to one of the two coasts, where much of the defense production was going on. Some women saw an opportunity to earn more money than was possible in the lower-paying, more traditional "women's" jobs of that period.

As critical as money was for most workers, the desire to help the United States win the war was equally important. Women responded to the nation's urgent call for help. In one poster, three women are featured in stateside jobs and at the bottom are identified as "Soldiers Without Guns." "Women in the War: We Can't Win Without Them" cried another poster. These were among thousands of flyers plastered in banks, department stores, post offices, on high school bulletin boards, and in magazines. Women on the home front wanted to bring their husbands, boyfriends, and brothers home as quickly as possible, and in a few instances, made financial sacrifices to do so. In other cases, the women sacrificed sleep, comfort, and time at home with their children.

Earning More than Money

Often, women discovered advantages to working outside the home that went beyond their paychecks. They enjoyed a camaraderie with each other and with their male co-workers that was a completely new experience after being isolated at home as housewives. Their confidence and self-esteem increased as they saw how well they could perform their work, conquering new, and sometimes frightening, tasks and circumstances.

They overcame discrimination, harassment, gritty working conditions, unfamiliar machines, acrophobia, transportation glitches, and homesickness. With gas rationing in place and all transportation systems overloaded, home-front workers had to find creative ways to get to work, either carpooling, walking long distances, or taking the few available buses.

Denying their preference for looking pretty and feminine, women factory workers grudgingly donned men's work clothes or uniforms, covered their hair with the hated "snoods" or bandannas, and tromped around in steel-toed leather boots. Women in office positions had it a bit easier.

Rosie the Riveter

During World War II companies like Westinghouse produced posters like the one below for the War Production Co-ordinating Committee to encourage the participation of women in the war effort. Rosie the Riveter was a symbol of patriotic womanhood— a strong, competent woman dressed in overalls and bandanna.

J. Howard Miller, "We Can Do It!" National Archives and Records Administration Still Picture Branch (NWDNS-179-WP-1563) http://www.nara.gov/exhall/powers/women.html.

But with the shortage of nylons, they had to use leg makeup that streaked in the rain, and with cotton and wool reserved for the defense industry, their clothes were created with rayon and other less desirable fabrics.

In talking about these hardships, though, women laughed more than complained, pleased with their ability to adapt. Many wore their welding leathers with pride and found carpooling fun. Superimposed on the tragedy of the war was the energetic lightheartedness of what were, for the most part, young women. As with most people in their early twenties, they were thrilled to be out in the world—working, getting together with friends, dancing at the United Service Organizations (USOs), which were charitable social groups for servicemen. Almost apologetically, women said they had fun working during the war.

Stepping Aside

With the end of the war, the jobs that had been created specifically for the nation's defense disappeared. Plants closed or were converted to peacetime work. Employment preference was now given to returning veterans. Many women did not question the men's right to return to their jobs. They stepped aside willingly, delighted to return home to their families or to start creating families in the midst of the marriage boom that followed the armistice.

"I wanted to be home with those kids. They were too precious," said Lillie Cordes Landolt of Des Moines, Iowa. She and her husband both worked in an ordnance plant during the war while a retired school teacher cared for their five children.

But for other women, the veterans' return entailed wrenching change, forcing them angrily back to "women's work," with its accompanying reduction of responsibility and pay. They had proven they could do the work and were frustrated not to be allowed to continue.

"The guy came back to my specific job," said Vera-Mae Widmer Fredrickson, who was operating a punch press in Minneapolis, Minnesota. "It was union and the punch press was a man's job and had always been. They never had women on it. They put me to work putting labels on switches and I quit. I was furious. I went to the union about it, too. Didn't do a bit of good."

Women came forward for their country and in doing so were accepted into the men's work world as riveters, welders, geologists, mail carriers, pilots, crane operators, and truck drivers. They learned faster and produced better than their male bosses anticipated. Their performance was extraordinary. But for nearly two decades after that, most women accepted the supporting role of homemaker and mother, not venturing into the workplace.

In 1994, with 57.3 percent of American women working outside their homes, compared to about 37 percent in 1950, women are taken for granted in some of the professions that were considered daring during the war. And in others, women still are in a minority.

Most women who participated in the workforce during the war consider it one of the highlights of their lives and retain the same pride and sense of accomplishment they felt half a century ago.

"When I show my grandchildren, I have a wonderful feeling of pride," said Jennette Hyman Nuttall, a crane operator during the war. "I say, 'See that crane way, way up there? Grandma used to run a crane like that during the war.'"

The Internment of Japanese Americans

Diane Yancey

The internment in relocation centers of Japanese Americans and Japanese who had immigrated to the United States represents one of the darker events to take place on the home front during World War II. In the following excerpt from her book *Life in a Japanese American Internment Camp,* Diane Yancey tells of the fear and paranoia that led to the Executive Order 9066, requiring the evacuation of "all persons of Japanese Ancestry, both alien and nonalien." Yancey details the chaos and confusion that resulted from the order, the embarrassment and humiliation of the assembly centers, the frustration and rebellion at imprisonment, and the courage and optimism that characterized many internees. According to Yancey, despite the mistrust of a misguided government, most internees maintained their faith in democracy and loyalty to the United States.

The bombing of Pearl Harbor on December 7, 1941, stunned Japanese Americans just as it stunned millions of others across the United States. Many had scoffed at the idea that a tiny nation like Japan would dare attack a world power. Others had believed that the United States would be able to foresee any Japanese strike and would therefore take steps to prevent or defeat it.

With the surprise attack and the president's declaration of war, however, Japanese Americans could not help but worry. All knew that many white Americans believed them to be loyal to their homeland and its emperor. Now that Japan and America were at war, they were unsure what the future would hold.

Reaction to Suspicion

The Issei, who were Japanese citizens and could possibly be suspect, reacted with fear. Many hastily destroyed anything they owned that might be judged suspicious or disloyal—Japanese flags, samurai swords, and books in Japanese—even if those possessions were cherished family mementos. After that, they stayed off the street, listened to their radios, and waited.

The Nisei were cautious but more confident. They were U.S. citizens. America was their country; nothing bad could happen to them there. To prove their loyalty, many went out and purchased war bonds. Some joined the Red Cross; others volunteered for civilian defense patrols. A number of young men decided to join the military even before they were drafted. Jack Tono, a Nisei born in San Jose, remembers, "All being citizens, a bunch of us were talking that we eventually would have to go. Go to the Army and defend the country, that was about the main thing."[1] And Charles Kikuchi, a Nisei college student living in San Francisco, wrote in his diary:

> Pearl Harbor. We are at war! . . . The Japs bombed Hawaii and the entire fleet has been sunk. I just can't believe it. I don't know what . . . is going to happen to us, but we will all be called into the Army right away. . . . I will go and fight even if I think I am a coward and I don't believe in wars. . . . If we are ever going to prove our Americanism, this is the time.[2]

Pro-Japanese?

Many Americans, especially those on the West Coast, believed that there was good reason to question the loyalty of

Japanese Americans. For instance, a great number of Issei belonged to *kenjinkai,* traditional Japanese associations made up of people from the same *ken,* or clan. Other Issei were involved in patriotic organizations, known as *kai,* that professed loyalty to Japan. Members of the Heimisha Kai in San Francisco regularly collected funds to be sent to Japan to help the War Ministry. The Togo Kai was named after a hero of the Russo-Japanese War; its purpose was to collect funds for the Japanese navy.

In addition to membership in Japanese organizations, many Issei subscribed to newspapers printed in Japanese containing news of the homeland. They sent their children to Japanese language schools to ensure they could speak Japanese. Some Japanese Americans even celebrated holidays that involved worship of the Japanese emperor, who was traditionally considered a god in Japan.

In the eyes of white Americans, such pro-Japanese associations indicated loyalty to Japan. It seemed logical that those who were loyal to Japan would be anti-American, willing to express their animosity through sabotage and espionage.

Loyal to America

Americans need not have worried so much about the Japanese in their midst. Only a few months before Pearl Harbor, a State Department official, Curtis B. Munson, had filed a report that included information on possible danger from West Coast Japanese. Munson found that, although the Pacific states were poorly protected against enemy attack, the great majority of Japanese Americans were wholeheartedly loyal to America and posed no threat in time of war. Munson pointed out that the physical characteristics of Japanese would make them easily identifiable if they attempted undercover work, and noted that few had the opportunity to spy or commit sabotage. "The Japanese here is almost exclusively a farmer, a fisherman or a small business man. He has no entree to plants or intricate machinery,"[3] he wrote.

Munson's report was the result of interviews with army

and naval intelligence officers, businessmen, university professors, farmers, and religious groups on the West Coast. Had it been widely published, fears about Japanese Americans might have been dispelled. "As interview after interview piled up," Munson wrote, "those bringing in results began to call it the same old tune. . . . There is no Japanese 'problem' on the Coast. There will be no armed uprising of Japanese."[4]

Unfortunately, Munson's report remained almost secret, as were similar reports filed by Kenneth D. Ringle, one of several naval officers stationed in southern California in 1941 whose job it was to keep an eye on the Japanese community. Ringle reported that over 90 percent of the Nisei and 75 percent of the Issei were completely loyal to the United States.

"Enemy Aliens"

Not willing to take any chances, FBI agents began their own roundup of three thousand suspected "enemy aliens" just hours after the bombing of Pearl Harbor. About half of those arrested were people of German and Italian descent, individuals who by their ancestry, behavior, and associations were judged hostile toward the United States. World War II had been raging in Europe for two years, with America's allies, Britain and France, pitted against Hitler's Germany and Mussolini's Italy.

The rest of the suspects were Japanese. Often without warning, wives and children came home to the disturbing discovery that a loved one had been taken for questioning, as Yoshiko Uchida describes:

> When I got home, the house was filled with an uneasy quiet. A strange man sat in our living room and my father was gone. The FBI had come to pick him up, as they had dozens of other Japanese men. . . . In spite of her own anxiety, Mama in her usual thoughtful way was serving tea to the FBI agent. . . . I couldn't share [her] gracious attitude toward him. Papa was gone, and his abrupt custody into the hands of the FBI seemed an ominous portent [sign] of worse things to come.[5]

Uchida's father worked for a Japanese import-export firm, reason enough to make the FBI suspicious of him. Many of the men arrested were chosen simply because of their occupations—heads of Japanese organizations; executives of Japanese businesses, shipping lines, and banks; and Japanese language teachers and journalists. Some suspects had expressed views that were pro-Japanese, but others were merely community leaders. Some pastors and Sunday school teachers were included. So were commercial fishermen, who were in a position to make contact with enemy ships.

Those men who were judged a threat to their country

A group of young Japanese Americans await relocation to an internment camp. The relocation of thousands of Japanese Americans, many of them U.S. citizens, was an act that the U.S. government later regretted.

were taken to special internment camps overseen by the Justice Department, located in North Dakota and Nebraska. There they remained, sometimes for many months. Eventually, those who proved innocent were allowed to rejoin their families, most of whom had meanwhile been sent to relocation camps.

With the arrests, the FBI was satisfied that danger from internal treachery was all but eliminated. Members of anti-Japanese organizations, however, were not convinced that the FBI had done enough to ensure the safety of the West Coast. They began calling for the removal of all Japanese Americans. Groups who competed economically with Japanese Americans also added their voices. "We're charged with wanting to get rid of the Japs for selfish reasons," stated a spokesperson for the Grower-Shipper Vegetable Association in California. "We might as well be honest. We do."[6]

"Yellow Journalism"

The "yellow journalism" press, which thrived on rumors and unverified speculation, was also busy stirring up public fears. Journalists whose job it was to be unbiased often expressed opinions that were one-sided and unfair. Derogatory terms such as "Japs," "Nips," "yellow men," and "yellow vermin" were used interchangeably when referring to Japanese and Japanese Americans. Unfounded articles with titles such as "Jap Boat Flashes Messages Ashore" and "Map Reveals Jap Menace" appeared in California newspapers.

Not even the Nisei, who were citizens, were exempt from the accusations. For instance, one journalist for the *Los Angeles Times* wrote, "A viper is nonetheless a viper wherever the egg is hatched—so a Japanese-American, born of Japanese parents—grows up to be a Japanese, not an American."[7] And renowned journalist Edward R. Murrow remarked to a Seattle audience in January 1942 that if Seattle was ever bombed, they "[would] be able to look up and see some University of Washington sweaters on the boys doing the bombing."[8]

Rejected and Threatened

Government and civic leaders were also responsible for whipping up anti-Japanese feeling through racist remarks and speeches. Members of Congress and senators such as Mississippian John Rankin and Tom Stewart of Tennessee denounced all Japanese and Japanese Americans as cowardly and immoral. In February 1942 the mayor of Los Angeles gave a speech calling for the roundup of all Japanese Americans before they could harm America. Even Earl Warren, later to become California's governor and influential chief justice of the U.S. Supreme Court, stated, "I have come to the conclusion that the Japanese situation as it exists today in this state may well be the Achilles heel of the entire civilian defense effort."[9]

Not surprisingly, such remarks led many ordinary people to react negatively. The reactionaries were a minority of the population; a public opinion poll taken during this period indicated that only 20 to 40 percent of the population supported action against Japanese Americans. Nevertheless, as a result, many Japanese Americans lost their jobs or were forced out of positions they occupied. The Los Angeles County Board of Supervisors fired all its Nisei employees. Officials in Portland, Oregon, revoked the licenses of all Japanese nationals doing business in the city.

Other reactions were more personal. Neighbors made threatening phone calls. Houses were stoned. Japanese passersby were attacked and spat on in the streets. In some places, beatings and lynchings occurred. To prevent mistaken attacks, Chinese Americans began wearing pins that stated "I am a Chinese." Yoshiko Uchida writes, "I wasn't aware of any violence against the Japanese in Berkeley, but there were many reports of terrorism in rural communities, and the parents of one of my classmates in Brawley were shot to death by anti-Japanese fanatics."[10]

One of the most influential government officials to believe the worst about Japanese Americans was General John DeWitt, in charge of the army's Western Defense Command stationed in San Francisco. DeWitt, a sixty-one-year-old army bureaucrat, was increasingly convinced by every rumor that the United States stood in grave danger from the thousands of Japanese Americans living on the West Coast.

DeWitt conscientiously passed on the "facts" to his superiors. In one memo he wrote that "there were hundreds of reports nightly of signal lights visible from the coast, and of intercepts of unidentified radio transmissions."[11] In another, that "for a period of several weeks following December 7th, substantially every ship leaving a West Coast port was attacked by an enemy submarine. This seemed conclusively to point to the existence of hostile shore-to-ship (submarine) communication."[12]

Most of the information DeWitt chose to believe was exaggerated or untrue. Japanese submarines attacked ships off the California coast extremely rarely and one report existed of a Japanese air attack on oil tanks near Los Angeles, but none of these had involved Japanese Americans. DeWitt's signal lights turned out to be farmers burning piles of brush. "Enemy" radio signals were, in reality, army transmissions. And thousands of guns, ammunition, dynamite, radio receivers, and cameras that had reportedly been confiscated proved to have been gathered from a licensed gun shop and a warehouse. According to Justice Department and FBI reports:

> We have not found a single machine gun, nor have we found any gun in any circumstances indicating that it was to be used in a manner helpful to our enemies. We have not found a single camera which we have reason to believe was for use in espionage.[13]

In fact, there never was a proven case of shore-to-ship signaling or any other sabotage or fifth column activity by Japanese Americans on the West Coast.

To the President

General DeWitt ignored these truths and earlier reports by Munson and Ringle and continued to express his belief that

Japanese Americans should be removed from the West Coast. Eventually, his arguments for relocation reached Secretary of War Henry L. Stimson. Stimson was aware of the strong anti-Japanese feeling in California, and he supported the establishment of zones around military installations, oil fields, dams, airports, and other sensitive operations from which Japanese Americans could be excluded. Still, he was reluctant to take the drastic and complicated step of relocating over a hundred thousand people if it was not necessary.

Then, on February 14, 1942, DeWitt sent Stimson a recommendation entitled "Evacuation of Japanese and Other Subversive Persons from the Pacific Coast." The report, and DeWitt's odd logic, apparently helped convince the war secretary of the military necessity for relocation:

> [A]long the vital Pacific coast over 112,000 potential enemies, of Japanese extraction, are at large today. There are indications that these are organized and ready for concerted action at a favorable opportunity. The very fact that no sabotage has taken place to date is a disturbing and confirming indication that such action will be taken.[14]

DeWitt's rationale was extremely weak; he based his argument that sabotage would take place on the fact that it had not yet occurred. After meeting with several War Department officials who also favored internment, however, Stimson went to President Roosevelt to urge relocation.

Earlier, Roosevelt had cautioned his country to guard against discrimination aimed at innocent citizens. However, when Stimson presented DeWitt's recommendations and requested that the president authorize the army to relocate all persons of Japanese lineage as well as others who might threaten the security of the country, Roosevelt agreed. On February 19, 1942, ten weeks after Pearl Harbor, he signed Executive Order 9066.

The order made no mention of any particular race, but it was directed at Japanese Americans. Relatively few persons of German and Italian descent were incarcerated, even though the United States was now also at war with Germany and Italy. Officials argued that German and Italian loyalty was easily determined, while that of Japanese Americans was not.

Although some of his advisers viewed the decision for relocation as extreme and without precedent, the president reasoned that in times of war and for reasons of national security such bold steps often had to be taken. Attorney General Francis Biddle, who opposed the order, later observed:

> I do not think [Roosevelt] was much concerned with the gravity or implications of his step. . . . What must be done to defend the country must be done. . . . The military might be wrong. But they were fighting the war. Public opinion was on their side. . . . Nor do I think that constitutional difficulty plagued him—the Constitution has never greatly bothered any wartime President.[15]

Voluntary Relocation

On March 2, DeWitt announced the designation of Military Areas 1 and 2 and warned that, in the near future, certain people might be excluded from those regions. Military Area 1 covered the western halves of Washington, Oregon, and California and the southern half of Arizona. Military Area 2 included the rest of these states.

Relocation had already begun, however, with a call for volunteers. As early as December 1941, Japanese Americans patriotic (or fearful) enough to disrupt their lives and leave their communities had been asked by Justice Department officials to move out of certain sensitive areas around military installations.

The result was chaos and confusion. Rumors of internment camps and mandatory evacuation were rampant; families asked themselves if they should go or stay and risk imprisonment. Jeanne Wakatsuki Houston, whose father had been arrested by the FBI, writes, "I remember my brothers sitting around the table talking very intently about what we were going to do, how we would keep the family together."[16]

Most families who decided to cooperate were faced with trying to dispose of their property and possessions in a short period of time, usually at a huge monetary loss.

Decisions had to be made about where to go, how to get there, and how to make a living on arrival. Some families decided to make the move as short as possible. For instance, many from Los Angeles relocated to Fresno. (In June 1942, DeWitt declared all California a prohibited zone, so these families had to move again.) Many decided to move to neighboring states, such as Nevada and Idaho. The most daring—usually Nisei with excellent language skills—went farther east, either to try and make a life for themselves on their own or to join the rare family member who had left the Pacific Coast.

"Japs Keep Moving"

Not surprisingly, people living in such states as Idaho and Wyoming believed that their dams, airports, and military installations were just as vulnerable to sabotage as were those in Pacific states. Almost as prejudiced as Californians, many were outraged by the influx of Japanese Americans who arrived from the West Coast expecting to resettle.

Refugees were met with hostility and with signs like "Japs Keep Moving. This is a White Man's Neighborhood." Some were turned back at state borders by armed and angry men; some were thrown in jail. Community leaders worried that mob violence was imminent.

By the end of March, over three thousand Japanese Americans had cooperated with the government, but nearly one hundred thousand still remained in Military Areas 1 and 2. Those numbers, coupled with increasing tension throughout the West, forced DeWitt to declare voluntary relocation a failure. Now the move would be compulsory. In a new policy outlined in late March, the general announced that all persons of Japanese lineage were to be evacuated from Military Area 1 in the near future. This included not only full-blooded Japanese, but anyone who had Japanese blood, "no matter how small the quantum."

A number of Koreans, Hispanics, and Blacks, married to Japanese, chose not to be separated from their spouses and children; they were relocated, as well.

Canada and Hawaii

The United States was not the only country to take such forcible steps against its Japanese American population. Feelings against the Japanese ran high throughout North, Central, and South America during the course of the war. In cooperation with the U.S. State Department, a few Latin American countries sent Japanese citizens living in their nations to U.S. internment camps, from which they were later used as bargaining chips in diplomatic exchanges with Japan. In Alaska and Canada, the entire West Coast Japanese population was relocated to camps in a move similar to that in the United States.

Ironically, the U.S. territory of Hawaii, deep in the war zone, did not imprison most of its Japanese both because Hawaiians were more racially tolerant and because Japanese made up a large percentage of its workforce. Locking them up would have had a devastating effect on the local economy. Thus, most were allowed to remain in their homes and jobs for the course of the war.

"Why Us?"

The evacuation announcement was no surprise to the Japanese American community, but all were hurt and humiliated by the decision. They had done nothing to warrant such unfair treatment. As former internee Emi Somekawa asked, "Why us? I felt like we were just being punished for nothing."[17]

Despite these feelings, leaders of the JACL, one of the few organizations to represent Japanese Americans, urged cooperation with authorities. "You are being removed only to protect you and because there might be one of you who would be dangerous to the United States. It is your contribution to the war effort. You should be glad to make the sacrifice to prove your loyalty."[18]

Many Japanese, particularly the Nisei, were critical of the JACL's compliant stance. They accepted the fact that the Issei, who were Japanese citizens, might justly be incarcerated as enemy aliens in times of war. But imprisoning American citizens threatened the constitutional freedoms of all Americans. Jack Tono remembers, "I just couldn't understand the whole atmosphere of the whole thing, being a citizen. I could see it if I was an alien. You have no choice but to face things like that. But at the JACL meeting when . . . nobody resisted . . . it was more shocking than the goddarn Pearl Harbor attack. It really frosted me."[19]

Veterans of World War I were equally outraged. They felt betrayed by the country for which they had fought and despised anyone who cooperated with the government. One veteran, Joe Kurihara, believed that all should fight against relocation "to the bitter end." "These boys claiming to be the leaders of the Nisei were a bunch of spineless Americans," he declared, referring to the JACL. And regarding the government: "Having had absolute confidence in Democracy, I could not believe my very eyes what I had seen that day. America, the standard bearer of Democracy, had committed the most heinous crime in its history."[20]

Other Nisei argued that uprooting hundreds of loyal and peaceable persons to remove a few potentially dangerous individuals from the West Coast was unnecessary and unjust. And to the government's argument that relocation was for their own good, to protect them from public violence, another Nisei pointed out, "The government could have easily declared Martial Law to protect us."[21]

Despite their criticism, few Japanese Americans actively resisted relocation. Prior to the Executive Order, some had signed petitions and attended meetings at which they begged their country to act fairly. Once the order was signed, however, their traditions and upbringing led them to obey authority. They had no leaders who encouraged their defiance. Thus, most expressed their disillusionment privately or not at all.

To some Japanese Americans the order to relocate came as

something of a relief. Since Pearl Harbor they had lived with uncertainty. Many Issei had had their bank accounts frozen and had lived in poverty for months. Some believed that deportation to Japan was just around the corner; others feared violence. "[T]o be unable to go out in the streets, or just to the corner store without the fear of being insulted," remembers one evacuee, "and being all tense inside with that same fear, was one of the most humiliating things." [22]

Thus the notion of going into a camp, away from a hostile and threatening world, seemed to some like a step toward stability. The camps would provide shelter, food, and protection. There everyone would be of Japanese lineage. As that same evacuee admitted, "I think some of us were a little relieved to be away from the minor irritations, the insults, slander, and the small humiliations unthinking people heaped upon us after Pearl Harbor." [23]

Model Citizens

The great majority of Japanese Americans on the West Coast were model citizens, as Jack Tono observes:

> [T]here was no ethnic group as straitlaced as the Japanese because of their historical background.... [W]e're all brought up with honor, shame, dignity; the moral code of standards is nothing but the best. When you talk about delinquency and other crime, for us there was nothing but traffic tickets. [24]

In fact, many people recognized the community's good qualities and deplored the injustice of the relocation decision. They pledged continued support of their Japanese American neighbors and colleagues. They urged unity and cooperation between races. Some expressed their views by letter to President Roosevelt. One asked, "Do you think the President . . . could find it suitable and wise, at a press conference or even in a fireside talk, to say a word of praise for the American citizens of Japanese descent, loyal and of good record, who . . . have endured and are enduring no little hardship?" [25] Another wrote, "Has the [government] really power to intern American citizens? Is it reasonable for Japanese-Americans to be interned and Germans and Italians, not? Is not the very essence of our democracy that we are made up of all races and colors?"[26]

As events continued to unfold, however, even the most concerned had to face the fact that the government was not going to consider or protect Japanese American rights. All the evacuees could do was make the best of their situation—by proving their loyalty to America, by following government directives, and by packing up their families and moving into the unknown. "We took whatever we could carry," one Nisei recalled later. "So much we left behind, but the most valuable thing I lost was my freedom."[27]

If the weeks after the bombing of Pearl Harbor were difficult for Japanese Americans, the days leading up to relocation were a nightmare. The government tried to disguise the fact that it was sending them into prison camps by using euphemisms such as "non-aliens," "protective custody," and "reception centers."

Reality was different, however. Beginning in late March 1942 and continuing throughout the summer, terse commands called Civilian Exclusion Orders appeared on telephone poles and shop windows in Japanese communities, directing all persons to prepare to move within the week. Those who did not comply faced severe penalties including arrest and imprisonment. Those who obeyed reported to a Civil Control station in their community, where they were registered and given a number by which they would be known during internment. One recalls, "I lost my identity. . . . The WRA [War Relocation Authority] gave me an I.D. number. That was my identification. I lost my privacy and dignity."[28]

An Agonizing Process

Preparing to move was an agonizing process. Families were directed to bring only a minimum of belongings to camp, but were responsible for their own clothing, eating utensils, towels, and bedding—blankets and sheets. Most also packed tea kettles, hot plates, books, and other small, personal items. Yoshiko Uchida writes:

> In one corner of my mother's room there was an enormous shapeless canvas blanket bag which we called our "camp bundle." Into its flexible and obliging depths we tossed anything that wouldn't fit into the two suitcases we each planned to take. We had been instructed to take only what we could carry, so from time to time we would have a practice run, trying to see if we could walk while carrying two full suitcases.[29]

Unsure of their final destination, adults worried about packing appropriate clothes for their families. If they went to the mountains, winter clothing would be a necessity. In warmer climates, heavy sweaters and coats would only take up valuable space. One woman remembers, "They said 'camp,' so we thought about going up in the mountains somewhere. I even bought boots thinking we would be up in the mountains where there might be snakes. Just ridiculous all the funny things we thought about."[30]

Adults also worried about disposing of household goods they could not take along. Most people were not wealthy, but the majority had a car or truck and a houseful of furniture. Each family member also had his or her own prized possessions—porcelain tea sets, houseplants, trunks of family mementos and heirlooms—most of which had to be left behind.

Finding homes for family pets was another difficult task. Families sometimes left their animals with friends. Others resorted to giving pets away. Yoshiko Uchida recalls the fate of the family dog. "Although the new owner of our pet had promised faithfully to write us in camp, we never heard from him. When, finally, we had a friend investigate for us, we learned . . . that Laddie had died only a few weeks after we left Berkeley."[31]

Storage and Sales

Since taking everything to camp was not an option, most families sold some of their more valuable household items, usually at a small fraction of their value. The *Los Angeles Times* wrote that "junkmen and second-hand furniture dealers" were preying on many who were desperate for money. Nearly new washing machines sold for $5; refrigerators for $10. Rather than sell her family furniture for a few dollars, one woman made a bonfire and burned everything. Another who had been offered $17 for a set of china worth over $300, smashed her delicate cups and saucers in front of the dealer who had made the offer.

Businesses and homes were also sold at a loss by families who had no one to act as caretaker. One woman observed, "We sold the store for a thousand dollars the day before we left. We had done an inventory, and the contents of the store were worth ten thousand. Our machines alone were worth eight thousand—that's what we paid for them. And we sold the whole store for a thousand dollars."[32]

But not every American was out to take advantage of the Japanese community. Many generous people offered to oversee homes and farms that had to be abandoned, and to store boxes of possessions that could not be taken to camp. Yoshiko Uchida remembers, "We were close to our neighbors and they both extended the warmth of their friendship to us in those hectic days. We left our piano and a few pieces of furniture with one, and we piled all the miscellaneous objects that remained on the last day into the garage of the other."[33]

E-Day

In late March, nervous but obedient Japanese Americans began reporting to the control centers on their assigned evacuation day (known as E-Day). As they gathered, dozens of volunteers, many from neighboring churches, helped them cope with children, suitcases, boxes, and bags. Some volunteers handed out coffee, tea, and doughnuts, so that no one would begin the trip on an empty stomach. In San Francisco, the Quakers set up a canteen offering, besides the usual refreshments, hot plates to heat baby bottles, string to tie up boxes, and tissues for those who could not hold back their tears. Many volunteers went so far as to drive the sick and aged to assembly centers so they would not have to cope with a difficult train or bus ride.

Once the journey into the unknown began, however, the atmosphere became less friendly. Stark signs of mistrust were all around. Armed guards were ever present. In some rail cars, windows had been papered over to prevent passengers from looking out. Former internee Miyo Senzaki remembers, "We got on, and as we traveled, I noticed that wherever we hit a town, the MPs [military police] would tell us to pull the shades down and we'd be curious, because we didn't know where we were going." [34]

Resistance and Despair

Most Japanese Americans cooperated when it came to relocating, but some tried to evade the move. One Nisei went into hiding and was found, near starvation, three weeks later. Fred Korematsu, a young Californian who eventually challenged the constitutionality of evacuation in court, underwent plastic surgery and successfully posed as a Spanish-Hawaiian for a time until he was arrested by the FBI.

For a few, the relocation process was too humiliating to be borne. Rather than shame himself and his daughter, a father afflicted with a medical condition that would have been revealed in the public atmosphere of the camps committed suicide. A World War I veteran did the same, dying with his Honorary Citizenship Certificate in his hand. The certificate had been awarded in "honor and respect for your loyal and splendid service to the country in the Great World War." [35]

Assembly Centers

Once begun, the process of relocation was so rapid that few permanent relocation centers had been built before internees began arriving at control stations, suitcases in hand. Until the centers were completed, therefore, most families were sent to one of twelve temporary reception centers, officially known as assembly centers. Manzanar and Poston Relocation Centers were the exceptions; both were close to completion, so some evacuees went directly into them from their homes.

Army officials in charge of this phase of relocation chose existing facilities such as racetracks and fairgrounds as sites for the assembly centers, since these public places had been designed to hold large numbers of people and were already equipped with electricity, water, and bathroom facilities. The addition of barbed wire and armed guards around the perimeters ensured that residents would not try to escape.

Within the centers, grandstands, livestock stalls, and stables were turned into apartments for the residents. The rooms were drafty and cold during bad weather and oppressively hot on sunny days. Dividing walls were paper thin and sometimes did not reach the ceiling. The floors of many stalls were only scraped out and covered with boards, so that, in the summer heat, the smell was overpowering. As Yoshiko Uchida describes,

> The stall was about ten by twenty feet and empty except for three folded Army cots lying on the floor. Dust, dirt, and wood shavings covered the linoleum that had been laid over manure-covered boards, the smell of horses hung in the air, and the whitened corpses of many insects still clung to the hastily white-washed walls.[36]

Other residents were housed in hastily built barracks—shacks with tar paper roofs—dubbed "chicken coops" because of their low ceilings and lack of windows. A bare lightbulb hung from the ceiling, and furniture consisted of army cots and mattress tickings that had to be stuffed with straw before they could be used. On arrival, stunned residents could do little but unpack their meager possessions and wonder how long they would be forced to live in such conditions.

A Lasting Impression

Living quarters were not the only disheartening and demeaning features of camp life. On rainy days, walkways turned into ankle-deep mud as thousands of residents tramped from apartments to mess halls and back again. Plumbing in laundries and bathrooms periodically backed up due to overuse. Conditions in the mess halls were unappetizing and unsanitary, and hundreds of residents suffered from food poisoning because food was incorrectly stored and handled. Former internee Minoru Yasui remembers his experiences in the Portland assembly center, where many families lived in the livestock pavilion.

> My lasting impression of the dining area was that it was festooned with yellowish, spiral flypaper hung from posts and rafters. Within a short time the paper would be black with flies caught in the sticky mess. There were horseflies, manure flies, big flies, little flies, flies of all kinds. . . . Flies, after all, usually inhabited livestock barns.[37]

Nonexistent Privacy

With thousands of people crowded into each assembly center, residents immediately discovered that every moment of the day was shared. Families were constantly thrown together in their tiny one-room apartments. Neighbors were so close that even the smallest sounds were detectable. Minoru Yasui remembers, "Because of the thinness of the three-ply wood, any noise—any coughing or sneezing, crying of babies, family arguments, boisterous conduct, laughing, or any shouting or yelling—could be heard throughout the hall."[38]

Meals were communal. Three times a day, residents carried their eating utensils to noisy mess halls, where lines were long, food was served cafeteria style, and everyone ate at crowded picnic tables.

Bathrooms and showers were also communal, and this was one of the most disturbing discoveries. Older Japanese, who habitually finished their day with the private luxury of a hot, relaxing bath, now found themselves compelled to shower shoulder-to-shoulder with strangers in an open room intended for horses. Women were horrified at the sight of rows of toilets, ranging back-to-back down the middle of the room. As one remembers, "For us women . . . it was just a shock. I remember we got sick . . . we couldn't go . . . we didn't want to go. . . . It was very humiliating."[39]

Some tried to solve the problem by carrying newspapers, behind which they could at least hide their faces and pretend to read. Some chose to use the bathrooms in the dead of night; others erected portable cardboard partitions around themselves. Eventually, carpenters constructed wooden partitions (without doors) around each toilet, but, as Yoshiko Uchida observes, "To say that we all became intimately acquainted would be an understatement."[40]

Relocation

There were many aspects of the centers that challenged the residents who were used to the privacy and comfort of their own homes. Yet, with persistence and creativity, most soon began to adjust to their new surroundings. They made new friends, settled into their apartments, and established new routines. Just as they did so, however, center officials made a disturbing announcement. Construction of the relocation centers was nearly complete. Barracks had been erected, water supplies developed, sewage systems built, and power lines strung. Internees would soon be transferred into them, and the assembly centers would close.

The news created fresh anxiety and added to the uncertainty of everyone's already unsettled lives. They had already given up their homes and property and begun anew. Now they were being told to repack their few possessions and begin all over again. They wondered when they would be leaving, what the permanent centers would be like, and if they would remain together as families. Charles Kikuchi wrote in his diary: "The suspense of getting our order [to move] is getting me down. I know that it is coming soon, but when? I hope that they will give us two or three days of advance notice so that we can pack."[41]

Notice was accordingly given, and between June and the end of October 1942, residents were transferred to one of ten relocation camps, located on federally owned land and run by the War Relocation Authority (WRA), an agency established by President Roosevelt for that purpose.

Dusty and Desolate

The relocation centers were located in desolate regions of the country, far from towns, highways, and railroads, since many Americans rebelled at the thought of treacherous "foreigners" living near them. Jerome and Rohwer camps were built on Arkansas swampland infested with malarial mosquitoes. Poston's three wards, or blocks of barracks, known as Poston, Toastin', and Roastin', were set in the sun-scorched Arizona desert. Topaz center was located in a barren Utah valley and recorded temperatures that ranged from 106°F in the summer to below freezing in winter. Manzanar, located in the dry Owens Valley in eastern California, also experienced similar temperature extremes. Jeanne Wakatsuki Houston, who lived in Manzanar, writes, "Some old men left Los Angeles wearing Hawaiian shirts and Panama hats and stepped off the bus at an altitude of 4000 feet, with nothing available but sagebrush and tarpaper to stop the April winds pouring down off the back side of the Sierras." [42]

Residents at Manzanar, Topaz, Minidoka, and Heart Mountain also suffered through dust storms, clouds of swirling grit that regularly turned day into night and shut down all activity for hours at a time. Even in calm weather, dust constantly filtered up through cracks in barrack floorboards, defying all efforts to sweep it away. One former Manzanar resident remembers, "The desert was bad enough. . . . The constant . . . storms loaded with sand and dust made it worse. . . . Down in our hearts we cried and cursed this government every time when we were showered with dust. We slept in the dust; we breathed the dust; and we ate the dust." [43]

Towns Surrounded by Barbed Wire

The relocation centers were not brutal concentration camps like those established in Nazi Germany for the Jews, but they were prisons nevertheless, surrounded by barbed wire fences, guard towers with machine guns, and searchlights. Wards were arranged side by side with military precision. In a typical center, there were nine wards—four blocks per ward, sixteen to twenty-four barracks per block. Each block had a kitchen, mess hall, laundry, bathrooms, and showers. Empty barracks were used as meeting halls, recreation rooms, churches, and schools. The centers were also equipped with a hospital, fire station, staff houses, and storage warehouses. Acreage within center boundaries was usually cultivated and crops were used to feed the residents.

The barracks themselves, usually partitioned into six apartments, were flimsy structures made of boards and covered with black tar paper. Each apartment was about twenty by twenty feet, the size of a small living room. None had running water. Heat was provided by an oil-burning stove, and furniture consisted of one army cot and two blankets per person. An average family was usually assigned to one apartment; couples and single persons were sometimes made to share an apartment, and larger families were allotted two.

Improvements

In dozens of irritating ways, internees were reminded that they were little better than criminals, but they soon realized that life in the camps was an improvement over the months spent in the assembly centers. Privacy was still at a premium—apartments were cramped and bathrooms and laundries were communal—but most of the camps covered thousands of acres, so now there was space for residents to walk around outside. Jeanne Wakatsuki Houston remembers, "[I]t was an out-of-doors life, where you only went 'home' at night, when you finally had to: 10,000 people on an endless promenade inside the square mile of barbed wire that was the wall around our city."[44]

Barracks were poorly built, with cracks in the floorboards and walls that allowed icy wind and sand inside, but they were an improvement from stables and "chicken coops," and residents soon made them more homelike. Within weeks, curtains hung at most windows, lids of tin cans covered knotholes in the walls, and homemade furniture, vases of flowers, and throw pillows brightened the stark rooms. After a time, sheetrock and linoleum—maroon, black, and forest green—were installed in most barracks, making them more weatherproof and more attractive.

Food was again served cafeteria style in mess halls, but its quality gradually improved, especially after residents began growing their own vegetables and raising poultry. From the beginning, as in the assembly centers, meals were "American" and included such items as hot dogs and hamburgers, which pleased members of the younger generation. Charles Kikuchi wrote in his diary, "There can no longer be conflict over the types of food served, everybody eats the same thing, with forks."[45] In time, fish, rice, and other foods preferred by older Japanese were added to menus in most centers.

Controlled and Supervised

Despite these improvements, internees never forgot that their every move was controlled and supervised. Each camp had a director, appointed by the national director of the War Relocation Authority, first Milton Eisenhower and later Dillon Myer. A few directors were men who lacked the tact and understanding needed for dealing with the complexities of camp life. For instance, Ray Best, head of Tule Lake Relocation Center, allowed radical nationalist internees to dominate and intimidate innocent Tule Lake residents for months.

Most directors, however, were responsible, businesslike individuals who tried to cope fairly in the midst of difficult situations. Ralph Merritt, head of Manzanar, often went out of his way to aid residents. Paul Robertson of the Leupp Isolation Center (a high security facility for troublemakers) treated his prisoners with respect and even corresponded with several after internment ended.

Each director had a staff who helped run the camp. In the beginning, all were Caucasian. As time passed, however, Japanese Americans proved ready and able to take over many assistant positions and do most of the work in offices and mess halls. There were Caucasians on the staff who were bigoted and unhelpful, but overall the group was dedicated and hardworking, saw the internees as equals, and treated them with understanding and tolerance. One internee testified to his supervisor's kindness: "He did not like to have me say that I was working for him, for he said we were working together for the good of 10,000 people. We worked night and day, but I did not mind, for I was working with a man who could not have been finer."[46]

A Constant Presence

Army soldiers who served as guards and sentries were a constant presence in every center. Since internees showed little or no desire to escape (at Topaz, internees themselves erected the fences and towers after they arrived), a minimum detail of officers and enlisted men was assigned to each camp. During times of disturbances, more soldiers were brought in.

Guarding the centers was boring duty for those who were away from their families and had little to do during the long months they served. Charles Kikuchi observed in his diary, "Sort of feel sorry for the soldiers. They are not supposed to talk to us, but they do. Most are nice kids. They can't get leaves and so have nothing to do."[47]

Kikuchi was more accepting of his captors than most of the internees. To them, the guards represented the army and the government, which all now hesitated to trust. And while some guards were sympathetic, others were not. As one WRA official reported, "[Lt. Buchner] explained that the guards were finding guard service very monotonous, and that nothing would suit them better than to have a little excitement, such as shooting a Jap."[48] In fact, in several incidents, guards wounded and even killed internees, one of whom had only carelessly wandered too close to a perimeter fence. Thus, it is not surprising that the sentries' attempts to be friendly were politely ignored by most internees.

High Security Camps

While most center residents were law abiding and required a minimum security presence, certain internees came to be seen as troublemakers and were sent to special camps where they could be more carefully guarded.

One of the highest security facilities for such troublemakers was located in Moab, Utah. Overseen by the WRA, this camp was populated by Nisei from mainstream camps who had been judged guilty of crimes ranging from organizing work stoppages, strikes, and protests, to having pictures of Japanese soldiers pinned in their apartments. In some cases of mistaken identification, innocent internees were held and given no chance to return to their families even when the mistake was discovered.

Life at Moab was grim; administrators there paid little attention to the comfort or preferences of the prisoners. Rules were strict; guards were ordered to shoot to kill; and the most dangerous men were under constant guard, even in showers and bathrooms. Predictably, internee morale was low, as one inmate's words reveal: "The life here has been worse than a prisoner's life. . . . In the event that our internment will be until after the war, there may be much bitter disillusionment brewing from this cruel camp life."[49]

In April 1943, WRA authorities closed Moab and transferred its inmates to a similar camp in Arizona. Located on a desolate Navaho reservation, Leupp Isolation Center proved to be an improvement over Moab, thanks to its humane director, Paul Robertson. Under Robertson, camp conditions were no worse than in mainstream centers, and prisoners were given greater freedom than they had experienced at Moab. Leupp was closed in December 1943 when its fifty-two inmates were transferred to Tule Lake camp, which became the new center for disloyal citizens.

Justice Department Camps

Moab and Leupp held Japanese American citizens; certain Issei identified as dangerous "enemy aliens" were incarcerated instead in camps operated by the Justice Department, located in Santa Fe, New Mexico; Bismarck, North Dakota; Missoula, Montana; and Crystal City, Texas. Almost all internees in these camps were men—generally older—who were suspected by the FBI of having ties with Japan. A large number were Japanese who had been transferred from Central and South America. Some were diplomats. Also interned were those individuals of German and Italian descent who had been judged a threat by the FBI early in the war.

Although under high security, internees in these camps lived similarly to internees in WRA relocation camps. All were housed in barracks, provided with an adequate diet, and allowed to develop recreation, education, and work programs. Their greatest single concern was for their families, from which they were often separated for years. Inmates at Crystal City Center were spared this hardship, since women and children were allowed to voluntarily join husbands and fathers, but, as one historian writes, "for the majority of the internees, there would be no family reunion for the duration, and no relief from this anguish."[50]

Patient Endurance

Whether internees lived in mainstream relocation camps or high security centers, every aspect of their lives was colored by the fact that they were not free. The fact that they had been suspected and presumed guilty by their government and their fellow Americans was not easily overlooked or forgotten.

However, most had been taught to bear hardship patiently, to put their personal feelings aside, and to work for the common good. They had endured prejudice and discrimination before the war. Now they were ready to do all they could to make the best of their days, even though the future appeared difficult and uncertain.

1. Quoted in John Tateishi, ed., *And Justice for All*, New York: Random House, 1984, p. 168.

2. John Modell, ed., *The Kikuchi Diary*. Urbana: University of Illinois Press, 1973, pp. 42–43.

3. Quoted in Commission on Wartime Relocation and Internment of Civilians, *Personal Justice Denied*. Washington, DC: GPO, 1982, p. 52.

4. Quoted in Michi Weglyn, *Years of Infamy*. New York: William Morrow, Quill Paperbacks, 1976, p. 45.

5. Yoshiko Uchida, *Desert Exile*. Seattle: University of Washington Press, 1982, pp. 46–47.

6. Quoted in Commission on Wartime Relocation, *Personal Justice Denied*, p. 69.

7. Quoted in John Armor and Peter Wright, *Manzanar*. New York: Times Books, 1988, p. 38.

8. Quoted in Roger Daniels, *Prisoners Without Trial*. New York: Hill & Wang, 1993, p. 38.

9. Quoted in Page Smith, *Democracy on Trial*. New York: Simon & Schuster, 1995, pp. 120–21.

10. Uchida, *Desert Exile*, p. 52.

11. Quoted in Armor and Wright, *Manzanar*, p. 20.

12. Quoted in Armor and Wright, *Manzanar*, p. 21.

13. Quoted in Armor and Wright, *Manzanar*, p. 22.

14. Quoted in Commission on Wartime Relocation, *Personal Justice Denied*, p. 82.

15. Quoted in Smith, *Democracy on Trial*, p. 127.

16. Jeanne Wakatsuki Houston and James D. Houston, *Farewell to Manzanar*. Boston: Houghton Mifflin, 1973, p. 13.

17. Quoted in Tateishi, *And Justice for All*, p. 147.

18. Quoted in Smith, *Democracy on Trial*, p. 146.

19. Quoted in Smith, *Democracy on Trial*, p. 146.

20. Quoted in Weglyn, *Years of Infamy*, p. 122.

21. Quoted in Weglyn, *Years of Infamy*, p. 122.

22. Quoted in Smith, *Democracy on Trial*, p. 151.

23. Quoted in Smith, *Democracy on Trial*, p. 151.

24. Quoted in Tateishi, *And Justice for All*, p. 169.

25. Quoted in Weglyn, *Years of Infamy*, p. 104.

26. Quoted in Weglyn, *Years of Infamy*, p. 103.

27. Quoted in Armor and Wright, *Manzanar*, p. 9.

28. Quoted in Commission on Wartime Relocation, *Personal Justice Denied*, p. 135.

29. Uchida, *Desert Exile*, p. 63.

30. Quoted in Tateishi, *And Justice for All*, p. 9.

31. Uchida, *Desert Exile*, pp. 61–62.

32. Quoted in Tateishi, *And Justice for All*, p. 215.

33. Uchida, *Desert Exile*, pp. 60–61.

34. Quoted in Tateishi, *And Justice for All*, p. 102.

35. Quoted in Weglyn, *Years of Infamy*, p. 78.

36. Uchida, *Desert Exile*, p. 70.

37. Quoted in Tateishi, *And Justice for All*, p. 73.

38. Quoted in Tateishi, *And Justice for All*, pp. 73–74.

39. Quoted in Tateishi, *And Justice for All*, pp. 12–13.

40. Uchida, *Desert Exile*, pp. 72, 75.

41. Modell, *The Kikuchi Diary*, p. 222.

42. Houston, *Farewell to Manzanar*, p. 25.

43. Quoted in Smith, *Democracy on Trial*, p. 245.

44. Houston, *Farewell to Manzanar*, p. 35.

45. Modell, *The Kikuchi Diary*, p. 82.

46. Quoted in Smith, *Democracy on Trial*, p. 249.

47. Modell, *The Kikuchi Diary*, p. 107.

48. Quoted in Commission on Wartime Relocation, *Personal Justice Denied*, p. 175.

49. Quoted in Weglyn, *Years of Infamy*, p. 127.

50. John J. Culley, "The Santa Fe Internment Camp and the Justice Program for Enemy Aliens," in Roger Daniels, Sandra C. Taylor, and Harry H.L. Kitano, eds., *Japanese Americans: From Relocation to Redress*. Seattle: University of Washington Press, 1986, p. 62.

CHAPTER 4

The Rise and Fall of the Motion Picture Industry

Hollywood Goes to War

Allen L. Woll

Hollywood was preparing for war long before the first bomb was dropped on Pearl Harbor in December 1941. When staunch isolationists accused Hollywood of producing propaganda films that planted interventionist ideas into the minds of naive Americans, Hollywood countered that it was speaking for the majority of Americans who opposed the Nazi regime, writes film historian Allen L. Woll in the following excerpt from his book *The Hollywood Musical Goes to War*. According to Woll, these interventionist films took two forms: The metaphorical film used historical parallels to advocate the defense of democracy, and the contemporary film revealed the horror of Nazi activities to encourage opposition to Hitler. Once the United States entered the war, Hollywood did its part to support the war effort but struggled against censorship by the Office of War Information. Woll is a professor of history at Rutgers University in Camden, New Jersey.

Hollywood entered the second World War almost three years before Washington, D.C. While the nation wavered between a sympathy for our European friends and a mistrust of outright intervention, film studios released a "flock of features to whip up enthusiasm for preparedness and the draft." *Variety*, the show business oracle, noted the

---

trend almost immediately and dubbed the new films "preparedness pix." By the end of 1940 film schedules were hastily revised to include thirty-six titles concerning "conscription, flying, and other phases of war and defense." With such films as *I Married a Nazi, Sergeant York,* and *British Intelligence,* Hollywood assumed an interventionist stance.

The Accusations from Washington

Hollywood's definitive commitment to the European war was looked on less fondly in the halls of Congress where isolationist forces, led by Senator Gerald Nye of North Dakota, had not yet been stilled. The so-called patriotism of Hollywood war films became mere propaganda in the eyes of those legislators who believed that the United States should avoid the terrors of war and leave European nations to fight their own battles. As a result, a subcommittee of the Interstate Commerce Commission met in September, 1941, to investigate "Motion Picture Screen and Radio Propaganda."

This investigation reflected Washington's long-standing distrust of the cinematic medium. The preponderant influence of the motion pictures in matters of morals had long been recognized, but not until the 1930s had fears erupted concerning the political uses of film. The Roosevelt Administration's use of the documentary film to support such projects as the Tennessee Valley Authority angered Congressional opponents who began to understand the political implications of the cinema. By 1941 these initial fears escalated to anger as the hearings swiftly revealed.

Senator Nye, the Committee's second witness, saw the presence of a vast conspiracy urging American entry into the war. Nye contended that screen propaganda was the most insidious of all: "Arriving at the theatre, Mr. and Mrs. America sit, with guard completely down, mind open, ready and eager for entertainment. In that frame of mind they follow through the story which the screen tells. If, somewhere in that story there is planted a narrative, a speech, or a declaration by a favorite actor or actress which seems to pertain to causes which are upsetting so much of the world today, there is planted in the heart and in the mind a feeling, a sympathy, or a distress which is not easily eliminated." He added that the public knew and expected propaganda from newspapers, but motion pictures took the audience completely by surprise. Nye placed blame for this mysterious conspiracy on Jewish interventionist interests. Although the Senator prefaced his comments with a perfunctory "some of my best friends are Jews," he repeatedly criticized Jewish radio commentators, columnists, and publishers for their attempt to deceive the American people.

Making the Moguls into Monsters

Senator Bennett C. Clark of Missouri agreed with his colleague's charges, and specifically condemned the film industry for the dissemination of interventionist propaganda. He contended that "not one word on the side of the argument against the war is heard." This was due to the "fact that the moving picture industry is a monopoly controlled by a half dozen men dominated by hatred, who are determined in order to wreak vengeance on Adolf Hitler, a ferocious beast, to plunge this nation into war on behalf of another ferocious beast." Clark's list of those in charge of the film media included Nicholas Schenck, Darryl F. Zanuck, Alexander Korda, and Henry Luce, who was responsible for the "March of Time" series, which "poisons the minds of the American people to go to war."

Clark found fuel for this argument in a government study of theatrical booking practices which investigated the motion picture industry and found a monopolistic situation. Eight major companies (Paramount, Loew's, RKO, Warner Brothers, Twentieth Century-Fox, Columbia, Universal, and United Artists) dominated the business. This situation caused Clark to fear that Hollywood moguls had gained complete control of the media in America.

While Clark and Nye found supposed evidence for their cause in this government report, their talent as film critics was found lacking. Nye in particular saw few of the films in question and the ones he did see he was unable to recall. Senator Ernest McFarland searched Nye's recent speech in St. Louis for all references to objectionable films:

SEN. MCFARLAND: Did you see *Convoy*?

SEN. NYE: I think I did.

SEN. MCFARLAND: Do you remember anything in that picture that was particularly objectionable?

SEN. NYE: I am at a loss to call to mind any particular feature about it that led me to draw the conclusion which I have drawn.

Nye then admitted that he did not see *Flight Command* (1941), *That Hamilton Woman* (1941), or *Sergeant York* (1941). He was unable to differentiate between *Confessions of a Nazi Spy* and *I Married a Spy* ("For the life of me I could not tell you which was which"). The only film Nye remembered was Charlie Chaplin's *The Great Dictator,* which he claimed was a "portrayal by a great artist, not a citizen of our country . . . that could not do other than build within the heart and mind of those who watched it something of a hatred, detestation of conditions and of leadership that existed abroad."

Defending Hollywood

Wendell L. Willkie, at that time with the Washington law firm of Willkie, Owen, Otis, and Bailly, supported Hollywood's interests before the Committee. Unlike other investigations of the activities of the motion picture industry, representatives of Hollywood presented their positions with valiant fervor, and made no attempt to hide the attitudes that caused them to make films favoring American entry into the war. Willkie sent a letter to Clark before the investigation began. He believed that the Committee sought to inquire whether the motion picture industry, as a whole, and its leading executives, as individuals, were opposed to the Nazi dictatorship in Germany. If this were the case, reasoned Willkie, there need not be an investigation, for "the motion picture industry and its executives *are* opposed to the Hitler regime in Germany."

Willkie explained that the attitude of the film industry represented the "great overwhelming majority of the people of our country." Indeed, Hollywood was just following the opinions of the nation. He contended that the "motion picture industry, like other American industries, is composed of sincere, patriotic citizens." These men admit that the industry "gladly and with great pride, has done all in its power to present to the American public a picture of our Army, our Navy, our Air Corps, and their equipment." Nevertheless, Willkie explained that Hollywood was accomplishing this task on its own volition, and not at the behest or with the assistance of the current administration. Indeed, "the motion picture industry would be ashamed if it were not doing voluntarily what it is now doing in the national defense."

Willkie also decried the anti-Semitic attitudes of the isolationist forces. He noted that the industry included "Nordics and non-Nordics, Jews and Gentiles, Protestants, Catholics, and native and foreign born." This demonstrates, added Willkie, that "the motion picture industry despises the racial discrimination of nazi-ism and is devoted to the cause of human freedom both in this country and abroad."

The Moguls Speak

Willkie called a long and distinguished list of important Hollywood representatives to lend credence to his arguments. Harry M. Warner, then president of Warner Brothers, was one of the first witnesses. Warner presented his position as unequivocally as possible:

> I am opposed to nazi-ism. I abhor and detest every principle and practice of the Nazi movement. To me, nazi-ism typifies the very opposite of the kind of life every decent man, woman, and child wants to live. I believe nazi-ism is a world revolution whose ultimate objective is to destroy

our democracy, wipe out all religion, and enslave our people—just as Germany has destroyed and enslaved Poland, Belgium, Holland, and France. I am ready to give myself and all my personal resources to aid in the defeat of the Nazi menace to the American people.

Warner then explained that his firm produced a wide variety of entertainment films designed to give the public what it wanted to see. He then presented detailed descriptions of *Confessions of a Nazi Spy, Sergeant York, Underground,* and *International Squadron,* by which he hoped to convince the Committee that his films were based solely on fact, as recorded in the daily newspapers, and were therefore not spurious attempts at propaganda.

Darryl F. Zanuck, then vice-president in charge of production at Twentieth Century-Fox, followed Warner on the witness stand. He detailed his Methodist background in Wahoo, Nebraska, (population 891) and recounted his adventures in the U.S. Army during World War I, where he rose to the rank of private first class. His testimony followed that of Warner's fairly closely. Zanuck explained: "In the time of acute national peril, I feel that it is the duty of every American to give his complete cooperation and support to our President and our Congress to do everything to defeat Hitler and preserve America. If this course of necessity leads to war, I want to follow my President along that course."

Zanuck's testimony met with stirring applause from the Senate audience, as he explained that pictures are so "strong and powerful that they sold the American way of life, not only to America, but to the entire world. They sold it so strongly that when dictators took over Italy and Germany, what did Hitler and his flunky, Mussolini, do? The first thing they did was to ban our pictures, throw us out. They wanted no part of the American way of life."

The Committee moved to recess after testimony from Barney Balaban, president of Paramount Pictures. The Committee never resumed its meetings. A small column in the *New York Times* announced its demise, since, after the bombing of Pearl Harbor, the isolationist position swiftly dissolved. America entered the war, and Hollywood was now able to use all the facilities at its disposal to help America win the war.

The Intervention Films

There seemed to be no way that Warner, Zanuck, or Schenck could deny that Hollywood had been producing films encouraging American entry into the war since early 1939. Whether it was propaganda seemed questionable to the film moguls. As Zanuck claimed: "I usually find that when someone produces something that you do not like, they call it propaganda." Rather, they argued that they were presenting motion pictures which advocated a particular political position. They reasoned that others, given the rights of free speech, might produce films that supported isolationist ideas. In reality, however, no one did so.

The films which preceded American entry into the war were of two types: the metaphorical and the contemporary. The metaphorical films deliberately avoided the current European conflict. They often looked to history for valid analogies to the present political situation. These motion pictures argued that the American people should learn from the lessons of history that war was often necessary in order to defend democracy and the American way of life.

The Metaphorical Films

As a result the camera wandered through time and place to discover parallels of current events. For example, *Juarez* (1939) exalted a nineteenth century Mexican president, because he defended his nation against the dictatorial Napoleon III and supported democracy for Latin American nations. The rhetoric of the film bordered on the contemporary, causing Frank S. Nugent, critic for the *New York Times,* to note "that it is not at all difficult to read between the lines."

Perhaps the most popular film of this historical genre

was an excursion into the American past with Howard Hawks' *Sergeant York*. Producers had attempted to film the life of this World War I hero since Jesse Lasky broached the idea in 1919. After years of negotiations, York finally allowed his biography to be filmed. Alvin York remained on the set during the entire filming, and later praised Warners for its historical accuracy.

Despite York's claims of the film's veracity, *Sergeant York* became yet another motion picture which advocated the taking of arms in the defense of democracy. The young Alvin York (Gary Cooper) finds religion after a misspent youth. He reads the Bible diligently, and when drafted, refuses to fight, since he believes "Thou shall not kill." An army major admires York's ability with a rifle but cannot understand his reluctance to support the war. He gives York a *History of the United States,* so the new recruit can learn what the Founding Fathers and the great American heroes once fought for. ("Daniel Boone wanted freedom. That's quite a word, *freedom*.") York retreats to a mountainside to ponder the major's message. A wind blows the pages of the Bible open to a quotation fraught with meaning: "Render therefore to Caesar the things that are Caesar's, and to God the things that are God's." A divine light shines on York's face, and he realizes that he must fight to preserve America's freedom. York has learned from history and from the Bible that pacifism is irrelevant when the defense of freedom is concerned. Warner Brothers hoped that the audience would learn the same lesson.

The Direct Approach

The majority of films of this period avoided the indirect approach and considered contemporary society. Some, such as *Confessions of a Nazi Spy,* revealed Nazi activities on the homefront. This factual account starred Edward G. Robinson as the assiduous American agent who uncovered a vast Nazi spy ring in the United States. The story itself was lifted from trial records, as well as a series of the *New York Post* articles written by Leon G. Turrou, a former F.B.I. investigator.

Other films concerned German society and the rise of the Nazi party. These films lacked the gritty reality of *Confessions of a Nazi Spy,* but attempted to fictionalize the horrors of Hitler's Germany. *The Mortal Storm* (1941) is typical of this genre. The family of Professor Roth (Frank Morgan) is brutally destroyed as Nazi power is concentrated. Roth's daughter, Freya, (Margaret Sullavan) defends the ideals of freedom, while the male children actively support the Nazi cause. Professor Roth, an anatomist, is ousted from the university because he refuses to support theories of Aryan superiority. He is then arrested and sent to a concentration camp. Roth's family attempts to emigrate, but Freya is detained. She eventually attempts to flee through the Austrian mountains with her lover, a young idealist, portrayed by James Stewart, but she is shot by Nazi troops led by her former boyfriend (Robert Young).

Four Sons, I Married a Nazi, and *So Ends Our Night* also followed this pattern of the breaking of family ties in the face of the Nazi menace. Other films which considered Germany were primarily of the espionage type *(Man Hunt, Underground),* but they maintained a firm anti-Nazi position.

What remained a minor trend before American entry into the war, soon became a torrent after Pearl Harbor. No longer was there any attempt to limit films opposed to Nazi Germany or those praising American ideals. In the next four years, Hollywood produced countless films which attempted to win the war in the hearts and minds of American citizens.

Hollywood at War

Life changed behind the screen as well. The active support of Washington's war policy was not only evident in the finished film product. Producers, directors, stars, extras, musicians, electricians, and carpenters gave more to the war effort than motion pictures. Hollywood's nightlife collapsed, and many restaurants remained open only on weekends. The carefree life of the previous decade dimmed considerably as the denizens of the film capital flocked to assist the war effort.

Volunteer organizations flourished shortly after Pearl Harbor. Stars joined every possible committee: the Volunteer Army Canteen Service, Bundles for Bluejackets, the Aerial Nurse Corps, the Women's Ambulance Defense Corps, and the Civil Air Patrol. They even became air raid spotters and wardens.

More than five hundred actors joined the Actors' Committee of the Hollywood Victory Committee for Stage, Screen, and Radio. This organization, headed by Clark Gable, arranged benefit performances for the Red Cross, Navy Relief Fund, and other wartime organizations. Others began cross-country tours to sell defense bonds. Carole Lombard was killed on one of these trips. Dorothy Lamour, known as the "Sweetheart of the Treasury," completed Lombard's itinerary and travelled more than ten thousand miles on visits to defense plants and shipyards.

Even film studios volunteered their services. The most noteworthy of these efforts was the contribution of half of the Walt Disney studios for films concerning defense projects. Donald Duck and Mickey Mouse thus appeared gratis in films for the Treasury Department and the Office of Inter-American Affairs.

General Lewis Hershey declared that the film industry was "essential" during wartime. As a result, he allowed studios to apply for draft deferments for irreplaceable workers. Despite the government's permission for major stars, directors, and writers to remain safely in Hollywood, many luminaries decided to enlist. Frank Capra, John Ford, Garson Kanin, William Wyler, and Darryl Zanuck offered their film-making talents to the War Department.

Actors also joined the exodus. Clark Gable departed soon after the death of his wife, Carole Lombard. James Stewart gained ten pounds so he could pass the physical and become a private. The numbers of leading men that deserted Hollywood during the war led to a crisis, as capable male actors became impossible to find for many new films.

In this fashion, Hollywood became a major ally to Washington. While the film capital was seen as an antagonist in the days before Pearl Harbor, government advisors began to realize that the film industry could be of major help in the war effort. Leo Rosten, the novelist and a deputy director of the Office of War Information (OWI), explained the value of the motion picture to the American audience:

> The movies can give the public information. But they can do more than that; they can give the public understanding. They can clarify problems that are complex and confusing. They can focus attention upon the key problems which the people must decide, the basic choices which people make. They can make clear and intelligible the enormous complexities of global geography, military tactics, economic dilemmas, political disputes, and psychological warfare. The singularly illuminating tools of the screen can be used to give the people a clear, continuous, and comprehensible picture of the total pattern of total war.

The motion picture seemed the ideal medium to fulfill OWI goals. Established in June 1942 by executive order, the OWI was designed to "disseminate war information" and facilitate the understanding of the "policies, activities, and aims of the Government" during World War II. Motion pictures could therefore play a vital role in this effort.

Despite Hollywood's willingness to help on a voluntary basis, it was no secret that the leaders of the film industry feared the imposition of government censorship. They were somewhat surprised when Lowell Mellett, head of the Bureau of Motion Pictures (BMP) of the OWI, explained to an audience of film producers that he was "hoping that most of you and your fellow workers would stay right here in Hollywood and keep on doing what you're doing, because your motion pictures are a vital contribution to the total defense effort." At first this statement bewildered the assembled film producers. When one asked Mellett if the industry should make "hate pictures," Mellett replied, "Use your own judgment. We'll give you our advice if you want us to."

Advice or Censorship

Yet, the OWI was not going to sit passively on the sidelines. Mellett explained that his office would fulfill two functions. First, he would attempt to advise Hollywood about Washington's attitudes concerning future films. Producers could submit their ideas voluntarily to his office, which would then determine proper policy after discussion with the State Department. In this manner film plots concerning Russia or China, for example, would follow official foreign policy decisions. Despite Mellett's calming tone, the fine line between advice and censorship was often cloudy. Within a short time, Mellett's office would be perceived as the enemy as it began to insist that both scripts and dialogue be changed to suit the needs of the government.

The BMP also coordinated Washington's entry into the film production game. Although the government had produced official films as early as 1900, wartime production reached new highs. The OWI could approve, reject, or request revisions in the multitude of government films designed for theatrical showing. Such motion pictures as *Tanks* (narrated by Orson Welles), *Bomber* (with commentary by Carl Sandburg), and *Army in Overalls* appeared in the nation's theatres. In the midst of these documentaries, a Donald Duck cartoon, *The New Spirit,* became one of the most popular films produced by the government.

Government policy affected not only what appeared on the screen, but also what occurred behind it. The War Production Board (WPB) issued a series of decrees in 1942, which were designed to control the profligate practices of the major studios, so that vital war materials might be conserved. The first ruling limited to $5,000 the amount that could be spent on sets for any one picture. The Board also suggested a sharp curtailment in film use. Budget analysts suggested the elimination of all filmed rehearsals and the use of single takes for rushes. One engineer even suggested that projection speeds be slowed from ninety to sixty-seven feet of film per minute. Although he claimed that more than 500 million feet of film would be saved each year, it would have meant that previously produced films could not be shown on these new projectors.

Hollywood took many of these suggestions to heart. When Frank S. Nugent visited the studios in 1942, he was stunned by the change:

> Say this for Hollywood: it rarely does things by halves. If it was magnificently extravagant a few years ago, it is being a magnificent miser today. Studio incinerators used to roar twenty-four hours a day. Lumber, doors, scaffolds, trim, paneling—enough for a real estate subdivision—were tossed to the furnaces. Nowadays, the lumber burned wouldn't build a respectable dollhouse. Sets are dismantled as carefully as time bombs: a carpenter who splits a board virtually is made to stand in the corner. . . . Hairpins—another vital product in a glamour creating town—are practically checked in and out of the dressing rooms, sterilized after each use.

One studio even tried to invent a nail straightening machine in order to recycle no. 8 nails which were in great demand by the wartime industries.

Thus, both before and behind the screen, Hollywood life was greatly affected by the coming of war. The massive changes in American society pervaded the industry, coloring the films produced during this era both consciously and unconsciously.

Doing Our Part: Celebrities Support the War Effort

Otto Friedrich

In the excerpt that follows, the late journalist Otto Friedrich tells stories of romance and tragedy while Hollywood's elite tried to do their part. While Jimmy Stewart, Clark Gable, and Henry Fonda joined the military, Hedy Lamarr and Carole Lombard sold war bonds for a kiss, and Bette Davis headed the Hollywood Canteen where servicemen bound for combat in the Pacific could meet and mingle with the stars, Friedrich writes. Although Hollywood had to deal with shortages that often made filmmaking difficult, there was no shortage of war movies featuring stars like Ronald Reagan, Fred Astaire, Greer Garson, and John Wayne. Friedrich was formerly the editor of the *New York Daily News* and an essayist for *Time*.

Jimmy Stewart quietly began putting on weight so that he could meet the army's physical requirements, and then he enlisted as a private (he soon became a bomber pilot and eventually a lieutenant colonel). Robert Montgomery joined the navy and ultimately commanded a destroyer at the invasion of Normandy. Tyrone Power abandoned both his wife and his male lover to join the marines; he became a transport pilot in the South Pacific. William Holden joined the army as Private William F. Beedle, Jr. Henry

Excerpted from *City of Nets: A Portrait of Hollywood in the 1940s,* by Otto Friedrich. Copyright ©1986 by Otto Friedrich. Reprinted by permission of HarperCollins Publishers, Inc.

Fonda, who was thirty-seven years old and had three children, waited only until the final shooting on *The Ox-Bow Incident* and then enlisted as a sailor. He got as far as boot camp in San Diego, where the shore patrol picked him up and sent him back to Los Angeles. "Why?" Fonda still bristled at the memory forty years later. "Because Darryl F. Fuck-it-all Zanuck had pull in Washington and demanded, 'I want Henry Fonda for a picture I'm planning. It's for the war effort and I need him.' And he had enough weight to swing it."

The Celebrities Get Involved

Zanuck, who was thirty-nine himself, also had enough weight to get a commission as a colonel in the Army Signal Corps so that he could, as Otto Preminger sardonically put it, "photograph the war." Zanuck spent his last weeks at Fox firing off a whole broadside of patriotic films—*To the Shores of Tripoli, Secret Agent of Japan, Immortal Sergeant, Crash Dive, Tonight We Raid Calais*—and when he went off to war, he donated his entire string of twenty Argentine polo ponies to West Point. Colonel Zanuck's mogul style remained unique. Sent to London to coordinate training films, he took up residence at Claridge's and duly accompanied a team of British commandos on a real night raid on Calais (actually, it was Saint-Valery). Sent to North Africa to produce a documentary, he took to carrying not only a .45 automatic but a tommy gun, and when he saw a German plane flying overhead, he began firing wildly. "I probably did no damage," he acknowledged, "yet there was always the chance that a lucky shot might strike a vital spot."

Each celebrity's call to colors was a major event in his studio's publicity department, and in the fan magazines that fed at the studio publicity trough. Ronald Reagan, despite his poor eyesight, had long been a lieutenant in the cavalry reserve, so he was summoned early in 1942 to report to Fort March in San Francisco. "It's Jane's war now," began an account by Cynthia Miller in *Modern Screen*.

This story was entitled "So Long, Button-Nose," which was apparently Reagan's nickname for his wife, Jane Wyman. The story reported that she had "seen Ronnie's sick face bent over a picture of the small swollen bodies of children starved to death in Poland. 'This,' said the war-hating Reagan, 'would make it a pleasure to kill.' That night he'd stood a little longer beside the crib of Button-Nose the Second, who'd inherited both the nose and the name from her mother. She'd known Ronnie would go, that he'd probably have enlisted after Pearl Harbor if he hadn't been a member of the Cavalry Reserve." And so on.

By October of 1942, some 2,700 Hollywood people—12 percent of the total number employed in the movie business—had joined the armed forces. But it was impractical and unrealistic for the celebrities to pretend that they were just ordinary citizens eager to do their patriotic duty. As a grizzled navy petty officer said to Fonda when he volunteered for service as a gunner's mate. "You know what the fuckin' gunners' mates do in this man's fuckin' Navy? They get killed! . . . You're too smart to be some fuckin' gunner's mate." The stars' value to the war effort obviously lay not in becoming cannon fodder but in exploiting their stardom, in making propaganda films, entertaining the troops. selling war bonds.

Selling War Bonds

Women were especially good at that, selling war bonds. Hedy Lamarr offered to kiss any man who would buy $25,000 worth of bonds. She once sold more than $17 million worth of government paper in a single day. Lana Turner's price for the promise of a kiss was $50,000, and she recalled that she "kept that promise hundreds of times," adding that she "appeared in so many cities that they're all blurred together in my mind." Dorothy Lamour was perhaps the most successful of all. The people who kept track of such things estimated that she once sold $30 million worth of bonds in four days, and ended with a total of $350 million, with and without kisses.

It was all very organized. Treasury Secretary Henry Morgenthau chose M-G-M's publicity director, Howard Dietz, to promote the sale of bonds, state by state. Dietz sent his plans to Clark Gable, who had been asked to head the actors' division of the Hollywood Victory Committee. Among those plans was a proposal that the bond drive in Indiana be launched that January by one of the state's most popular citizens, Carole Lombard, who was also Mrs. Gable. Dietz warned her and all his other recruits to avoid airplanes, which he considered unreliable and dangerous, so Miss Lombard set off by train, selling bonds at various stops en route to Indianapolis. Gable had to stay behind to start work with Lana Turner on *Somewhere I'll Find You*. Miss Lombard left in Gable's bed a pneumatic blond dummy, as a substitute for Miss Turner, with a note that said, "So you won't be lonely." Gable chortled at her ribaldry. ("I'm really nuts about him," Miss Lombard had once said to Garson Kanin. "And it isn't all that great-lover crap because if you want to know the truth, I've had better.") He spent three days building a male dummy, expectantly erect, to welcome her home.

Miss Lombard sold two million dollars' worth of bonds, then couldn't wait for the train on which she already had a ticket and a reservation. On the night of January 16, she boarded a TWA DC-3 bound for home. A few minutes after takeoff from Las Vegas, the plane somehow strayed off course. Beacons that might have warned the pilot had been blacked out because of the continuing anxiety about Japanese bombers. The plane smashed into a cliff near the top of Potosi Mountain. The first reports to reach Hollywood said only that the plane was missing, but somehow everyone knew what had happened. M-G-M publicity agents mobilized, chartered planes, organized searches. A dazed Gable asked to join the search parties but was persuaded to wait in Las Vegas. It was Eddie Mannix, the studio's general manager, who accompanied the stretcher-bearing mules up into the snow-covered mountains and retrieved the charred and decapitated corpse of Carole Lombard.

Recruiting Clark Gable

Gable was distraught for months. "Why Ma?" he kept asking. (He and his wife had called each other Ma and Pa.) He bought a motorcycle and drove wildly through the canyons north of Hollywood. He refused to speak to anyone, or else talked compulsively about his dead wife. Of the many diamond pieces he had given her, only one mangled fragment was found at the site of the crash, and he wore that around his neck. But there was now a war on, and the army was keenly aware of the promotional value of Clark Gable. On January 23, 1942, at a time when the Japanese were conquering the Philippines and advancing through much of Southeast Asia, a telegram from Lieutenant General H.H. Arnold, chief of staff of the Army Air Forces, informed Gable that "we have a specific and highly important assignment for you," and announced that an aide would soon arrive in California to "discuss my plans with you." The only thing more remarkable than General Arnold's devoting any effort at such a time to recruit a movie star was that M-G-M intercepted his message and repressed it. "Wire to Gable received but not giving it to him as do not think it advisable to discuss with him at present time." Howard Strickling of the M-G-M publicity department cabled back to Washington.

The movie studio's goal, apparently, was to keep Gable at work before the cameras as long as possible (*Somewhere I'll Find You* did get made), but Gable could hardly work at all. He brooded. He drank. Joan Crawford invited him to dinner and listened to him talk about his dead wife until three in the morning. "One night," she recalled, "I said, 'Clark, you have got to stop this drinking, you've got to.' He started to cry, and said, 'I know I must.'" So Gable went to the air force recruiting office that August and enlisted as a private. But an M-G-M cameraman named Andrew McIntyre enlisted at the same time and never left the star's side, and when the two of them were shipped to Miami Beach for training, an Army officer remarked, "Gable is the only private in the history of the Army who had his own orderly." On his first day in camp, in Miami Beach, Gable was asked if he would mind if photographers took pictures of him shaving off his famous mustache. "I'll probably be cooler anyway," he was quoted as saying. Within two months, he was commissioned a lieutenant and sent with McIntyre to Colorado to make a training film about "the day-to-day activities of a typical heavy bombardment group."

The Hollywood Canteen

Los Angeles was a major point of departure for young servicemen bound for combat in the Pacific, and they all wanted to see the sights before they left. The main sight was Hollywood and Hollywood naturally wanted to oblige. It wanted to be patriotic; it also wanted its patriotism richly publicized. John Garfield was apparently the man who conceived the brilliant idea of organizing the Hollywood Canteen where the boys could meet all the glittering stars and the stars could play at being the girl next door. Garfield also had the no less brilliant idea of recruiting the tireless Bette Davis as president. She found and leased a former livery stable at 1451 Cahuenga Boulevard, just off Sunset, and then dragooned studio workmen into volunteering to paint the walls, install the lights, and turn this refurbished barn into the social center of Hollywood.

Miss Davis also went to her agents at MCA and persuaded the firm's reclusive president Jules Stein, to push a few buttons. As a start he proposed a gala opening night in October, with seats at $100 in the surrounding bleachers. "The canteen made $10,000 that night from the bleacher seats," Miss Davis recalled. "It seemed thousands of men entered the canteen. . . . I had to crawl through a window to get inside." But that was only the beginning of Jules Stein's button-pushing. Lo, Harry Cohn of Columbia suddenly felt inspired to donate to the canteen the $6,500 in proceeds from the premiere of *Talk of the Town* (Ronald Colman, Jean Arthur, Cary Grant). Stein even persuaded Warners, which happened to be Miss Davis's studio, to make a movie entitled *Hollywood Canteen* and to donate a share of the proceeds to the operation of the canteen.

Bette Davis worked the phone. She called, for example Hedy Lamarr.

"Sure . . . but what can I do?" asked Hedy Lamarr, according to her own account.

"We need help in the kitchen," said Bette Davis, perhaps not without malice. But then she became more expansive. "You can sign autographs and dance with the boys. And there are a hundred other things. You'll see when you get there."

A Place Where Celebrities Met

Hedy Lamarr remembered herself as being docile. "I couldn't cook. I was a mess in the kitchen. I would wash dishes gladly. . . . This was my adopted land and it had been good to me." She recalled later that she went to work two nights every week in the kitchen of the canteen, which "was always hot, noisy, and swinging." Her chief memory of the place was that the canteen was "where I met my third husband."

He was John Loder, who was wearing a tweed suit with a pipe in the breast pocket as he dried stacks of dishes. The canteen was like that—a social center for even those celebrated stars who often had nowhere to go in the evening, but also a social obligation for those same stars, who knew that their celebrity depended on imagery. Betty Grable, too, met her future husband, Harry James, while he was conducting the orchestra there.

Gene Tierney considered it perfectly natural that someone should call her "to remind me that I had not appeared at the Hollywood Canteen lately to entertain the GIs." She "felt guilty about that," even though she was pregnant and suffering "spells of being tired," so she promised to appear the following night. Miss Tierney was a somewhat unusual figure in Hollywood, a girl of considerable beauty but without either great talent or that animal ambition that vivified a Joan Crawford or a Barbara Stanwyck. Her beauty itself was slightly waxen, like that of a debutante, which was natural enough since her father was a prosperous New York insurance broker, and she had gone to Miss Porter's and made her debut at the Fairfield Country Club. Her father actually filched much of her Hollywood income (he was her trustee until she was twenty-one) but the whole family nonetheless disapproved profoundly of her marrying Oleg Cassini, a rather sleek-looking costume designer at Paramount, who posed as an aristocrat because his mother had once been a Russian countess. After Pearl Harbor, Cassini joined the Coast Guard, then somehow transferred to the cavalry. That took him to Fort Riley, Kansas, and thus took Gene Tierney there too.

Gene Tierney's Sacrifice

Just before she left Hollywood, though, and just after her appearance at the Hollywood Canteen, she came down with German measles. She postponed her trip a few days until the red spots were gone, then joined the migration of women to army camps. "My first room was in the post guest house, where the walls were made of beaverboard and you could hear everything that went on in the rooms on either side . . ." she said later. "After a week you had to look for housing. . . . I rented a dumpy little place that I soon discovered was inhabited by mice. . . ."

Her daughter was born prematurely, weighed two and a half pounds, and had to have eleven blood transfusions. She was named Daria. When she was about a year old, it became clear that her sight and hearing were impaired, and that there were even worse prospects. It was only beginning to be known in those days that German measles in early pregnancy could seriously damage an unborn child. "I would not, could not, accept the idea that Daria was retarded or had brain damage," Miss Tierney recalled.

The Cassinis struggled on for a time, then agreed on a divorce and consigned their hopelessly retarded daughter to a school in Pennsylvania. Then, at a tennis party on a Sunday afternoon in Los Angeles, Miss Tierney was approached by a young woman who smiled and said they had met at the Hollywood Canteen.

"Did you happen to catch the German measles after that night?" she inquired. Miss Tierney was too startled to answer. "I probably shouldn't tell you this" the woman went on. She had been in the women's branch of the Marine Corps, she said, and her whole camp had been swept by an epidemic of rubella. "I broke quarantine to come to the canteen to meet the stars," she said, smiling cheerily. "Everyone told me I shouldn't, but I just had to go. And you were my favorite."

Miss Tierney stood silent for a moment, then turned and walked away. "After that," she recalled, "I didn't care if I was ever again anyone's favorite actress." She was already beginning to crumble, and the crumbling would lead her to a mental institution, to attempted suicide, to a sense of nothingness and despair. Her lost child, Daria, she wrote in her memoirs, was a war baby, born in 1943. "Daria was my war effort."

Attracting Audiences

These were individual episodes, but there remained always a collective Hollywood, an array of low-lying buildings and streets and people on the northern edge of Los Angeles, a community that was partly an industry, partly a technology, partly a style and a quality of mind, partly a negation of all those things, partly just a hunger for money and success. The war was good for Hollywood. It brought in big grosses, big profits. Hollywood expected as much. One of its first reactions to Pearl Harbor had been a race to register movie titles that might attract audiences to the box office: *Yellow Peril, Spy Smashers, Wings over the Pacific, V for Victory*. . . . (The songwriters were more imaginative, for it took very little time to churn out such novelties as "Goodbye, Momma, I'm Off to Yokohama" or "Slap the Jap Right Off the Map" or "To Be Specific, It's Our Pacific" or "When Those Little Yellow Bellies Meet the Cohens and the Kellys.")

There were problems, though, with film scripts suddenly outdated. What could M-G-M do with an Eleanor Powell musical entitled *I'll Take Manila* when the city was actually being threatened by the Japanese army? At Warners, the *Maltese Falcon* gang—Huston, Bogart, and the rest—was in the midst of filming *Across the Pacific,* which was supposed to be about a struggle to thwart an unthinkable Japanese plot to bomb Pearl Harbor. That was hastily changed to an unthinkable plot to bomb the Panama Canal. More complicated was the fact that Huston was suddenly called to

During World War II, Hollywood celebrities did all they could to support the war effort, from selling U.S. bonds to entertaining the troops. Actress Rita Hayworth donated her car's bumpers to the war effort.

duty as a lieutenant in the Signal Corps. As a going-away prank, he decided to leave Warners a movie that was not only unfinished but virtually unfinishable. He filmed Bogart tied to a chair in a house filled with Japanese guards. "I . . . installed about three times as many Japanese soldiers as were needed to keep him prisoner," Huston recalled with satisfaction. "There were guards at every window brandishing machine guns. I made it so that there was no way in God's green world that Bogart could logically escape. I shot the scene, then called Jack Warner, and said, 'Jack, I'm on my way. I'm in the army. Bogie will know how to get out.'" Bogie didn't know, and neither did anyone else. Warner's assigned the mess to one of its more reliable professionals, Vincent Sherman, and he or some nameless underling had to concoct an escape. "His impossible solution," Huston gloated, "was to have one of the Japanese soldiers in the room go berserk. Bogie escaped in the confusion, with the comment, 'I'm not easily trapped, you know!'"

Dealing with Shortages

The material demands of the burgeoning war effort caused far greater problems. The windows that heroes used to leap through had been made of sugar, which was now rationed. The chairs that they smashed over each other's heads had been made of balsa wood from the Philippines, now under attack by the Japanese. Harmlessly breakable whiskey bottles suitable for barroom brawls had been made of resin, and that, too, was now needed for military production. Film itself was made of cellulose, which was required for explosives (and for the metastasizing production of official military training and propaganda movies). The amount of film available to Hollywood was cut by about 25 percent. Even the flow of money—Hollywood's lifeblood—was restricted. The War Production Board issued a decree on May 6 limiting the use of new materials for stage sets to $5,000 per picture. James F. Byrnes, the Director of Economic Stabilization, even ordered that all salaries be held to $25,000 as of January 1, 1943 (Louis B. Mayer's salary for the previous year was reported to be $949,766), but Congress soon canceled that unseemly gesture of austerity.

The restrictions had some unexpectedly beneficial results. The assembly-line production of trashy B pictures, required for the double features that had become standard during the Depression, had to be curtailed, and a Gallup poll showed that 71 percent of the supposedly insatiable viewers approved of the curtailment. Overall, Hollywood's output decreased from 533 pictures in 1942 to 377 in 1945. Because of the shortage of film, directors could no longer shoot dozens of takes of each scene, so they devoted more time and effort to rehearsals before filming. And because of the tackiness of sets that relied on painted canvas to substitute for scarce metals and lumber, they began exploring the possibilities of moving out of the sound stages into the real world. Alfred Hitchcock even took the daring step of filming *Shadow of a Doubt* entirely on location.

One shortage was unique: the lack of Japanese villains who could sneer at a captive Bogart or gibber and gesticulate on the bridge of an imperial battleship as the forces of retribution started dropping bombs. All starring parts were played by Caucasians, of course (wasn't Peter Lorre perfectly credible as John Marquand's Mr. Moto, after all, and hadn't Paul Muni and Luise Rainer been admirable as Chinese peasants in *The Good Earth?*), so the only problem was to round up some non-Japanese Orientals to play the secondary Japanese villains. Thus a former beer salesman named Richard Loo and a poet named H.T. Tshiang suddenly found themselves making around a thousand dollars per week in *The Purple Heart*. "The leading Oriental villains (if we exclude J. Carroll Naish) were Sen Yung, Chester Gan and Philip Ahn," as Richard Lingeman wrote in his witty history of this period, *Don't You Know There's a War On?* "Gan specialized in portraying stolid brutal Japs. Sen Yung was the treacherous, English-speaking Japanese, whose mastery of American slang he turned back on Americans in such films as *Across the Pacific* and *God Is My Co-Pilot* ('OK, you Yankee Doodle Dandy, come and get us . . .'). Philip

Ahn, a Korean, was perhaps the most sought-after villain of all, with his flat voice and his mask-like face that looked as if it had been carved out of India rubber. Ahn eventually tired of his type-casting and refused any more Japanese roles, saying he wanted to play romantic Chinese leads. . . . There were no romantic Chinese leads.". . .

The War Movies

Like Detroit, Hollywood was by now producing war movies on an assembly line. It requisitioned Ronald Reagan back from the Army training-film center known as Fort Roach to star in Irving Berlin's *This Is the Army*. It saluted American pilots in *Air Force* and *Destination Tokyo,* and Marines in *Guadalcanal Diary,* and merchant seamen in *Action in the North Atlantic,* and army nurses in *So Proudly We Hail.* Some of these films made a dogged pretense at realism, like *Wake Island,* in which William Bendix and Robert Preston fought gallantly against overwhelming hordes of Japanese. Some were shamelessly sentimental, like *Mrs. Miniver,* in which the beautiful Greer Garson seemed to save the entire British army from Dunkirk. Some were primarily thrillers, like Hitchcock's *Saboteur,* with that unforgettable finale of the villain dangling by his sleeve from the hand of the Statue of Liberty—and then the sleeve starting to tear. Even the movies that were purely escapist, like *You Were Never Lovelier,* in which Fred Astaire found his new dancing partner in Rita Hayworth, or *Reap the Wild Wind,* in which John Wayne, Paulette Goddard, and Hedda Hopper were all upstaged by a giant squid—even these were escapes from the war, and the war remained in the anxieties of everyone who watched them.

Postwar Hollywood: From All-American to Un-American

Robert Sklar

The anti-Communist crusade turned Hollywood against itself, creating an atmosphere of fear that stifled the creativity of the motion picture industry, writes historian Robert Sklar in the following excerpt from his book *Movie-Made America: A Cultural History of American Movies*. Sklar explains that despite Hollywood's heroic efforts during World War II, old enemies found new ways to attack the movie industry. Hoping to defend the industry from Communist infiltration, conservative movie workers provided the House Un-American Activities Committee (HUAC) with witnesses to testify against their colleagues. Although industry leaders who fought the HUAC opposed blacklisting, to suggest any other alternative was to make them suspect as well, and to avoid adverse publicity and empty theaters, the studios refused to take a stand. When some in Hollywood were cited for contempt and served prison terms for failing to state whether they were or had been members of the Communist Party, industry members began to turn against themselves, and the industry crumbled. Sklar is a professor and historian of twentieth-century American culture and society at the University of Michigan in Ann Arbor.

Excerpted from *Movie-Made America: A Cultural History of American Movies*, by Robert Sklar. Copyright ©1975 by Robert Sklar. Reprinted by permission of Random House, Inc.

"I have never," said Colonel K.B. Lawton, chief of the Army Pictorial Division of the United States Signal Corps, "found such a group of wholehearted, willing, patriotic people trying to do something for the government." He was speaking in 1943 about Hollywood motion-picture producers and their employees, in testimony before Harry S. Truman's Senate committee on the war effort, and of course no one on the committee believed a word of it. The committee wanted to know, among other things, how some of the moguls and their staff had wangled officers' commissions, how much the movie industry was profiting from the production of military training films, and whether the major studios exercised monopolistic control over government-contract filmmaking. No one gave a thought to the value of Betty Grable's pinup picture for GI morale or to movies like *Wake Island* (1942), the first of many to dramatize American war heroics for the home front. In war, as in peace, Hollywood served as a convenient and vulnerable villain.

Hollywood Faces a Suspicious Government

Once again the motion-picture producers could not seem to do the right thing. There they were, providing essential recreation and entertainment for civilians and soldiers alike by offering feature films and live appearances by stars in Army camps and at war fronts. There they were, making dozens of skillful propaganda films depicting enemy evil and supporting the fortitude of America's British, Russian and French allies. There they were, many of them volunteering along with hundreds of their employees for military service to perform the critical tasks of battlefield and instructional filmmaking.

And to what response? Among others, the suggestion by Senator Ralph O. Brewster of the Truman Committee that "recent citizens" were not appropriate filmmakers for the war effort, that the War Department should hang out a sign saying only "seasoned citizens" may apply. His words implied a belief similar to the one Senator Gerald P. Nye had expressed in 1941: that the moviemakers were insufficiently American in origin, intellect and character.

The unkindest cut came soon after the war, when the cry of Communist infiltration of Hollywood was once again raised. This time the House Un-American Activities Committee (HUAC), under new leadership, prepared the ground more carefully. It aimed not for a few headlines but at a thorough purge of radically oriented workers from the entertainment field.

In 1947, HUAC found the industry a surprisingly softer touch. Though their films had attained their peak of popularity, the producers—twice burned by the Senate investigations of 1941 and 1943, apprehensive about the outcome of the government's antitrust suit against them, made cautious by the advent of home television programing and lacking the experienced political leadership of the recently retired Will H. Hays—felt themselves in a peculiarly weak position. Under pressure from the congressional investigators, they devoured their own, and Hollywood began to destroy itself. . . .

A New Strategy for Hollywood's Enemies

The postwar attack on Hollywood could not have got off the ground had it been merely a renewal of old enmities. The familiar charges against moviemakers, although couched in moral terms, had never fully succeeded in masking ethnic, religious and class antagonisms. In the aftermath of a war against Nazism, these traditional complaints began to appear base and repugnant. When Congressman John Rankin of Mississippi denounced Hollywood in 1945, his blatant anti-Semitism was a disturbing embarrassment to the movie industry's antagonists. The more rational among them knew they had a far stronger case against the movies on ideological grounds.

Hollywood had always put up a united front against criticism, protesting that it was being used as a scapegoat by people unwilling to look honestly at other modes of communication, and least of all at themselves. This stance did not hold up before the postwar method of scrutiny. It was made clear that the investigation of Communists in Hollywood was no special harassment but only an early step in a thorough purging of "subversive" influence from every institution in the land (indeed, before the House Un-American Activities Committee got around to Hollywood, the loyalty-security program for government employees had already begun). Hollywood itself was deeply divided on the issue, and no one could say that HUAC was prejudiced against Jews or the foreign-born, since members of those categories were among its most ardent supporters.

The grounds for suspicion no longer consisted principally of wild charges by publicity seekers and right-wing cranks. In 1945 the Chamber of Commerce of the United States published a report on *Communist Infiltration in the United States,* warning that Communists were seeking to gain control of entertainment and information media. They already dominated the Screen Writers Guild in Hollywood, the report claimed. The way to stop this Communist plot, it suggested, was to expose it.

The new prominence of respectable businessmen among Hollywood's critics may have been the principal reason why the producers picked the Chamber's president, Eric Johnston, to succeed Will Hays as their industry's front man. Johnston was expected to influence his former colleagues on Hollywood's behalf, as Hays had influenced politicians a quarter century before.

Neither Johnston nor anyone else, however, could stop the effort to expose "un-Americans," and the movie community was the obvious place to launch the crusade. Its critics had always been able to abuse it with impunity. Its enormous popularity gave its accusers access to wide national publicity. Its product was not constitutionally protected under the First Amendment guarantees of free speech and free press (the *Mutual Film* decision of 1915 still defined the movies' constitutional status). And nearly everyone believed, in those pre-television days, that movies had a greater influence on public values than any other medium. Only a few observers and the victims themselves recognized that the attack on Communism in Hollywood, if successful, would achieve what special-interest groups had been seeking for half a century—effective outside control over movie content and personnel.

A Divided Hollywood

In 1947, when the House Un-American Activities Committee returned to Hollywood, the movie community had gone through great changes since Martin Dies' visit, seven years before. Ideological lines had been drawn between political extremes. Major strikes had further exacerbated old conflicts. The man who in 1940 accused movie workers of Communist leanings had not been connected with the industry; the producers had resisted his charges, and the persons named had been given a chance to clear themselves in private. In the drastically altered postwar atmosphere, the accusers were important figures in the movie community; the attitude of the producers was uncertain, and the accused were called to defend themselves in the glare of floodlights and before a bank of movie cameras.

The crack in Hollywood's united front began in 1944 with the formation of the Motion Picture Alliance for the Preservation of American Values (MPA), an organization of politically conservative movie workers who proposed to defend the industry against Communist infiltration. Congressman Rankin praised its members as "oldtime American producers, actors and writers," which may have been more revealing of Rankin's prejudices than the Alliance's, since the group included Jews and immigrants of conservative persuasion.

The MPA provided HUAC with something no outside critics ever had, a body of supporters within the industry willing to testify publicly against their colleagues. For more than a decade there had been left-wing political activity in the movie community, but Communist party members and their sympathizers had basically formed alliances and sought influence within already established organizations, like labor guilds and unions. Their opposition, therefore, had come largely in the context of intraorganizational debates—for example, within the Screen Writers Guild. The sole purpose of the Alliance, however, was to combat Communism in general, and it gave the anti-Communist forces more concentrated purpose than the Communists themselves possessed. . . .

Stepping Up the Pressure

HUAC may not have been willing to venture into Hollywood without the encouragement of influential supporters within the industry, but the goals of HUAC and of Hollywood's anti-Communist front were not always the same. The committee made its strategy apparent in March 1947—nearly two months before it took secret testimony from "friendly" witnesses—when it interrogated Eric Johnston.

The committee pressed Johnston along the path of logic the U.S. Chamber of Commerce pamphlet had only partially laid out. The first premise was that every Communist party member was an agent of a foreign ideology seeking to overthrow the American form of government and substitute its own, and that any such person employed in the entertainment and information media would undoubtedly use his or her position to attack American principles and put forward Communist ideals. Therefore, the congressmen maintained, the motion-picture industry should get rid of every Communist it employed. Johnston balked at this final step in the argument. "There is nothing," he protested, "which will enable us to discharge a person in Hollywood because he is a Communist." He reiterated the Chamber of Commerce position that exposure of Communists would be sufficient. Yet he could not bring himself, any more than the Chamber report could, to spell out the consequences of exposure. If audiences knew an actor was a Communist, Johnston faintly suggested, they could show their displeasure by staying away from his films.

Johnston was caught in an unpleasant trap. He did not want to fire Communists, but the alternative he seemed to advocate, a selective boycott, invited economic disaster for the industry he represented. Moreover, his solution was open to the criticism that the allegedly most dangerous subversives were writers whose work was not as obvious to the moviegoing public as that of actors. Johnston's dilemma was to become all too familiar to liberals in many fields during the years of anti-Communist oppression. Once one accepts the basic anti-Communist premise—that Communists are disloyal—then any conclusion short of dismissal is merely a squeamish refusal to face the consequences of one's judgment.

As usual, Rankin put the committee's aim most bluntly: "Everyone whose loyalty was questioned I would certainly get them out of the moving-picture industry." Various other committee members tried to mount their favorite hobbyhorses during the hearings: Chairman J. Parnell Thomas, persisting in his efforts to show that the New Deal was Communistic, tried unsuccessfully to prove that the Roosevelt Administration had twisted arms in Hollywood to get pro-Russian movies produced during the war, in particular *Song of Russia* (MGM) and *Mission to Moscow* (Warner Bros.). "Large numbers of moving pictures that come out of Hollywood carry the Communist line," Rankin had said on the floor of the House, and the investigators occasionally talked grandly of documenting that assertion, though it's clear they never tried.

But all the issues the hearings raised—the lack of anti-Communist films made by Hollywood (this was Congressman Richard M. Nixon's singular interest) and the possibility that Communists sidetracked such projects; the role of high-salaried Hollywood Communists in contributing funds to the party; efforts by Communists to deprive anti-Communists of work—were subordinated to the committee's central purpose, the barring of all Communists from Hollywood employment. This, in a single stroke, would solve all problems.

The Blacklist

The witnesses, "friendly" and "unfriendly," knew from the beginning they would have to take a stand on the committee's demand for an employment blacklist. On the eve of the October public hearings in Washington, Johnston told attorneys for the nineteen "unfriendly" witnesses who had been subpoenaed, "As long as I live I will never be a party to anything as un-American as a blacklist." The industry's stance appeared firm when Jack L. Warner opened the hearings as the first "friendly" witness. In his secret May testimony he had boasted of having thrown more than a dozen Communist writers out of his studio. In October he said, "I have never seen a Communist, and I wouldn't know one if I saw one," and he explicitly opposed the suggestion of a blacklist. Robert Stripling, the committee's chief investigator, inserted Warner's May testimony into the record to demonstrate the disparity between Warner's private views and his public adherence to the official industry line.

Louis B. Mayer would not compromise his conservative principles: he vowed that MGM would not employ any Communist party members. Among the remainder of the "friendly" witnesses there was no obvious unity on the question of a blacklist. Adolphe Menjou, the actor, said he saw no reason for a producer to fire a Communist writer: "He could be very carefully watched; this producer could watch every script and every scene of every script. We have many Communist writers who are splendid writers. They do not have to write Communistically at all, but they have to be watched." Other "friendly" witnesses pleaded that it was the responsibility of Congress to make laws authorizing private employers to fire employees for political beliefs, since what the committee wanted the movie industry to do was in all likelihood illegal.

All told, twenty-three "friendly" witnesses appeared over a week's time, headed—at least in the eyes of the public crowding the hearing room—by stars like Gary Cooper, Robert Taylor, Robert Montgomery, Ronald Reagan and George Murphy. Their motives were varied. Some wanted to square old grievances, defend past decisions, get even with old enemies, advance their own careers or causes.

More often than not their testimony was petty, mean, craven, even stupid. But some had also come to share a purpose they had not had in mind when they encouraged HUAC to enter their world: they wanted to limit the damage the committee was inflicting on their industry. If the wrath they had helped to unleash could be deflected toward the "unfriendlies," perhaps their industry could still survive the hearings with its powers and prerogatives intact. . . .

The Hollywood Ten

Nineteen "unfriendly" witnesses were subpoenaed from Hollywood by the committee Eleven were called to testify during the second and final week of the motion-picture hearings. One, Bertolt Brecht, the German playwright, answered the committee's questions, denied he was a Communist and shortly thereafter returned to Europe, where he became one of the leading figures in East Germany The others refused to answer whether they were then or had ever been members of the Communist party (the writers also refused to state whether they belonged to the Screen Writers Guild). They were cited for contempt of Congress, and after carrying their appeals unsuccessfully through the federal courts, two of them served prison terms of six months; the other eight served a full year. These are the "Hollywood Ten" of fact and legend. . . .

By refusing to state whether they were or had been members of the Communist party, they risked a contempt citation from Congress—this was the path they chose, and conviction and imprisonment were the result. Had they answered the questions negatively, they were likely to have been indicted for perjury (it is probable that all the Hollywood Ten had at one time been party members). There was a third alternative, and some later commentators have strongly condemned them for not telling the truth. If they had admitted party membership, it is argued, perhaps their candor and courage would have disarmed HUAC and rallied public support behind them. That prospect seems far-fetched. Had they confessed their party affiliations, it is far more likely they would have been grilled endlessly to name every other Communist in Hollywood and would not themselves have escaped reprisals unless they recanted their political beliefs.

Given the intransigence of HUAC and the evidence in newspapers and opinion polls indicating public disapproval of the committee's assault on civil liberties, their strategy to attack the committee's basic purpose as an unconstitutional infringement of First Amendment rights of free speech and free assembly was both expedient and high-principled. The committee responded that Communists had forfeited their right to constitutional protections. "At this ultimate point of conflict," Dalton Trumbo wrote in a pamphlet, "either the Committee or the individual is bound to be destroyed."

The committee survived, and ten men went to jail. The crux of nearly all later criticism of the Ten centers on their demeanor before the committee. They behaved, it is said, in a manner Communists have traditionally taken before such tribunals, turning the attack around against their accusers, filling the air with windy rhetoric, pugnacious belligerence and lofty incredulity that they should be suspected at all. There seems to be no question but that their performance on the witness stand cost the Ten critical support within the industry. But it must be remembered that during the first week of hearings, they had been forced to sit silently and observe Chairman Parnell Thomas' contempt for them, his raging temper, his own windy rhetoric and pugnacious bombast. It did not seem likely that even a saintly serenity could avail in the face of the committee's wrathful purpose. More than ever a tenacious offense appeared to be the most effective defense. . . .

Sacrificing a Few

Less than a month after the hearings, Twentieth Century-Fox announced it would "dispense with the services" of Communists and all other persons who refused to answer questions about Communist party affiliation. On November

24, 1947—the same day the House of Representatives voted overwhelmingly to approve HUAC's contempt citations for the ten "unfriendly" witnesses—the motion-picture producers association met at the Waldorf-Astoria Hotel in New York to discuss the fate of the Ten and formulate a policy on blacklisting. The following day they released a statement pledging, "We will not knowingly employ a Communist or a member of any party or group which advocates the overthrow of the Government of the United States by force, or by any illegal or unconstitutional method."

The producers specifically deplored the behavior of the Ten: "Their actions have been a disservice to their employers and have impaired their usefulness to the industry." They stated that they all would be discharged or suspended without pay pending the outcome of their cases.

It has frequently been said that the decision to institute a blacklist came not from Hollywood but from Wall Street bankers and the movie industry's New York business-office heads, but the distinction between East Coast moneymen and West Coast moviemen is in this case not worth drawing. The Hollywood producers' strategy under Will Hays's leadership had always been to avoid outside interference, keep power in their own hands and surreptitiously circumvent unpalatable declarations of principle as need required and circumstance permitted. Clearly, the blacklist policy was designed to further the same goals: if the Waldorf declaration could head off further congressional attacks on the industry, and particularly Thomas' announced probe into motion-picture content (as it seems to have done), then the sacrifice of a few heretofore valued employees might not seem such a high price to pay. Much the same thing had happened before, in the Arbuckle scandal and other such events.

But the movie industry's old bulwarks had never experienced such a storm as struck them in the postwar period on the issue of Communist infiltration. "In pursuing this policy," the producers said in their Waldorf statement, "we are not going to be swayed by any hysteria or intimidation from any source." In all the history of hollow Hollywood words, few were emptier than these. The producers were more prophetic when they went on to say: "We are frank to recognize that such a policy involves dangers and risks. There is the danger of hurting innocent people, there is the risk of creating an atmosphere of fear. Creative work at its best cannot be carried on in an atmosphere of fear. Those words read a little like an epitaph.

A Perverse Democracy

The problem was not so much the producers, whose limitations by then were well known, but the times and the nature of their antagonists. The period of anti-Communist madness in American life was a time when accusations without proof were immediately granted the status of truth; when guilt was assumed, and innocence had to be documented. Though anti-Communism was a tactic both major political parties used in pursuit of foreign policy and electoral goals, it was one that "respectable" people could not control. A perverse kind of democracy was practiced: all accusations, no matter from whom, were taken equally seriously. A housewife or a grocer, a "nobody," could by simply writing a letter jeopardize the career of a wealthy, glamorous movie star. When national organizations like the American Legion set themselves up as judges of the movie industry's ideological purity, the threat of a boycott, of picket lines before movie theaters, so frightened producers that they were willing to capitulate to any and all outside demands.

The anti-Communists were hard taskmasters. Myron C. Fagan, playwright and author of *Red Treason in Hollywood* (1949) and *Documentation of the Red Stars in Hollywood* (1950), made clear that he wanted to clean far more than Communist party members out of Hollywood. "As far as we are concerned," he said, "any man or woman who is a fellow traveler, or belongs to a Red front organization, or has supported Communism with financial or moral support . . . or has come out in open support of the ten branded men who defied the Parnell Thomas investigation, or associates with known Communists, openly or in secret is just as guilty of treason, and just as much an enemy of America as any outright Communist. In fact, more so! I have no fear of the known Communist! It is the rat that masquerades as a good American but who secretly nourishes the Communist's slimy cause, who is our greatest menace."

As far as Fagan was concerned, to have joined the Committee for the First Amendment was an act of high treason. His list of "Stalin's stars" ran to almost two hundred—a figure close to the number of persons estimated to have been blacklisted over the years from the late 1940s to the mid-1960s. He was also, of all things, critical of the conservative Motion Picture Alliance, accusing it of being a tool of the producers. Of the producers themselves he was deeply suspicious, expressing the view that they really wanted the Communists to remain in movie work (he was already aware that some studios were using blacklisted writers working under pseudonyms, although he did not mention that the writers were receiving a fraction of their former salaries). He himself was duped by producers, he wrote, who asked him to go easy with his charges, on the argument that if movie attendance dipped too far, studio managements would be replaced, and the new bosses wouldn't be as experienced at getting rid of Communists as the old. But he concluded that their plea was one more Red-tainted ruse.

Attacking the Stars

It was a dark and difficult season for the industry. The anti-Communists naturally delighted in naming not little-known figures, like screenwriters, but big box-office stars. Actors and actresses, unlike writers, could not continue working under pseudonyms. Various groups in the movie community saw the necessity for a systematic procedure to deal with the many unsubstantiated charges pouring in from free-lance Red hunters. Gradually a system of "clearance" evolved. When faced with an accusation that might wreck a career, a person could, rather than flounder in ignorance, learn which conservative colleagues to approach, in order to begin the process of satisfying the accuser's demands. (Some accusers were never satisfied, but if the American Legion or HUAC approved, that was good enough.) For non-Communists, "clearance" required repudiating all liberal opinions and associations; former Communists were required to perform a humiliating public ritual of expiation by naming names of other Hollywood Communists.

The behavior of the studios during this period was contemptible, but given their unwillingness to take a stand on principle (along with nearly every American university, newspaper, radio and television station and the vast majority of intellectuals), what choice did they have? They might invest several million dollars in a movie, release it to the public and find that because its star—or writer or director or producer—had once signed a petition in the 1930s attacking Nazi Germany, the American Legion was ready to throw up picket lines throughout the country. To avoid adverse publicity and empty theaters, they quickly gave in.

Even so, the damage to Hollywood was very nearly fatal. For the first half-century of American movies the industry had had a fascinating and curious relationship with the American public. It had always stood slightly aslant the mainstream of American cultural values and expressions, seeking to hold its working-class audience while making movies attractive to middle-class tastes, and therefore never quite in step with other forms of cultural communication. Movies were always less courageous than some organs of information and entertainment, but they were more iconoclastic than most, offering a version of American behavior and values more risqué, violent, comic and fantastic than the standard interpretation of traditional cultural elites. It was this trait that gave movies their popularity and their mythmaking power.

And it was this trait that the anti-Communist crusade destroyed. Creative work at its best could indeed not be carried on in an atmosphere of fear, and Hollywood was suffused with fear. It dared not make any movie that might arouse the ire of anyone. One of the Payne Fund authors, Charles C. Peters, had argued in his *Motion Pictures and Standards of Morality* (1933) that movies ought not to challenge or deviate from prevailing moral norms. In the Cold War atmosphere of the late 1940s and 1950s, Hollywood went far beyond the standard Peters had asked of it: the studios tried to avoid making movies that would offend any vocal minority. As a result they lost touch both with their own past styles and with the changes and movements in the dominant culture at large. Let it not be said that television killed the movie industry: the movie industry must take that responsibility itself.

CHAPTER 5

Emerging Trends in Popular Culture

Television Takes Off

Harry Castleman and Walter J. Podrazik

The number of TV sets operating in America increased more than 2,000 percent in 1947, write Harry Castleman and Walter J. Podrazik in their book *Watching TV: Four Decades of American Television*. Not until 1948, however, did the networks make serious efforts to provide Americans with significant programs. According to the authors, during 1947, TV networks faced many problems, including difficulties adapting to an audience who would view programs on a small screen. However, the authors explain, in 1948, the networks began to use ratings to guide their programming decisions. At first, many program ideas came from radio broadcasting, including talent shows, situation comedies, and sporting events, but new programs were evolving such as the children's show *Puppet Television Theater*, which made *Howdy Doody* into a permanent after-school superstar. Broadcast of the political conventions and the presidential race added a new dimension to politics, but the most successful form of programming during 1948 was the variety show, and a successful nightclub comedian, Milton Berle, hosted the *Texaco Star Theater*, which was television's first smash hit.

I n September, 1926, RCA placed a full page ad in the nation's major newspapers announcing the birth of NBC and the beginning of network radio broadcasting:

Excerpted from *Watching TV: Four Decades of American Television*, by Harry Castleman and Walter J. Podrazik. Copyright ©1982 by Walter J. Podrazik and Harry Castleman. Reprinted with permission from the authors.

The day has gone by when the radio receiving set is a play-thing. It must now be an instrument of service. . . . The purpose of [NBC] will be to provide the best program[ing] available for broadcasting in the United States.

Only two years later, NBC began operating an experimental television station, but it was not until January 5, 1948, that the follow-up ad appeared, announcing network TV:

1948—TELEVISION'S YEAR

. . . an exciting promise is now an actual service to the American home. After twenty years of preparation, the NBC television network is open for business.

NBC proudly spoke of the four TV stations already programming its network material, with stations in Boston and Baltimore to open soon. In 1947, it was pointed out, the number of TV sets operating in America had increased by more than 2,000 percent, from 8,000 to 170,000.

Nineteen forty seven marked the end of television's interim period. Nineteen forty eight marks TV's appearance as a major force.

In almost awe-struck tones the ad concluded:

The greatest means of mass communications in the world is with us.

Launching New Programs

The excitement that followed Kraft's commercially successful entry into TV in the summer of 1947 had continued into the fall as more and more sponsors invested money in television entertainment. Throughout the fall, the networks launched new television vehicles and the quality of their programming began to rise noticeably. In October, the Du-Mont network presented gossip columnist Jack Eigen in a nightclub setting, surrounded by glamour girls. For fifteen minutes, Eigen talked about the latest showbiz rumors and chatted with whatever celebrity he could corral. (Both Frank Sinatra and Fred Allen were on the show, but only via a telephone hookup.) In November, NBC brought Mutual radio's popular *Meet the Press* interview program to TV, after convincing a sponsor, General Mills, that the show was not too controversial for television. Fred Coe enlisted help for his NBC Sunday night drama presentations from two respected Broadway organizations, the Theater Guild and the American National Theater Academy (ANTA). In December, DuMont restaged "A Christmas Carol," using twelve sets and a cast of twenty-two.

Still, it was another sports remote that produced the most exciting television in the Fall of 1947—baseball's annual World Series contest, the first to be televised. All eight TV stations on the East Coast coaxial cable broadcast the seven game "subway" series between the New York Yankees and the Brooklyn Dodgers, two bitter crosstown rivals. With Gillette and the Ford Motor Company as sponsors, CBS, NBC, and DuMont organized a "pool" coverage system in which the three networks each carried all of the games but took turns on the play-by-play and camera chores. Bob Stanton of NBC was the broadcast voice for games one and seven, Bill Slater took games two, five, and six for DuMont, and Bob Edge handled games three and four for CBS. Close-up cameras presented viewers at home and in bars with sharp, clear pictures of every phase of the game: the antics of baseline coaches giving complicated signals, the challenging stance by a batter waiting for a pitch, and the dejection on the face of a pitcher taken out of the game. Television, in effect, provided the best seats in the house and gave the dramatic championship match a greater sense of theater than ever before as the Yankees won the series, four games to three.

Viewer response to the World Series was even greater than the reaction to the Joe Louis-Billy Conn fight of the year before. The TV audience was estimated to be at least 3.8 million, and retailers reported a sharp increase in TV set sales during early October. Welcome as this news was, the World Series was merely another short-term special event. The TV networks were still searching for regular weekly hit series to solidify their position as the primary source of video programming. They were a bit anxious to find such material because the very concept of national live TV networks was under attack from the West Coast.

The Networks Stall Syndication

In June, 1947, Jerry Fairbanks, a former producer of film shorts at the Paramount studios in Hollywood, announced that he was setting up a TV film unit. He promised to supply regular weekly filmed programs to individual stations directly through the mail for airing at their pleasure (a process called "syndication"). Not only did this represent a considerable saving when compared to the potential cost of using AT&T's coaxial cable, but, with coast-to-coast network TV hookups still years away, Fairbanks offered a ready supply of programs to new TV stations not yet connected to the cable. He filmed seventeen episodes of a crime drama series, *Public Prosecutor* (at the unconventional length of twenty minutes per episode), but the networks were able to pressure the local TV station managers into ignoring the service. The networks feared that if local stations began to obtain filmed shows directly from a syndicator, they might eventually decide not to use network programming at all. Stressing that television should be *live*, not filmed, the networks assured the locals that once the cable connections were made, stations would receive much better material if aligned with a national network. In the meantime, for those in the hinterlands, DuMont supplied the stopgap solution when it announced development of a method of preserving live TV shows by filming them directly from a television monitor. These kinescope recordings, popularly known as "kines," meant that while a local station waited for the arrival of live network TV in its area, it could still obtain network programs, albeit delayed a week or two. Though the kines were often grainy and hard to hear, they allowed the TV networks to beat Fairbanks at his own game. Finding no buyers, Fairbanks dropped the idea and, as a result, his *Public Prosecutor* series stayed on the shelf until the early 1950s.

The success of the networks in scuttling the Fairbanks film proposal had as much to do with the standoffish attitude of Hollywood to television, and vice versa, as their own influence on the locals. All the major film studios considered TV to be a prime competitor for the future, and they refused to allow any of their feature films, producers, directors, or stars to appear on television in any form. Consequently, they also gave Fairbanks no support in his scheme. Their strategy was to treat the upstart television with disdain and not give it any help or support, hoping that it would just fade away. . . .

As television continued to expand through the fall and winter, though, that situation was rapidly changing. Applications for stations, which had been crawling in at one or two per month the year before, averaged three a week by the end of 1947. Set sales were climbing and the January, 1948, declaration by NBC that network television had arrived served as a signal that the time had come for serious efforts at regular weekly programming.

Less than two weeks after the NBC ad, DuMont revived the long-successful radio variety standard, *The Original Amateur Hour.* Major Edward Bowes had run the series on radio from the early 1930s until it ended in 1945, just before he died. Bowes had assumed a wholesome, fatherly, yet realistically critical role introducing new talent to the nation. The possibility of rags-to-riches stardom had made the show very successful on radio and DuMont had high hopes for the TV version. Ted Mack, who had worked under the tutelage of Bowes, took charge, adopting the same approach in welcoming the aspiring performers. Though DuMont took a chance and slotted the program earlier than practically anything else then on (Sunday night, 7:00–8:00 P.M.), it became a very popular video hit. But how popular?

Television was being run by people familiar with radio formats and strategies and, as they began to develop more expensive new video series, they felt the need for program ratings just as in radio. Less than one month after *The Original Amateur Hour* premiered, the Hooper organization, radio's most respected-ratings service, conducted the first television rating sweep, in New York City. Ted Mack's show walked away with the number one slot, registering a 46.8% rating (that is, of the televisions in the homes contacted, 46.8 percent were on and tuned to *The Original Amateur Hour*). The J. Walter Thompson agency, an early believer in TV advertising, was the first ad agency to subscribe to Hooper's rating service.

In early 1948, NBC also found itself with a hit show, though it took a while longer to catch on. *Puppet Television Theater* had begun at Christmastime, 1947, as a one-hour children's show running Saturday afternoons at 5:00 P.M. By April, 1948, two weekday episodes were added and the series was renamed *Howdy Doody* after the main puppet character. The idea behind the show was simple: a few kids, a few puppets, a clown, and some music. What made it click was the personality and verve of the program's ringmaster, "Buffalo" Bob Smith, a former New York disk jockey who had previously been the host of a relaxed Arthur Godfrey-type morning radio show for adults. Smith seemed to enjoy the children present in the "peanut gallery" and his efforts to entertain them came out in an ingratiating but not condescending form. He supplied the voices to most of the puppets (such as Howdy Doody, Phineas T. Bluster, and Captain Scuttlebutt), giving each an individual personality. The live characters such as Princess Summer-Fall-Winter-Spring and the mute clown Clarabell (played by Bob Keeshan, later renowned as Captain Kangaroo) shared his enthusiasm and helped make the humans as warm and friendly as the puppets. By the fall of 1948, the program aired Monday through Friday.

Howdy Doody was one of television's first superstars. Small fry seized control of the family TV set in the late afternoon and demonstrated that they could become quite devoted to a television character. Mothers were not upset because, when the kids were occupied with *Howdy Doody*, they could relax. In the postwar baby-boom era, television had a practical function—it was an excellent babysitter. As a result, the late afternoon and very early evening "after school" time slots were recognized as prime "kidvid" hours—perfect for programming geared toward children, whose parents were still too busy to settle down and watch.

Stepping Up the Competition

Television was becoming an item of interest to more and more households. Newspapers began accepting the medium as a fact of life and grudgingly agreed to print daily broadcast schedules for no charge—just as they did with radio. CBS, which had been airing only remote telecasts for almost a year, realized that NBC and DuMont had seized the initiative in television programming. Having attracted only a few sponsors for its outdoor broadcasts, the network conceded defeat in February, 1948, by announcing that it would soon reopen and greatly enlarge its studios at Grand Central Station. ABC, which had abstained from TV production for a year while waiting for its home base in New York to be constructed, decided not to wait until the August completion date but geared up instead for a mid-April kick-off, using its affiliates on the East Coast.

All the networks realized that if their new program drive was to go anywhere, they would need live music. They at last came to terms with James C. Petrillo's American Federation of Musicians and the total ban on live television music ended. Within hours, CBS and NBC staged a nip-and-tuck race to be the first network to present live music on television. CBS won by ninety minutes. Eugene Ormandy and the Philadelphia Orchestra hit the air at five in the afternoon on March 20, while Arturo Toscanini and the NBC Orchestra weighed in at 6:30 P.M. These orchestral presentations, however, were not really representative of the future of live television music. Soon, pop-oriented musical programs appeared, modeled after the popular radio music shows, which showcased singers in either an all music format (usually a fifteen-minute slot) or more elaborate musical-variety shows (a half-hour or an hour long).

Though CBS was far behind NBC in developing studio entertainment programming and signing up new TV stations as affiliates, once it decided in earnest to reenter in-studio commercial television the network quickly became the chief competitor to NBC, leapfrogging the competition. This was a reflection of CBS's radio strength. It was a very strong number two in radio behind NBC and the two were generally regarded as the powerhouses of broadcasting. As television stations decided to align themselves with a network, it made sense to go with one of the two biggest in radio.

CBS's only holdover from its all-remote concept was the network's first effort in theatrical drama, *Tonight on Broadway*. Producer Worthington Miner took TV cameras to New York theaters in order to present hit Broadway plays, beginning with "Mr. Roberts," starring Henry Fonda. Miner treated the series like any other remote event and positioned the cameras so that the entire stage was visible at all times on the TV screen. While dead center, thirty-five rows from the front, might have been perfect for a patron at the theater, it was disastrous to viewers at home who tried to follow the action on their eight-inch screens (opera glasses were not much help). The tiny figures were lost in the open expanse of stage, but it was felt that this was the only way to correctly convey the feel of theater. The cameras were there to present the event exactly as a member of the audience would see it. Home viewers were, in effect, sneaking in for free.

The resurrected ABC also dabbled in drama with its first new series in April, *Hollywood Screen Test*. Originating at first from Philadelphia, the program was a combination drama-anthology and talent show in which two performers who had Broadway experience, but who were not yet stars, appeared in a scene with a celebrity veteran. Just as in *The Original Amateur Hour* there was the lure of seeing stars-in-the-making, but the overall quality of production was much higher. The show was set up as if it were an actual West Coast "screen test," which not only served as an innovative format but also covered up the lack of expensive scenery. The series lasted five years for ABC, with veteran Neil Hamilton acting as host for all but the first few months.

The Radio Influence

Through the spring of 1948, the networks' TV schedules expanded tremendously to include elementary versions of basic entertainment formats that were popular on radio. NBC presented *Barney Blake, Police Reporter,* starring Gene O'Donnell as a reporter-as-cop. On DuMont, real-life husband and wife Johnny and Mary Kay Stearns faced the humorous trials and tribulations of married life in the appropriately titled situation comedy, *Mary Kay and Johnny.* Kyle MacDonnell, one of the first singing stars to make a name on television, hosted a series of pleasant fifteen-minute musical vehicles for NBC: *For Your Pleasure, Kyle MacDonnell Sings,* and *Girl About Town.* All the networks had quizzes such as *Americana Quiz* and *Charade Quiz.* DuMont offered the imaginative *Court of Current Issues,* in which actors would argue a case in a courtroom setting and the studio audience acted as jury. This seemed the perfect setting for a television discussion show.

While television developed its selection of entertainment vehicles in an effort to duplicate some of the attraction of network radio, a dramatic—and symbolic—change took place in radio programming. On March 21, the day after the Petrillo ban ended for television music, *Stop the Music* premiered on ABC radio. It was a musical quiz show conceived by Louis G. Cowan, directed by Mark Goodson, and slotted in one of the toughest time periods of the radio week: Sunday night against Edgar Bergen and Fred Allen. Surprisingly, within months, Fred Allen, a member of radio's top ten for a decade, had dropped to thirty-eighth place. By the end of the year, Edgar Bergen took his Sunday night show off the air for a season. *Stop the Music* had beaten them both. . . .

The giveaway quiz show fad did spill over into TV in mid-1948, but none of the programs became big hits. Video production budgets were still relatively small so the

TV quiz programs looked cheap rather than magical and glamorous. The shows simply did not appear as visually exciting as the equivalent radio programs sounded. They remained just one more experimental format for television programmers in search of hit shows and prestige events.

Television and Politics

The 1948 presidential race provided the networks with an excellent opportunity to boost television's stature. President Harry Truman, who had assumed office when Franklin Roosevelt died, was running for his first elected term and the Republicans felt certain they could beat him. As the race heated up through the spring and summer, the networks devoted as much air time as possible to the various campaigns. Most of the stories appeared on the fifteen-minute nightly newsreel shows that the networks had established over the previous year in an effort to upgrade the image of their news departments. DuMont had been first in the summer of 1947 with Walter Compton's *News from Washington*. NBC soon followed with *Camel Newsreel Theater*, a ten-minute collection of newsreels completely produced by Fox-Movietone (which even took responsibility for hiring the show's off-screen announcing trio of Ed Thorgensen, George Putnam, and Helen Claire). In April, 1948, as part of its return to in-studio broadcasts, CBS brought Douglas Edwards back on camera and retitled the daily program *Douglas Edwards and the News*. ABC joined the others in the summer with *News and Views*, which used a rotating anchor crew, including TV's first anchorwoman, Pauline Frederick.

In addition to coverage on the newsreel shows, that summer CBS gave thirty-minutes of time to a different presidential candidate each week on *Presidential Timber*. Republican Harold Stassen was the first to appear. At the time, the radio networks banned the "dramatization of political issues," so most political forays into radio were generally dull discussions and speeches by either the candidate or a chosen representative. Television had no such ban, so Stassen hired an ad agency to produce a thirty-minute film to run in his segment of *Presidential Timber*. Actually, the film did not spend much time on "the issues" at all, but instead served as a warm pictorial biography meant to promote Stassen as a "nice guy" rather than just a speechmaker.

Covering the Nominating Conventions

The planners of both party nominating conventions had noted the staggering growth of television set sales in 1947 and realized that a city connected to the Eastern coaxial cable network offered the opportunity for a tremendous publicity boost at convention time. Both parties chose Philadelphia and, by the time the first gavel fell, there were eighteen stations from Boston to Richmond sending out the proceedings to ten million viewers watching on 300,000 sets.

There was little to distinguish one network's convention coverage from another's because all four used the same pictures, provided by a common pool camera set up to focus on the main podium. There were no additional pickups from roving floor reporters, though NBC did set up a small studio off the convention floor ("Room 22") in which Ben Grauer conducted on-the-spot, off-the-cuff interviews with political bigwigs. To anchor coverage of the proceedings, the networks rotated among their top reporters. CBS featured Ed Murrow, Quincy Howe, and Douglas Edwards, while NBC had H.V. Kaltenborn and Richard Harkness. ABC made extensive use of Walter Winchell, while DuMont, which had no formal news staff, hired Drew Pearson as its main commentator.

The Republican convention was generally uneventful and dull as Governor Thomas Dewey from New York easily beat Harold Stassen, but the Democrats staged a drawn-out free-for-all. Minnesota's Hubert H. Humphrey, a candidate for the U.S. Senate, led a floor fight over inclusion of a civil rights plank in the party platform and, in response, Southern Democrats walked out and formed their own splinter party (popularly known as the Dixiecrats). The Democratic nominee, President Harry Truman, fell victim to the floor wrangling along the way and his acceptance speech was delayed until 2:00 A.M. By then most viewer-voters were asleep and consequently missed a truly electrifying presentation. Though Truman was a horrible reader of prewritten speeches, when he started speaking ad-lib from the heart, his oratory was close to perfection. This was the style he used for his acceptance address and it resulted in one of the best speeches of his life.

It was also a very good television speech. By not reading from a script, Truman could look the camera (and the voter) in the eye, without the distracting pauses and downward glances of most speechreaders. He came across on TV as a sincere natural man who was not so much the President as "one of the guys." Truman's speech vividly demonstrated the personal intimacy possible through television. Sharp politicians sensed that television might be even more important than first suspected, but they were not yet ready to incorporate the medium into a full-scale presidential campaign. That fall, Governor Dewey turned down an advertising agency's suggestion to concentrate on short "spot announcements" for television, and he and President Truman restricted their use of TV to a few live pickups of large political rallies. It was generally agreed that television played very little part in Truman's come-from-behind victory.

The Variety Show

While politicians were just beginning to experiment with television, the era of testing had passed for entertainment programming. The networks and sponsors were ready for a dramatic breakthrough to tie it all together. Kraft's McLaren Cheese promotion demonstrated how effective television advertising could be. The top-rated Ted Mack show proved that viewers liked variety. The vaudeville styled *Hour Glass* had attracted a devoted following in 1946 without any live music, and now the Petrillo ban was lifted. The total number of TV sets in the country was doubling every four months. It was time to move!

On pages 26 and 27 of the May 19, 1948, issue of the

entertainment trade weekly *Variety,* the William Morris talent agency placed a two-page ad with a large headline:

VAUDEVILLE IS BACK

The Golden Age of variety begins with the premiere of *The Texaco Star Theater* on television, Tuesday, 8:00–9:00 P.M. E.D.T., starting June 8 on NBC and its affiliated stations in New York, Washington, Boston, Philadelphia, Baltimore, Richmond, and Schenectady. WANTED—Variety artists from all corners of the globe. Send particulars to the William Morris Agency.

A radio version of *The Texaco Star Theater* had played since the fall of 1938, but that mixed variety and drama under a succession of celebrity hosts (including Ken Murray, Fred Allen, James Melton, Alan Young, and Gordon MacRae). The new television version was conceived as a throwback to the vaudeville houses (such as New York City's famed Palace Theater), which had thrived from the turn of the century until the advent of radio and talkies.

In vaudeville, a few acts would appear on stage, perform, and step off, beginning with the unknowns and working up to the headliners. An emcee would introduce the performers and attempt to give the show some continuity. NBC felt that a big budget television version of the vaudeville form might catch on, just as *Hour Glass* had done in its brief run. With imaginative production, a good selection of talent, and a strong host, *Texaco Star Theater* could be a big hit. Finding the right host was the most difficult part of the formula, so the network decided to spend the summer giving a few candidates trial runs. It quickly settled on Milton Berle to open the series. Berle was a successful nightclub comedian who had been a flop in numerous attempts to make it on network radio, but he had brought down the house on a heart fund auction program televised by DuMont on April 7. It seemed that the added visual nature of television was just the extra plus Berle needed and, on June 8, he stepped out for the first *Texaco Star Theater.* It was as if television had been reinvented.

The Return of Vaudeville

Reviewers were ecstatic: "Television's first real smash!" "Let the hucksters make way for the show folk!" As emcee, Berle delivered a cleaned-up version of his nightclub routine, with visual mannerisms impossible to convey over radio, then introduced a succession of acts (including Pearl Bailey). Yet that was just the beginning. Berle also had an amazing sense of timing and pacing. When he saw the show was lagging, he would dash on stage and ham it up, holding the program together with the force of his personality. Unlike old-time vaudeville and every other variety show previously on television, Berle's *Texaco Star Theater* opened fast, stayed fast and tight, and finished fast. Even the one commercial—known as the middle ad—was integrated into the act as a funny plug by pitchman Sid Stone, whose "tell ya' what I'm gonna do . . ." come-on soon became a national catch phrase.

Instead of staging the show for the studio audience, the producers were more interested in giving the viewers at home a sharp, clear picture. The camera was taken out of the infamous thirty-fifth row and placed on stage. The resulting closeups produced an immediacy and intimacy unmatched by radio and theater. This marriage of vaudeville and video techniques produced a new form, vaudeo. There had never been anything else like it on television.

NBC had hoped for success, but had not expected a hit of such proportions. After Berle's three appearances in June and July, a rotating group of emcees took over (including Henny Youngman, Morey Amsterdam, and George Price), but none could generate anything near the excitement of Berle. The format and his personality had meshed perfectly. After frantic importunings by NBC, Berle signed to become permanent host of *Texaco Star Theater* beginning in September.

Twelve days after Berle's June premiere, CBS unveiled its own television vaudeville show, *Toast of the Town,* with Ed Sullivan as host. Sullivan had been a Broadway newspaper columnist for almost twenty years and his Broadway contacts made him the perfect choice to head a variety show drawing on new talent. CBS producer Worthington Miner first spotted the somewhat dour, low-key Sullivan as a potential for television, and chose him to emcee the 1947 Harvest Moon Ball, staged and televised in Madison Square Garden by CBS and the *New York Daily News*. He used him again in a 1948 Easter Sunday variety benefit, and *Toast of the Town* soon followed.

Coming so soon after Berle's spectacular, Sullivan's June 20 debut suffered in comparison. He was judged by the same standards even though Berle had been chosen for his abilities as a performer and Sullivan for his skills as an off-stage producer who could unearth new talent. *Toast of the Town* itself was much closer to a traditional vaudeville set up than *Texaco Star Theater*, as Sullivan merely introduced a succession of acts and stepped aside. At first, even the camera placement was back at the thirty-fifth row.

Jack Gould of the *New York Times* called the selection of Sullivan as emcee "ill advised," saying: ". . . his extreme matter-of-factness and his tendency to introduce friends in the audience add up to little sparkling entertainment."

In a medium centered on performing talent and warm intimacy, Sullivan was the permanent exception to prove the rule—he had neither, but his knack for finding talent on the verge of making it big was uncanny. In fact, two of the seven performers on the opening show were the then unknown "zany comic" team of Dean Martin and Jerry Lewis (paid $200 for their appearance). Nonetheless, jokes about Sullivan's stage mannerisms never ceased, even after the show became a big success. Budding impressionists cut their teeth on mimicking his scrunched stance and his frequently repeated phrases such as "And now, right here on our stage . . ." and "really big shew." Husbands would turn to their wives in the glowing dark and opine, "He's got no talent. He'll never last." It was Sullivan who had the last laugh as his program ran for twenty-three years. Fred Allen explained the incongruity: "Ed Sullivan will stay on television as long as other people have talent."

The Belles of Baseball

Jack Fincher

In the following article, Jack Fincher, a feature writer for *Smithsonian* magazine, recalls the All-American Girls Professional Baseball League (AAGPBL). In 1942, Fincher writes, Philip K. Wrigley, owner of the Chicago Cubs, was concerned that World War II might shut down major league baseball, so he pulled the best players from amateur softball leagues for women who also represented all-American ideals of womanhood and divided them into four teams that traveled the country. To maintain their all-American image, Fincher explains, the players not only worked out all day, but attended charm school in the evening and were chaperoned to protect them from admirers and prevent them from drinking, gambling, or violating curfew. Despite these restrictions, these women with nicknames like "Pepper," "Moe," "Tiby," and "Ziggy" played the game with skill and intensity, gaining the respect of fans and professionals alike.

Visitors to the Baseball Hall of Fame in Cooperstown, New York, were mystified one weekend last fall to behold an ebullient throng of older women trooping around the place as if they owned it. Which, in a manner of speaking, they did. Once, those senior citizens were the glamorous Girls of Summer—stars of the only professional fe-

Excerpted from "The 'Belles of the Ball Game' Were a Hit with Their Fans," by Jack Fincher, *Smithsonian*, July 1989. Reprinted with permission from the author.

male baseball league this country ever had. Playing for teams with such unabashedly sexist names as the Chicks, the Peaches and the Lassies, they swung for the fences, barreled down the base paths and signed autographs for their adoring fans just like big-league ballplayers. But they weren't merely shadows of their male counterparts. They added dash and excitement to the national pastime and, in so doing, made it uniquely their own. Sportswriters dubbed them the "Queens of Swat" and the "Belles of the Ball Game." They called each other "Moe" and "Tiby," "Nickie" and "Pepper," "Jeep" and "Flash." They rode stuffy buses from city to city, played six games a week and doubleheaders on Sunday, and dreaded the day in September when the grueling season would come to an end. Now, aging in body but ageless in spirit, they were in town to attend the unveiling of a new permanent exhibition in their honor.

Dedicated to "Women in Baseball," the intriguing collection of uniforms, photographs and trophies salutes the 545 athletes from the United States, Cuba and Canada who were part of the All-American Girls Professional Baseball League (AAGPBL) from its inception in 1943 to its demise 12 years later. It is an impressive tribute, and one so richly deserved that most of the heretofore unsung heroines can't understand what took so long. As one of them pointedly noted in Cooperstown: "It doesn't say 'Men's Baseball Hall of Fame,' does it?"

The Memorable Games

No, it most assuredly does not. But then, the Girls of Summer didn't always play as if they were destined to be enshrined in *any* hall of fame, men's or women's. Take, for example, the chilly night in June 1943 when the Racine, Wisconsin, Belles took the home field against the South Bend, Indiana, Blue Sox.

The setting was Horlick Field, a windy old wooden stadium near Lake Michigan with a hand-posted scoreboard and dim floodlights. At that early stage of the league's development, the girls were playing modified softball, not hardball. The distance between the bases was a little longer, there were nine players on a side (instead of the usual ten), and a runner was allowed to take a lead off base and steal. The Racine and South Bend pitchers pinned the high-hemmed skirts of their one-piece uniforms, so as to take nothing away from their speed and control, but they still had trouble getting the ball over the plate and holding runners on base. The fielders had problems, too, and when the comedy of errors was over, the Blue Sox had drawn nine walks and two wild pitches, made seven miscues, stolen 17 bases and won 12 to 6. "A crowd of 683 cash customers turned out despite the cool weather," reported the *Racine Journal Times,* "but the temperature was nothing compared to the chill they received from the two hours and 35 minutes of how *not* to play."

That, as it turned out, was the exception to the rule. The league went on to include as many as ten teams and attract more than a million enthusiastic fans a season. The pitching shifted to overhand in 1948, the ball got smaller, the base paths got longer and the caliber of play got better and better. Max Carey, a Pittsburgh Pirates Hall of Famer who managed the Milwaukee Chicks and was the league president for six years, called a 14-inning contest between the Rockford, Illinois, Peaches and the Racine Belles the "greatest" game he had ever seen, male or female.

It was the final meeting of the 1946 championship series. Pitcher Carolyn Morris of the Peaches had a no-hitter going for nine innings, but in the 12th inning Rockford manager Bill Allington took her out. Pitching for the Belles was Joanne Winter, who had survived one close call after another. "I was getting banged all over the place and watching my teammates make these tremendous plays behind me," recalls Winter, who in 1988 was teaching golf in Scottsdale, Arizona. "They got 13 hits off me but never scored." The game was decided in the bottom half of the 14th inning when the Belles' scrappy second baseman, Sophie Kurys, slid across home plate with the winning run. "I got a base hit, stole second and was on my way to steal third when Betty Trezza [the Belles' shortstop] hit it into right field and I slid into home," says Kurys, who in 1988 was a retired businesswoman also living in Scottsdale. "It was real close, but I was safe." Kurys stole 201 bases that year, a professional record no one in any league has even managed to approach.

Selling a Women's League

Ken Sells, the AAGPBL's first president, who in 1988 was a robust, 83-year-old retiree living in Paradise Valley, Arizona, not far from where several major-league baseball teams stage their spring training. He maintains that although female baseball players enjoyed themselves and made reasonably good money, they had a serious mission to accomplish. "They proved," he says, "that women didn't have to sacrifice their femininity to be standouts in what was then a man's world."

That's one of the things Philip K. Wrigley had in mind when he decided to start up a women's league in 1942. The chewing-gum magnate and owner of the Chicago Cubs baseball team was afraid the wartime draft might shut down the major leagues altogether; a number of minor-league teams had already been forced to suspend operations. If the big leagues did fold, Wrigley reasoned, it might be possible to transfer a professional women's league into those parks. But the major leagues got through the war years intact and consequently the AAGPBL remained in a number of smaller Midwestern towns and cities, where factory workers had money to spend but couldn't travel much because of gas rationing.

In the early 1940s, amateur softball leagues for women were thriving in thousands of communities all over the country. Wrigley decided to skim the best players off those teams, winnow the candidates down to a select few, and then use that reservoir of talent to set up his new play-for-pay league.

Wrigley contributed the major share of the start-up costs

and also footed half the operating expenses of each team. (Local supporters in the four charter cities—Rockford, Illinois; Racine and Kenosha, Wisconsin; and South Bend, Indiana—guaranteed the other half.) As a savvy baseball man and shrewd entrepreneur, he knew what he wanted and he understood how to go about getting it. He drew upon the Cubs organization for executive talent and scouts, and he persuaded his friend Branch Rickey, the respected general manager of the Brooklyn Dodgers (and later the Pittsburgh Pirates) to serve as an adviser and trustee.

All-American Girls

Wrigley also understood the importance of image. His league would have nothing to do with the kind of short-haired, mannishly dressed toughies then touring the country on several all-girl barnstorming teams. As one of Wrigley's associates put it, the new league's athletes would be expected to epitomize "the highest ideals of womanhood." The order went down to Ken Sells, the Cubs' assistant general manager and head of the AAGPBL: at the league tryouts in Chicago that spring, Mr. Wrigley expected to see nothing but healthy, wholesome, "all-American" girls.

In May 1943, more than a hundred of the best female softball players in North America registered at the Belmont Hotel in Chicago, and then assembled for tryouts and spring training at the Cubs' Wrigley Field. Most of them were underage, overawed, homesick and as green as the outfield grass. Jane (Jeep) Stoll, presently a resident of Phoenix, went to Chicago as a recent high school graduate from rural Pennsylvania. "I had never ridden on a train," she says. "I sat up all night in a Pullman car because I didn't understand how that seat was gonna be my bed."

Sophie Kurys was 17 when she showed up in Chicago, a taciturn Polish Ukrainian from Flint, Michigan. "It was raining when I got there. I told them I wanted to turn around and go right back home. They moved me in with some older girls, and probably told them to mother me a bit. The next day the sun was shining and I felt fine."

Girls. It was always "girls," never "women," and in their recollections it remains so today.

The players soon found that they were in for more than they had bargained for. After getting up at dawn and working out all day, they were required to attend charm school in the evening. The classes were conducted by representatives of the Helena Rubinstein cosmetics company, who taught the athletes how to put on makeup, get in and out of a car, and put on a coat with seemly grace. The girls also learned how to enunciate correctly and how to charm a date (look right at him and say: "Oh my, what nice eyes you have"). To avoid getting dirt under their fingernails when sliding on the base paths, they were told to scratch a bar of soap before the game.

Charm school fit right in with the league's so-called femininity concept. It produced a lot of good publicity but it was also a big pain in the neck—or knee, or calf. "It wasn't easy to walk around in high heels with a book on your head when you had a charley horse," remembers Lavone (Pepper) Paire Davis, who played shortstop and catcher for three teams and is now enjoying retirement in Van Nuys, California.

At the end of that first training camp, Wrigley's four managers selected the 60 best players and divided them up, as equally as possible, into four teams. Then it was time to "play ball." The players were paid between $65 and $125 a week. The 108-game "split" season lasted for three months, with the winner of the first half playing the winner of the second half in a championship series at the end.

A New Generation

That premiere season had barely gotten under way before a new generation and gender of baseball personalities began to shine. One of them was a statuesque redhead named Ann Harnett. She hit the ball well enough to finish as one of the league's best batters in 1943. Eventually the charismatic slugger became a nun and coached a boys' team at a Catholic school. One day, a former AAGPBL executive recalls, a nun dropped by and asked, "How're the boys upstairs?" She was referring, of course, to Wrigley and his associates.

For a decade, the AAGPBL teams—each consisting of 15 players, a manager, a chaperone and a driver—rattled around the heartland, trailblazing a path of equal opportunity where no women's professional sport had ever gone before. Everywhere they went, they won new fans—and kept them. "Maybe at first the men came out to see the legs," says Pepper Paire Davis. "But they stuck around when they realized they were seeing a darn good brand of baseball."

For managers, the league reached into the ranks of old-time ballplayers, many of whom came and went trailing faded dreams of glory. Bill Wambsganss of the Cleveland Indians, the only man ever to pull off an unassisted triple play in the World Series, always carried a yellowed press clipping to prove it. Others, the famous Red Sox slugger Jimmie Foxx, preserved their cherished memories in a bottle.

Chaperoning the Players

Chaperones protected the morals of the players at home as well as on the road. The girls were officially forbidden to drink, gamble, violate curfew, wear shorts or slacks in public, or go out on dates alone without permission and an interview of the prospective swain. A good thing, too. "My mother wouldn't let me play until I convinced her we'd be chaperoned," remembers Betty (Moe) Trezza of Brooklyn.

Quite a few of the girls were underage and the league kept a particularly close eye on them. Thelma (Tiby) Eisen, who was an outfielder with three different teams between 1944 and 1952, had an admirer when she was a rookie who followed her on a road trip. He checked into the same hotel one night and invited her up to his room before they went out to dinner. "I wasn't there three minutes before there was a knock at the door," Eisen says. "It was the house detective wanting to know what was going on."

Some chaperones knew their baseball; others did not. "We had one who was famous for yelling things like, 'Hit a home run, honey, and we win!'" Sophie Kurys recalls.

"The only trouble was, we would be four runs behind in the bottom of the ninth with two out and the bases empty." Some chaperones had other priorities. Shirley Jameson of Albuquerque remembers going to bat in a tense situation only to be restrained by her chaperone. "Oh, my dear," the woman exclaimed. "You don't have your *lipstick* on!"

Off the field, chaperones sometimes had their work cut

Jackie Robinson—Rookie of the Year

The following excerpt is taken from an article in the September 17, 1947, issue of the Sporting News *written by the legendary sportswriter J.G. Taylor Spink, who died in 1962, and reveals that Jackie Robinson did more than just break racial barriers in baseball, he was one of the game's greatest stars.*

In selecting the outstanding rookie of 1947, *The Sporting News* sifted and weighed only stark baseball values.

That Jack Roosevelt Robinson might have had more obstacles than his first-year competitors and that he perhaps had a harder right to gain even major-league recognition, was no concern of this publication. The sociological experiment that Robinson represented, the trail-blazing that he did, the barriers he broke down, did not enter into the decision. He was rated and examined solely as a freshman player in the big leagues—on the basis of his hitting, his running, his defensive play, his team value.

Robinson had it all and compared to the many other fine first-year men that 1947 produced, he was spectacularly outstanding.

Dixie Walker summed it up in a few words the other day when he said: "No other ballplayer on this club, with the possible exception of Bruce Edwards, has done more to put the Dodgers up in the race than Robinson has. He is everything that Branch Rickey said he was when he came up from Montreal."

J.G. Taylor Spink, "Rookie of the Year . . . Jackie Robinson," *Sporting News*, September 17, 1947.

out for them. Maddy English, a third baseman for the Racine Belles who now lives in Everett, Massachusetts, once told a sportswriter who wouldn't stop pestering her: "If you don't leave me alone, I'm going to jump in Lake Michigan." He didn't. She did, and had to be fished out. Other infatuations were less threatening. Sophie Kurys had a fan club of 11- and 12-year-old boys in Racine, one of whom invited her home for a porkchop dinner one afternoon before a game. Faye Dancer, an exuberant center fielder for the Fort Wayne Daisies who now resides in Santa Monica, California, got a letter from a G.I. in France after her picture appeared in *Life* magazine. "I am not proposing," he wrote, "but I have about $1,000 and an old jalopy in New Jersey, I am footloose and fancy free, and I can settle anyplace."

The Risks of Daring Plays

On the field, there were times when the Girls of Summer could have used some protection from one another. Action was replete with daring plays along the base paths, brushbacks at the plate and painful "strawberries" from sliding hard in short skirts. One day Dolly Pearson Tesseine was playing shortstop for the Daisies when the opposing pitcher came barreling into second base and spiked her. "Next time you do that, I'm gonna jam the ball down your throat," Dolly said. When Dolly came up to bat, the pitcher knocked her down instead. Nobody got hurt that time, but when Dolly was batting in an exhibition game one day, she was hit right behind the ear by a pitch.

The players acted like women on and off the field. Pretty June Peppas of the Kalamazoo (formerly Muskegon) Lassies performed a little shimmy when batting that her fans called the "Peppas wiggle." But sometimes in the heat of a game the girls played just as recklessly as men. Once Alma (Ziggy) Ziegler of the Grand Rapids Chicks was playing second base when the batter hit a ground ball to the shortstop with a runner on first. The shortstop tossed the ball to Ziggy for a force-out at second and Ziggy threw to first for the double play. The runner, however, came into second base standing instead of sliding; the ball smacked into her and she was called out for interference. "I didn't throw at her," Ziggy recalls innocently. "She ran into the ball."

So intense was the play, sometimes even the umpires weren't safe out there. Pepper Paire Davis will never forget the time she knocked down Lou Rymkus, a hulking future all-pro football player who was moonlighting as an umpire. After sliding in at second, she whirled around to protest Rymkus' call and her fist inadvertently caught him square on the chin. The big guy ended up flat on his back. "I guess you know, Pepper," Rymkus murmured apologetically as he looked up at her, "that I gotta throw you out." Pepper knew.

In the scant free time they had to themselves, the players managed to raise a little hell every now and then. Joanne Winter got together with a teammate one night and tried to pass off two ladies of the evening on their manager as the new rookies he was expecting. Pepper Paire Davis and Faye Dancer occasionally hoisted a few beers together in a local cemetery to escape the prying eyes of townspeople, who tended to regard the players as kid sisters. "We *were* just kids having fun," recalls Dottie Collins of Fort Wayne, Indiana. "Not until it was all over did we look back and realize we had been pioneers."

Skill and Polish

It is clear, too, that ultimately they played with great skill and polish. After watching shortstop Dorothy Schroeder of Sadorus, Illinois, work out one day, Cubs manager Charlie Grimm said, "If she was a boy, I'd give $50,000 for her." Wally Pipp, one of the best glovemen in the business when he played first base for the New York Yankees in the early 1920s, called Dorothy Kamenshek of Anaheim, California, "the fanciest fielding first baseman I've ever seen—man or woman." Fort Lauderdale of the Florida International Baseball League once tried to buy her contract from the AAGPBL. Not long ago, after watching rare film footage of the league at its peak, a member of the Society for American Baseball Research enthused, "The way they were throwing the ball was unbelievable. It looked as though they were as good as men."

They weren't quite. They lacked the requisite power. No one in the league ever hit more than 16 home runs (though, granted, the fences in most ballparks were never moved in). But some old-timers remember seeing Triple-A players take practice cuts at the plate against the likes of Jean Faut Eastman (who posted 140 wins in eight years with the South Bend Blue Sox and had a combined earned run average of 1.23) and come up empty.

The league's second year, 1944, was the last for Wrigley and Sells, since it became obvious the war wasn't going to close down the majors after all. Wrigley sold his interest to Art Meyerhoff, his Chicago advertising man, and gradually ownership passed on to local boards in each town. Franchises at first flourished but then attendance sputtered fitfully until after the Korean War, when televised big-league baseball finally killed the AAGPBL forever. Whereupon the players, most still in their athletic prime, put down their bats and balls and gloves, and went on to raise families and often to coach their children. (It has been said of Helen Callaghan St. Aubin's son, Casey Candaele of the Houston Astros, that he "runs just like his mother." That's a compliment. His mother played center field for the Daisies.) They also started energetic careers in everything from pro golf, pro bowling and school-teaching, to anesthesiology and statistical analysis.

The Politics of Popular Music

Lewis A. Erenberg

Before and during World War II, swing music represented ideals of tolerance and individualism, but internal fragmentation, drug use, and pressure from the conservative anti-Communist movement created public concern that popular music was a subversive influence on society, writes historian Lewis A. Erenberg in an excerpt from his book *Swingin' the Dream: Big Band Jazz and the Rebirth of American Culture.* Erenberg explains that because many musicians supported liberal New Deal ideals, they were often suspected of Communist association and were either blacklisted or forced to pledge their loyalty, naming their friends as Communists. Others believed that a war on drugs would restore order and security, Erenberg reveals, and many popular jazz musicians who used drugs were singled out as symptoms of society's decline. Furthermore, because popular music often promoted a message of personal freedom that appealed to America's youth, many believed that the music itself was a threat to the American way of life. Although big band jazz did not recover from this assault, bebop and small combos continued to appeal to alienated American youth, forever changing the face of popular music. Erenberg is a professor of history at Loyola University in Chicago, Illinois.

O ver and over during the late 1940s and early 1950s, jazz musicians found their names splayed across the headlines of the daily newspaper, the gossip column, the jazz press: Cops bust Billie Holiday . . . Goes to jail . . . Artie Shaw called before HUAC . . . Frank Sinatra a Red? . . . Aaron Copland a Red? . . . George Gershwin a Red? . . . Charlie Parker committed to Camarillo . . . Thelonious Monk arrested on drug charge . . . Anita O'Day and husband arrested . . . Gene Krupa arrested . . . Stan Getz arrested for narcotics . . . Barney Josephson a Red? . . . Lena Horne a Red? . . . Dope—the shameful U.S. jazz record . . . Who will escape this stigma? . . . The dope leeches . . . Weed out the weeders. If swing represented the rebirth of dreams, the postwar jazz world seemed stuck in a never-ending public nightmare.

A Divided and Vulnerable Industry

In order to understand the public concern with the subversive impact of modern jazz, we need to examine the unraveling of the swing synthesis in bitterness and recrimination during the tension-filled post-war years. By 1947, as swing fragmented into competing factions amid the band industry's decline, all forms of jazz had difficulty attracting a mass audience. The unprecedented internecine warfare in the jazz world led to the decline of common allegiances. Each faction blamed the others for the public's lack of interest, and intense self-doubt and introspection among musicians, critics, and fans replaced the former confidence in swing's ability to achieve wide popularity. Big band modern jazz (bebop) faced the longest odds of reviving the dance band industry, but all forms of jazz were thrown on the defensive, trapped between past and future. Indicative of this loss of momentum is that *Down Beat* mounted a contest in 1949 to find a replacement for the terms "Ragtime, Jazz, Boogie-Woogie, Dixieland, Swing, BeBop," which had "lost much of their original significance. . . . We need a new term to describe our music—ALL of our music, regardless of the school to which it belongs."

Lacking even a common terminology, the jazz world

proved vulnerable to outside enemies. Criticism of jazz as a racially alien and immoral influence on young men and women had waxed and waned in the music world since World War I. However, the economic and cultural weaknesses of the dance band industry and the splintering of a united front allowed critics to attack on moral and political grounds with a virulence and effectiveness hitherto impossible. Throughout the war, jazz musicians and critics had put aside stylistic and racial differences to make common cause against "Mickey Mouse" bands and attacks by moralists and reactionary politicians determined to paint jazz in the most lurid un-American colors. When Congress had attempted to denigrate boogie-woogie and swing during the war, for instance, black and white musicians and singers had stood together with a concerted argument that every facet of swing represented American culture. After the war, however, that common defense proved impossible against a rising fear that American institutions and values were being weakened from within by subversion at the very moment that the Cold War posed a threat from without.

Targeting New Deal Supporters

Like the other arts, the music industry found itself caught up in the anti-Communist attacks on subversive New Deal radicalism in American entertainment. The first inkling of trouble came in 1947 when *Down Beat* announced that a congressional subcommittee planned to subpoena "certain well known musicians and singers" for "being Communists." No evidence of specific hearings on the music business exists, but conservatives turned up many individuals associated with the "swing left" as part of their probe into the arts and entertainment in Hollywood and New York. The FBI, for example, probed pianist and revivalist critic Art Hodes's politics and tapped his phone because, he believed, "the wrong people were coming in to see *Jazz Record.*"

Conservative groups also targeted Frank Sinatra. Having experienced ethnic prejudice as a boy, he strongly supported FDR and the New Deal ethic of ethnic and racial pluralism. In January 1946, however, America Firster Gerald L.K. Smith told the House Un-American Activities Committee (HUAC) that Sinatra was "a Mrs. Roosevelt in pants" who "acts as a front" for Communist organizations. "The minute anyone tries to help the little guy," Sinatra noted, "he's called a Communist." In 1949 the California State Senate Committee on Un-American Activities labeled Sinatra a Fellow Traveler. When Robert Ruark linked this "savior of the country's small fry, by virtue of his lectures on clean living and love-thy-neighbor," to the mob in 1947, the twin sins of crime and Communism badly weakened his audience appeal. In a pattern common during the late 1940s, Artie Shaw was pressured to declare his loyalty to free enterprise and American compromises with equality. In 1948 he was attacked for supporting various Popular Front groups, and, living under "a haze of rumor," he agreed in 1953 to testify before HUAC. He told the committee that when he returned from the navy in 1945 he was angry at domestic reactionaries and black marketeers and set out to fight for the Fair Employment Practices Commission and other leftist causes as part of his conception of American war ideals. He confessed to being "duped" and pledged to "defend American institutions and American folkways" and never to sign any petitions or protest letters ever again. He also swallowed his anger at the anti-Semitism that had scarred his personality and the racism that had marred his attempts to integrate bands. Instead he expressed his gratitude for what the nation had done for him, "a member of a minority." Humiliated by having to repudiate his former beliefs, Shaw exiled himself to Spain.

The Dangers of Promoting Tolerance

While a number of musicians got caught up in congressional investigations aimed at Hollywood and New York, Barney Josephson and Cafe Society found themselves under attack as emblems of New Deal radicalism. Home to integrated jazz and humorous attacks on segregation and the upper classes, Cafe Society's uptown and downtown branches were pilloried by the entertainment columns. In his appearance before HUAC in 1948, Josephson's brother Leon, who had been involved in an attempt to kill Hitler in 1935, told the public—but not the committee—that he was a Communist and proud of his anti-Fascism; he was jailed for contempt. When Barney refused to condemn him, tabloid gossip columnists began a smear campaign. Westbrook Pegler, for example, implied that Leon was also a drug addict—"and there is much to be said about his brother Barney." He had welcomed black members of the audience and introduced inflammatory songs such as "Strange Fruit" and "The House I Live In." As a result of the campaign, business declined, Josephson was forced to sell both of his clubs, and by 1950 he was broke. The FBI and Congress also pressured those associated with Cafe Society: John Hammond, Ivan Black (the press agent), Hazel Scott, Teddy Wilson, Zero Mostel, Lena Horne, Jack Gilford, and Josh White. Black, Mostel, and Gilford were blacklisted in movies, radio, and television. In 1951, the Hearst press tried to bar Lena Horne from television too. Along with Josh White and Hazel Scott, she saved herself by pledging her loyalty to the United States and branding friend and former Cafe Society regular Paul Robeson, as well as Henry Wallace, as Communists. In this "hysterical political climate," *Down Beat* advised musicians, "if you're anywhere to the left of Rep. Rankin . . . just keep your views to yourself."

Yet the jazz community already was cutting its ties to the Popular Front. In 1946, when Soviet authorities censored and then jailed Eddie Rozner, their best-known swing bandleader, for playing decadent bourgeois music, Barry Ulanov editorialized in *Metronome* that "dictatorships inevitably get around to censuring, censoring or altogether forbidding jazz," just as Hitler and Japan had done. "Now Russia, logically suspicious of a musical form which is based upon spontaneity of expression, finds jazz offensive." Defending swing as the "peculiarly American" embodiment of freedom, he argued that jazz fans and musicians "should be proud of its low mark in totalitarian countries" and urged that "the large number of Communists and Fellow-travelers in American jazz should do some serious thinking about this latest cultural development in their shabby Utopia-by-the-Volga." Soon after, the swing ideology of jazz as freedom and tolerance was turned outward against the Communist world. In 1947, the State Department and the Voice of America chose Benny Goodman to broadcast America's best dance music to the USSR. After *Metronome*'s editors publicly quarreled with his selections, the State Department invited Ulanov, along with George Simon and the editors of *Down Beat,* to add modern jazz to these broadcasts. Sensitive to orthodox Communist attacks on modern jazz as formalistic, modernists were consistent in their criticism of the USSR's lack of creative freedom. Outside and inside the music world, the Cold War placed pressure on jazz to sever its ties to the Left.

Nevertheless, swing musicians continued to promote pluralism and tolerance at home during the late 1940s. Immediately after the war, black and white musicians performed interracial concerts and benefits to honor the memory of President Roosevelt. During this period Duke Ellington produced "Deep South Suite," his musical criticism of segregation and injustice, followed in 1947 by "Beggar's Holiday," a show of social protest that featured interracial casting. In early 1947, Goodman supported the United Nations because it fulfilled swing's dream of greater freedom for all. "Freedom gets around in this country, and it better," he urged. "It has to start on our own street—in our willingness to give the right guy a job—or let him into our free schools—no matter what his race, creed or nationality. It's either freedom for all of us or freedom for none of us—anywhere in the world." Meanwhile, *Down Beat* and *Metronome* challenged baseball to follow swing's example and integrate the major leagues. Lionel Hampton, moreover, linked swing to a growing national commitment to desegregation. A replacement for an ailing Goodman, Hampton happily joined Lena Horne and a host of white stars in January 1949 to play for the inauguration of Harry S. Truman, the first president to make civil rights a plank in his campaign platform and the president who ordered the desegregation of the armed forces. In the meantime, Shaw and Goodman publicly defied HUAC in 1947 to support the Committee for the First Amendment. After 1948, however, the red scare would make it difficult to move so boldly again on civil rights or to oppose the growing power of the right.

A War on Drugs

The red scare took its toll, but as *Down Beat* put it, "the real threat, to music today is not a red scare . . . it's a head scare." Although all players were affected, the boppers were the primary target of a growing antidrug crusade because their racial, generational, and personal rebellion symbolized the disturbing disruptions that the war had left in its wake. Many who had dreamed of an ordered world of security and domesticity during the war now found that ideal difficult to achieve amid strikes, inflation, and sexual and familial disjunctures. The result was a war on drugs from 1947 to 1954, the cultural equivalent of the red scare in the defense of middle-class values. Fear about the changes brought by war came to a head in the anxiety about juvenile delinquency: absent fathers and working mothers had created independence for teenagers, and they elaborated a youth culture filled with angst and alienation. Bop music, black and white zoot-suited hipsters, and promiscuous "victory girls" hanging out in jazz clubs reinforced unresolved wartime fears about the sexual activity of young women. The concern with social deviance was a way to police the boundaries of convention and squeeze recalcitrant men and women back into the mold of a secure and ordered family life. Moral and political authorities focused on the dangerous "hopped up" bopper in order to contain the spread of decay. Jazz and drugs were the means by which the American character was being weakened. At a time when the nation needed to be united and morally strong to fight the cold war, boppers and the ills they spread signified a threat that the war had unleashed.

Starting in 1943, federal and local authorities attempted to keep drugs and other forms of vice from weakening the war effort by demoralizing soldiers and civilians. In a sensational case that year, the crackdown nabbed Gene Krupa for possession of marijuana and for contributing to the delinquency of a minor—the band boy who supplied him with the pot—which was a felony. He served ninety days and lost his band, his livelihood, and his reputation. Shocked by the government's action against a common musician's habit—smoking marijuana—the swing world rallied to his defense. As George Simon charged, "One of the quickest ways to stamp out an evil is to make an example of somebody everybody knows. Everybody knows Gene Krupa and so he was picked on." Soon, federal and local agents clamped down on all prominent jazz venues, especially 52nd Street, Hollywood, Los Angeles's Central Avenue, and Chicago's Loop and South Side.

The concern with drugs and jazz musicians as causes and symptoms of individual and national demoralization rose dramatically as heroin surfaced and as fears about external and internal threats to the nation intensified. Arrests increased and national attention grew after 1947. Billie Holiday, for example, was arrested for heroin possession in 1949 and tried in U.S. District Court in Philadelphia. "It was called 'The United States of America versus Billie Holiday.' And that's just the way it felt," she wrote in her autobiography. She pleaded guilty and asked to be sent to a hospital to take "the cure," but the judge noted that she was a well-to-do entertainer and sentenced her to a year in jail. As she put it, "People on drugs are sick people. So now we end up with the government chasing sick people like they were criminals, telling doctors they can't help them, prosecuting them because they had some stuff without paying the tax, and sending them to jail." Arrests of musicians for marijuana also rose. In Hollywood, singer Anita O'Day and her husband Carl Hoff were arrested in 1947 by undercover police for possession of "tea," but this was only part of a larger crackdown. According to Assistant Chief of Police Joseph Reed, officers in Los Angeles set up roadblocks downtown to stop a "crime wave" and raided after-hours jazz clubs "in a new attempt to break up the breeding places of crime." In 1948, Akron police picked up several of Alvino Rey's musicians. Across the nation, George Simon noted, police were anxious to break up " tea parties," especially among prominent entertainers who acted as well-publicized examples of the wages of sin. All the while, the same tabloids and gossip columnists who spread the dirt on the political sins of celebrities fueled the drug furor with tales of secret moral decay in the popular arts. According to Simon, "sensation-mongering columnists" convinced the public "to look down upon musicians.". . .

A Musical Message of Personal Freedom

It had not been very long since optimistic visions of jazz's role in American culture still reigned. What is notable about the swing era is how its creators, promoters, and fans saw it as part of a cultural rebirth. Benny Goodman, for example, saw swing in the 1930s as part of a revival of larger American cultural traditions in the Great Depression. The innovations he helped promote were a vital dance music and a contribution to jazz, but they were much more. The improvisation that lay at the heart of the music, he said, was "the expression of an individual kind of free speech in music." Our "music ha[d] grown out of our brand of government," and if swing died, "it [would] die over the body of American freedom." It is not that musicians were politicians or that they had political platforms. But, as this language suggests, their music carried a message of hope for personal freedom as well as cultural regeneration. Certainly, as they entered the concert hall on a regular basis, swing bands and the dance band industry could hope that a true American music rooted in democratic culture had triumphed over European and hierarchical cultural forms.

Swing brought jazz to the center of American music and culture. As Paul Whiteman's mission of refinement gave way to the limpid Guy Lombardo style in the early 1930s, space opened for white and black musicians to accelerate the pace of exchange and appropriation on a regular basis. The depression wounded young men and women, weakened conceptions of individual potency and power, and dethroned the remaining hierarchical conceptions of American culture. Under these pressures, the modern swing band, rooted in the achievements of black jazz bandleaders and arrangers, became the dominant paradigm in popular music during the 1930s and 1940s. Part of the populist thrust of the era, this musical culture was less firmly rooted in the past than in new pluralist visions of American life. Swing was more racially and ethnically mixed than any other arena of American life. With New York once more music's vital cultural and business capital, swing held out a more utopian and cosmopolitan vision of swinging the American Dream. Although black bands continued to operate at a disadvantage, they also had the opportunity to aspire to national acclaim for the first time. They kept alive the Harlem Renaissance dreams of urban freedom during the dark days of the depression and added to this ferment a populist music from Kansas City that expressed the aspirations of ordinary black youth. This cultural pride interacted with the rebirth of leftist political forces in music and in American society to promote the advancement of African Americans as full-fledged Americans.

A Vision for America's Youth

Swing's appeal to a nation of youth turned it into a mass culture. Most accounts have missed how powerful young people became in the music market of the 1930s and why such "commercial forms" appealed to them. Looking back from the vantage of the postwar decline, Mike Levin noted that the "unified taste of the kids and the musicians was enough to swing large groups of the general public which normally wouldn't be interested in these bands." Because of mass interest in bands, black and white jazz musicians could dream of national acceptance and stable careers as popular idols, surpassing movie stars in the eyes of youth. As pianist-arranger Ralph Burns put it, "It was a fantasy world for us, because people thought differently about bands then, probably the way they think about rock groups now. . . . If you were a jazz musician playing with Woody Herman, you were almost like a movie star."

Swing bands offered young people powerful visions of personal freedom and generational solidarity, defined a mass youth style around music, dance, and fashion, and conveyed hopeful visions of the future. By combining and undergirding wounded male individualism with the encompassing support and security of the large group, these bands also created powerful models for young people eager to keep alive the personal and moral experimentations of the previous decade. While bands served as all-male families, the ritualized relationship of male band and female singer emphasized that women would help support male creativity. Playing a subordinate public role, the singers also offered young women models for how to adjust as romantic objects and working women in a man's world. In personal terms, swing dancing promoted the committed couple who improvised in a much more egalitarian way in the private realm. Swing was a public, democratic art that helped ease the gender and social tensions of the era.

As swing went to war, it did so with a divided legacy. As a relatively pluralist mode of expression, swing became a symbol of American culture in a war against Fascism and racial supremacy. For many black musicians and racial liberals, Hitler's defeat would also challenge segregation and second-class citizenship at home. While the war enabled black bands—and the African American population—to make substantial strides, it also increased racial and cultural tensions that undermined those advances. The war heightened and then exhausted swing as it brought the central tensions of the 1930s to a head. As swing became enmeshed in national purpose, it became more bureaucratic and sentimental. Although Glenn Miller supported pluralism, his orchestra was a whitened and corporate vision. In this, swing was part of a public culture that lionized the crowd and the group—on the stage and in the audience. During the war the popularity of sentimental ballads and singers expressed powerful individual demands for personal fulfillment and the security of ordered domesticity removed from the public sphere. This vision ultimately clashed with the demand by younger black—and some white—musicians that public life reflect the national ideal of a pluralistic and equalitarian society.

A Musical Critique of American Life

Young black jazz musicians nurtured on the tension between the utopian hopes of swing and the racial and commercial realities for black bands created a powerful critique of American life and music in the 1940s. Many of the most fervent swing fans followed the musicians into bop. They were drawn by the new style's intense musical vision and alienated from "whitened" big bands. Even more, however, it was a younger generation of black and white fans who supported bebop. This generation was born in the depression and came of age during the war, and as a result of the drop in marriage and fertility rates in the early 1930s formed the smallest generation cohort of the twentieth century. This generation was also one of the most alienated. The depression and the war had shown them that the world was not ordered; it was out of joint. Bebop expressed their reality: chance and spontaneity ruled a universe devoid of fixed guideposts. They would have to search for identity in an overly organized and bureaucratized world. Holding to an older racial and musical vision, traditional jazz musicians and leftist music supporters revolted against the homogenization of swing and of the music business. But they turned to an older form of collective improvisation and a paternalistic conception of the African American performer. At the same time, much of the older swing audience turned to fulfilling wartime swing dreams; they still loved swing, but they had neither the time nor the money to go dancing or even buy records. Washing machines, not record players, were first on their agendas. Swing bands and the dance band industry collapsed, and jazz bands split off from dance orchestras. Listeners and dancers also split, cults developed, and the jazz world broke down into musical, generational, and racial factions.

Returning to Outsider Status

Working in a declining band industry, promoting modern sounds and bohemian values, the boppers met with a storm of protest. Music expressed the fierce divisions in American culture as those who sought to re-create an ordered home front clashed with modern jazz musicians over the nature of music, new forms of personal freedom, racial assertiveness, and generational alienation. Given that modern jazz seemed to symbolize the disturbances unleashed by the war, it is no surprise that the mass audience was content to keep retreating toward private domestic fulfillment. The Cold War put the final nail in the coffin. At the same time that anti-Communists railed against subversive threats to the American "home front," police and civic authorities cracked down on drug use among jazz musicians as a way to contain the cancer of personal decay and alienation. Between 1947 and 1954, jazz returned to its culturally subversive outsider status; the big band industry never recovered. The hope of swinging the dream that coincided with the New Deal's attempts to create a more democratic society and culture came crashing down in bitterness and recrimination as entertainment institutions, the public, and the musicians went their separate ways.

Although the great public moment of the big bands faded, jazz remained very much alive. Bebop had established itself as the fountain of all modern jazz and as a key part of a new, more assertive African American identity. Despite tremendous obstacles, the new music continued to exert enormous influence throughout the early 1950s. When ballrooms no longer proved inviting to modern big bands, jazz clubs and lounges modeled on the listening rooms along Fifty-second Street and in the Royal Roost and Birdland spread across the country. In most jazz clubs outside the South, noted Leonard Feather, black patrons made up anywhere from 25 to 50 percent of the customers, and combos were made up of musicians of any race who chose to play together. On a smaller scale, jazz as the democratic art form continued, aided still by swing-era promoters such as Norman Granz, whose Jazz at the Philharmonic programs transported large numbers of musicians from city to city and demanded that auditoriums and halls be integrated wherever they played. Although audiences were smaller, they followed the music passionately and saw their interest in modern jazz as a declaration of personal independence from the tyranny of middle-class values that were now buttoning down America. As the hipster visual artists, poets, and novelists who came of age with modern jazz matured and took on the Beat mantle, they created works of art that drew on the spontaneity, movement, and experimentation of bop. The Beats also adopted the bop search for new identities removed from fixed social institutions and defined roles. For blacks and whites, jazz still carried powerful impulses and attractions as well as a critique of American life as uptight and racially rigid. Having lost their mass audience, jazzmen were freer to develop some of their best music in the mid- to late 1950s, once the cold war—cultural as well as political—abated. By this time, however, mass popularity had fallen to rock and roll, another mixture of black and white music blasting across the crazy landscape of American culture.

CHAPTER 6

The Cold War

AMERICA'S DECADES

The Soviet-American Rift: An Overview

Armin Rappaport

Although the United States and the Soviet Union had been allies during World War II, a rift began to develop between these nations during postwar negotiations, writes Armin Rappaport in the following excerpt from his book *A History of American Diplomacy.* The author explains that the ill will created by the disagreements between these two powers created a Cold War. When President Harry S. Truman suggested to Congress that the United States provide aid to European countries to avoid the spread of communism, a philosophy of Communist "containment" had begun that British Prime Minister Winston Churchill said created an iron curtain across Europe. The Soviets tested the resolve of the democratic western powers with their blockade of Berlin, which resulted in a massive air lift of food, clothing, and other supplies to the Berliners. Rappaport points out that the democratic powers recognized a need for a western military alliance, which culminated in the creation of the North Atlantic Treaty Organization (NATO). The late Armin Rappaport was a distinguished professor of history at the University of California at San Diego.

A t Potsdam, Germany, in July 1945, in full view of the ruins of Berlin, the leaders of the Big Three [British Prime Minister Winston Churchill, Soviet Premier Joseph

Excerpted from *A History of American Diplomacy,* by Armin Rappaport (New York: Macmillan, 1975). Copyright ©1975 by Armin Rappaport.

Stalin, and U.S. President Harry S. Truman], met for the last time. The war in Europe had ended nine weeks earlier and much had to be done to effect the transformation of the continent from war to peace. The atmosphere was friendly. Stalin invited Truman to preside and Truman played the piano for Stalin. That Soviet troops were in occupation of eastern Germany, Austria, Czechoslovakia, Hungary, Bulgaria, Rumania, Poland, Yugoslavia, and Albania did not seem to mar the benign climate. Nor did the successful testing on July 16, one day before the conference opened, of the first American atomic bomb in the New Mexican desert have an effect on the meeting. Some historians have claimed that Truman's spine was measurably stiffened by the news and that he was made bolder by it as he faced Stalin but there is no hard evidence to support the thesis. That the president was less amiable and more brusque than his predecessor in the White House was true but it was a reflection of personality differences, not the bomb.

Setting the Boundaries

The fixing of the details for the occupation of Germany constituted the central task of the conference. The European Advisory Commission had, in 1944, fixed the boundaries of the four zones. Now it was agreed that each power would administer its own zone with supreme authority to be placed in the hands of the military commander. An Allied Control Council to sit in Berlin was charged with coordinating matters affecting the whole of Germany; this coordination was chiefly economic for the decision was taken to treat the divided country as a single economic unit. Also, steps were taken to demilitarize, denazify, and democratize the nation as well as to bring its leaders to trial and punish those convicted of being war criminals, As for reparations, each power was to remove the necessary goods and property from its own zone.

Drawing up peace treaties for Hitler's allies—Italy, Rumania, Bulgaria, Austria, Hungary, and Finland—was referred to a newly created Council of Foreign Ministers representing the Big Four, [France, Great Britain, the Soviet Union, and the United States]. Finally, the western boundary of Poland was set temporarily at the Oder-Neisse line on the west pending the negotiation of a German peace treaty that would settle that country's borders permanently.

To President Truman, the conference gave indication that cooperation among the Allies was proceeding splendidly. He reported to Congress that the Big Three were more closely bound than ever in their desire for peace. To Secretary of State James Byrnes, however, Potsdam was a "success that failed." He saw too much evidence of an absence of cooperation and of seeds of discord. Too many issues had not been tackled; too many problems bad been left unresolved; too many Soviet demands had been made that augured badly for the future. Stalin's wish to control the Dardanelles, [a strait connecting the Black Sea and the Mediterranean], and to have a trusteeship over Italian colonies in north Africa revealed an ambition too great for comfort. His insistence that the United States and Great Britain extend recognition to the one-party governments in eastern and southeastern Europe gave little hope for the future of democracy there and his refusal to internationalize all European waterways raised the prospect of a closing of Soviet-held rivers and canals to western commerce.

The Soviet-American Rift

The events of the months following Potsdam reinforced Byrnes' dark forebodings and those of the year 1946 gave them credibility. During that time, Soviet-American relations worsened and disagreements were more frequent than agreements. Each of the two powers became more hostile and more suspicious where the other was concerned until between them there was so much enmity and ill-feeling that a "Cold War" was said to exist. By the spring of 1946, Churchill could say in a speech at Fulton, Missouri, rightfully and ruefully, "That from Stettin in the Baltic to Trieste in the Adriatic, an iron curtain has descended across the continent" separating the democratic part from the communist part controlled by Moscow.

The several meetings of the Council of Foreign Ministers between 1945 and 1947 reflected the growing Soviet-American rift. The first, at London, in September and October of 1945, was an exercise in futility. There was disagreement over Chinese and French participation in the making of the satellite peace treaties and over the terms of the treaties. There was a wrangle, too, over the Soviet demand for a voice in the peace treaty with Japan. At the second at Moscow in December of 1945 and the third at Paris, which met on two occasions between April and July of 1946, the differences were exacerbated and Soviet conduct was such as to elicit from President Truman after Moscow the exasperated comment, "I am tired of babying the Soviets" and to provoke Byrnes at Paris into telling Soviet Foreign Minister V.M. Molotov there would be no more unilateral concessions by the United States. At the second Paris session some progress was made on the satellite peace treaties; the ministers actually agreed upon terms on July 1. Those terms were quickly submitted to a conference of 21 nations, which Molotov, at Moscow, had consented to convening, to debate the drafts. The delegates—representing the Big Four and 16 other countries from both sides of the Iron Curtain that had contributed to the war effort—gathered in Paris on July 29, 1946. For eleven weeks they debated the terms and differed on many matters, chiefly along east-west lines, but finally drew up five treaties—with Finland, Bulgaria, Italy, Romania, and Hungary. They, in turn, were reviewed by the Council of Foreign Ministers meeting in New York in November and December of 1946 and approved but not without more Soviet-American disagreements. Byrnes considered Soviet demands and maneuvers so excessive and obstructionist that he told Molotov that "The United States government was not so interested in making the treaties that it would accept endless delays and new compromises suggested by the Soviet Union." Senator Arthur H. Vandenberg, who was on the American delegation, was pleased that "our 'surrender days' are over." The treaties were finally signed by Byrnes for the United States in Washington on January 20, 1947 and by the other nations in Paris on February 10.

Disagreement Within the United Nations

In the United Nations, too, from the very first session in London in January of 1946, the Soviet-American rift was apparent. The two powers differed on the composition of the military forces to be made available to the international organization for enforcement. The United States (and Great Britain) supported the idea of specialized force—Russia, ground troops; America and England, air power and navy—while the Soviet Union insisted on equal and similar forces from both sides. In the absence of agreement, no forces were established. Then there was the question of atomic control. On January 24, 1946, a United Nations Atomic Energy Commission was created to control atomic weapons. To it, on June 14, Bernard Baruch, the American member, presented a plan. It provided for the licensing and inspection of non-dangerous atomic energy and the ownership of "all atomic energy activities potentially dangerous to world security" by an International Atomic Development Authority. Inspection rights were to be unrestricted and no power would be able to veto punishment of any nation breaking the rules. Baruch promised that, once the authority were set up and operating, the United States would destroy its stockpile and cease further manufacture of atomic weapons.

Nothing came of the suggestion because of Russia's rejection of it. The Soviets would not accede to unrestricted inspection nor surrender the veto, yet they insisted that the United States, nonetheless, destroy its pile and manufacture no more. On September 23, 1949, President Truman announced the news of the detonation of an atomic bomb by the Soviet Union.

Disarmament, also, proved to be a source of conflict between the two great powers. In February of 1947, there was formed a United Nations Commission for Conventional Armaments to draft measures for reducing the forces of the victorious nations but 18 months of discussion resulted in failure only. So great was the mutual feeling of mistrust that neither power would accept a cut in their armies, navies, or air forces. There were other differences between the two nations—the admission of new members to the UN, choosing a neutral government for Trieste, and the evacuation of Soviet troops from Iran. At the Teheran Conference, the Big Three had promised to evacuate Iran six months after the end of the war, but when that time came, the Soviet Union retained its soldiers there. They stood in support of the communist Tudeh Party which, in November of 1945, raised a revolt in the Iranian province of Azerbaijan. When the Security Council, at its first meeting in January of 1946, referred the whole matter to direct negotiation between Iran and the Soviet Union, the latter demanded the right to station troops in the country indefinitely (as in eastern Europe), control of a Soviet-Iranian oil company, and autonomy for Azerbaijan (no doubt, as part of the Russian security belt, which was to stretch from the Baltic Sea to the Persian Gulf). When Iran refused, a crisis loomed but the United States put pressure on Stalin in the form, virtually, of an ultimatum and the Russian dictator capitulated. In May of 1946, he cleared his soldiers out of Iran. One historian, at least, dates the true beginning of the Cold War to the confrontation over Iran.

The German Question

Of all the problems and questions which separated the two wartime alliance and caused them to engage in the Cold War, Germany stood preeminent. Indeed, the German question constituted the core of the Soviet-American conflict. The two nations disagreed on that country's future. Both expected Germany to take its place eventually in the family of nations once again as a sovereign state, but there the agreement ended. Americans envisaged the new Germany a federal republic with all the trappings of democracy—free elections, competing political parties, parliamentary government, ministerial responsibility—purged of Nazism and dedicated to following a peaceful course in international affairs. The Soviets, on the other hand, looked to a Germany not unlike the other nations surrounding Russia—a centralized and unitary one-party state run by local communists and tied to the Soviet Union by treaty and by ideology.

Given such divergent views, it is not surprising that the Allied Control Council found itself in chronic deadlock on the matter of a common policy for the four zones and on the treatment of Germany as a single economic unit. There was no agreement on such important matters as reparations, land reform, foreign and internal trade, education, political parties, and labor organizations. In each of those matters, the Soviets went very much their own way in their own zone, acting unilaterally, secretively and in disregard of the needs of German recovery. They continued to strip their zone of crops, raw materials, finished products, machinery, and factories and to transport Germans to Russia for forced labor.

Byrnes, believing that the source of Soviet conduct was rooted in a fear of a military resurgence of a reunited and strengthened Germany, offered a four-power alliance, guaranteeing German demilitarization as a price for allied cooperation. He made the proposition in September of 1945 at the London Foreign Ministers' meeting, again at Moscow in December and, again, at Paris in April of 1946. Each time, Molotov found some fault with the plan. In exasperation, Byrnes, in May, had halted shipments of reparations to Russia from the other zones. Such shipments had been agreed upon at Potsdam: industrial equipment in exchange for food, coal, and other raw materials from the Soviet zone (which the Soviets had not been providing). Yet Byrnes continued to look for an accommodation. In July he suggested a merger of the American zone with the others and in September, in a speech in Stuttgart, Germany, he pushed the idea again—this time suggesting not only an economic union of zones but a political one organized into a federal government. The zones, he said, were not meant to be and should not be self-contained areas, and he warned the Soviets that the others would join their zones without Russia's. Once again, he proposed an alliance—this time for forty years. Once again, Stalin spurned the offer. Thereupon, Byrnes went ahead with his alternative. Arrangements were made to join the American and British zones and on January 1, 1947, "Bizonia" came into being. Shortly thereafter, the French zone was added to the two to make "Trizonia."

The Truman Doctrine

Germany was now divided into two parts and the division reflected the growing rift between the two wartime allies—one almost too great to be mended. Still, George C. Marshall, who in January of 1947 replaced Byrnes as secretary of state, made another effort to work with Russia. It came at the Council of Foreign Ministers' meeting in Moscow in March. The Soviet minister was willing to entertain the suggestion of German unity but at a price—$10 billion in reparations, a Russian share in control over the industrial Ruhr area located in the British zone, and a centralized government for a united Germany. For Marshall, the price was too high and he rejected it. The point of no return had been reached. Other efforts were to be made by the United States later in the year but they could not have been expected to bear fruit because the decision had already been made in March by the Truman administration to take such action as would seal the antagonism between the two countries and make them hostile rivals.

The action came on March 12, 1947 when President Truman appeared before a joint session of Congress to request an appropriation of $400 million for military and economic aid to Greece and to Turkey. He was responding to calls for help from those two countries, who were being threatened by the Soviet Union. Ever since December of 1944, the Greek royalist government had been fighting off communist guerrilla forces, which were receiving aid from neighboring communist countries. The British had been sending supplies and money to the Greeks but on February 24, 1947 they informed the United States that, as of March 1, that subsidy would have to stop. They had reached a grave crisis in their economy and were virtually bankrupt. Similarly, their aid to Turkey ended just at the time when the Russians were making demands on that country for land at the eastern end of the Black Sea and a voice in the control of the Dardanelles. Truman was proposing to assume the British burden; the eagle was replacing the lion.

In his message to Congress, the president enunciated a new policy for the United States—one that was to endure for the next twenty-five years. It was "to help free peoples to maintain their free institutions and their national integrity against aggressive movements that seek to impose upon them totalitarian regimes. I believe," he said, "that it must be the policy of the United States to support free peoples who are resisting attempted subjugation by armed minorities or outside pressure." Despite the liberal use of the word *free*, the message ought not be construed in ideological terms. Neither Greece nor Turkey could be considered "free" as the term was used in western democracies. Rather, Truman's position must be viewed as directed against the expansion of Soviet power and territory and influence. It was a call to contain the Soviet Union in its boundaries and permit no further expansion.

A Policy of Containment

The tactic of containment was most lucidly spelled out by George F. Kennan, in an article in *Foreign Affairs* for July 1947, entitled "The Sources of Soviet Conduct." In it, Kennan suggested that "the main element of any United States policy toward Soviet Russia must be that of a long-term patient but firm and vigilant containment of Russian expansive tendencies . . . by the adroit and vigilant application of counterforce at a series of constantly shifting geographical and political points corresponding to the shifts and maneuvers of Soviet policy." And that was exactly what Truman was recommending—counterforce in the eastern Mediterranean. Kennan bad for some time been urging strength and firmness by the United States. A close student of Russian language, history, and literature, he had served in the embassy in Moscow from where, in January of 1946, be had warned his superiors in Washington that "The Kremlin's neurotic view of world affairs is traditional." In February of 1947, Secretary of State Marshall brought him back to the Department of State as head of the newly created Policy Planning Staff.

Truman's request for funds (and for approval of his new policy) passed both branches of Congress handily—67–23 in the Senate and 287–107 in the House—but not surprisingly as the president had consulted the leadership of both parties in February. Still, there was rancorous debate in both chambers. From left and right, the policy was assailed. The left scorned the appellation "democracy" to Greece and Turkey, labelling them corrupt and tyrannical and claimed the action would provoke the Soviet Union and weaken the United Nations. The right objected to the deep involvement in international political affairs that the measure would demand. The great majority of legislators, however, saw no alternative. If the Soviet Union was to be halted, the United States would have to do it. A face-saving amendment proposed by Senator Vandenberg that the United States would turn over the task of aiding beleaguered countries to the United Nations as soon as that body proved capable helped assuage some uneasy consciences. President Truman signed the bill on May 22, 1947 and at once sent money, supplies, and military and civilian advisors to the two embattled countries.

In adopting so revolutionary a policy, both president and Congress were satisfied that they had widespread public support. For at least two years, as relations between the United States and Russia were deteriorating, there had been a good deal of public sentiment in favor of a hard line toward the Kremlin. There had, also, been some severe criticism of Truman's stiffening position, voiced most notably by Secretary of Commerce Henry Wallace. In a speech at a rally in Madison Square Carden in New York on September 12, 1946, Wallace castigated the Administration for meddling in eastern European affairs, which area, he said, was rightfully a Soviet sphere. "We must get out of eastern Europe," he stated. Five days later, Truman fired him from the Cabinet. Since that time, the supporters of a "get tough" policy had increased in number and by the spring of 1947 a Gallup poll on the Truman Doctrine, as the new policy came to be called, revealed only 4 per cent in favor of "hands off" in the crisis. What a far cry from the sentiment of the majority of Americans after the first great war when the vast majority *favored* "hands off!"

The Marshall Plan

The road from the Truman Doctrine to the Marshall Plan was short, logical, and inevitable. It was clear to American planners that Truman's aid to Greece and Turkey was, in one sense, a negative measure. That is, it was designed to meet a threat after one had been made. Steps would have to be taken, they believed, to create such conditions that would discourage a threat from being made. Specifically, the president and his advisors had in mind the state of Europe in the winter of 1946–1947. The old continent was on the verge of collapse. Drought, storms, snows, power shortages had brought it to the brink of ruin. Winston Churchill described it as "a rubble heap, a charnel house, a breeding ground of pestilence and hate." Shortages of food, clothing, shelter made for a desperate situation. And Marshall was convinced that Stalin regarded the imminence of Europe's collapse with equanimity. He recalled the Soviet dictator's remark at the Moscow conference in March of 1947 that delays in reaching agreement on European matters were not tragic to his country. Indeed, delay was to his advantage. If Europe continued its decline, its inhabitants, hopeless and hungry, despairing and debilitated, would fall victims to revolution and to communism. Obviously the answer was to strengthen Europe, to reconstruct it, to restore it to prosperity and well-being, thereby enabling its people to resist the twin menaces of communism and revolution. Such a scheme, Secretary of State Marshall unveiled in a speech at the Harvard University commencement on June 5, 1947.

The idea had been touched on the previous month in a little-noticed address by Undersecretary of State Dean G. Acheson in Cleveland, Mississippi. Acheson, substituting for the president, announced that the United States was ready to give long-range help "to aid free peoples to preserve their independence." The key word was *long-range.* The United States had, since 1943, contributed vast sums through the United Nations Relief and Rehabilitation Association to provide food, clothing, and other supplies to impoverished peoples. That help was, however, for relief, not recovery. The new program, elaborated by Marshall at Harvard, was designed to rebuild Europe's factories and farms, end unemployment, increase production, restore the cities, and make the countries self-supporting again with viable economies. "It is logical," he said, "to assist in the return of normal economic health in the world without which there can be no political stability or assured peace." He then invited the European nations to meet and to detail their needs, to which the United States would respond.

The European reception of Marshall's call was immediate and enthusiastic. British Foreign Secretary Ernest Bevin likened it to "a lifeline to sinking men." At once, he and French Foreign Minister Georges Bidault suggested to Soviet Foreign Minister Molotov that the three meet in Paris for preliminary discussions. The three men did meet in the French capital on June 27 but the Soviet minister stayed only long enough to attack the plan. Calling it a "new venture in American imperialism" and a Trojan horse calculated to extend America's capitalistic tentacles into the European markets, he spurned the offer of help. At the same time, he recommended strongly that the Soviet satellites follow Russia's lead, which they did. The Soviet refusal to participate in so useful a scheme has been ascribed mainly to two factors—the disinclination to reveal economic statistics and the danger of a successful Marshall Plan acting as a magnet drawing the satellite nations from the Soviet orbit. Whatever the reasons, Russia stood aloof, thereby adding one more dimension to the widening gulf between west and east.

Aid to Europe

Meanwhile, sixteen European nations met in Paris on July 12, 1947 as the Committee of European Economic Cooperation to discuss their needs. On September 22, they passed the estimate to Marshall—$19.1 billion from the United States and $3.1 billion from the International Bank of Reconstruction and Development (created in 1945 at an international monetary conference at Bretton Woods in New Hampshire) over a period of four years. On December 19, President Truman submitted to Congress a request for an appropriation of $6.8 billion to be funnelled to the European nations in the following fifteen months and $10.2 billion over the coming three years. The Foreign Assistance Act, passed by Congress in March of 1948 by 69-17 in the Senate and 329-74 in the House, provided $5.3 billion for the first twelve months and authorized $13 billion over a four-year period. The president signed the legislation on April 3, 1948.

The vote in Congress reflected accurately the sentiment of the country. To be sure, there was opposition. The left branded the measure "the martial plan" and claimed it was a warlike and provocative action; the right feared the expenditure would bankrupt the country and wondered, further, whether foreigners were worth helping. But to the vast majority of Americans, resistance to the program seemed naive and unrealistic and dangerous to American security in view of the nature of the Soviet response.

The Russian moves to counteract the Marshall Plan were violent and desperate. In a fiery speech, Andrei Zhdanov, a leading party ideologue and a deputy premier, called for a holy war against the Plan and at a meeting in Warsaw of the Communist Parties of Yugoslavia, Bulgaria, Rumania, Hungary, Poland, France, Italy, Czechoslovakia, and the Soviet Union in early October of 1947, a Communist Information Bureau (Cominform) was established to direct the campaign. Plans were laid to foment strikes in western Europe, to cripple industries, and to sabotage Marshall Plan projects. Particular attention was to be paid to France and to Italy, which had large and powerful Communist parties, to force those countries to renounce Marshall Plan aid. Meanwhile, the Soviet Union was tightening its hold on the satellites. In February of 1948, treaties of friendship and mutual assistance were signed with Rumania, Hungary, and Bulgaria and, in April, with Finland. In February, too, a Soviet-engineered coup in Czechoslovakia placed a communist government in power, thereby rounding out the ring of satellites protecting Russia. At the same time, Stalin was moving to clear Berlin of the western powers.

The Berlin Blockade

That city, it will be recalled, although lying entirely in the Soviet zone of Germany, was divided among the Four Powers. On March 31, 1948, the Soviet authorities in Germany began to take measures to seal Berlin off from the western zones. The first step was to subject freight, people, and baggage to delays and checks upon entering or leaving Berlin via the Soviet zone. That harassment culminated on June 24, in an edict halting all surface transportation to or from the city.

The options open to the United States, Britain, and France were two—abandon the Berliners under their jurisdiction to the Russians or fight their way through the Soviet zone to supply them. Fighting was not a really viable alternative; nor was leaving the Berliners to their fate. For, as the American commander in Berlin, General Lucius D. Clay, noted, "When Berlin falls, West Germany will be next. If we mean . . . to hold Europe against communism, we must not budge. . . . If we withdraw, our position in Europe is threatened. If America does not understand this now, does not know the issue is cast, then it never will and communism will run rampant. I believe the future of democracy requires us to stay."

America did stay. By means of a massive air lift, food, clothing, and other supplies were provided to the residents of Berlin. By September, 4,000 tons of goods were being flown in daily and by the spring of 1949, the figure had doubled. The Soviets could have intercepted the air delivery but they were not willing to risk a clash and on May 12, 1949, they ended the blockade. They had tested the resoluteness of the western powers and had found it firm. They capitulated for another reason. The blockade had been, in part, an attempt to frustrate the creation of a federal republic out of the three western zones of Germany. By the spring of 1949, they realized they could not frustrate or impede the movement. The three western powers were determined to form a government for Germany without Russia once they accepted the fact that the Soviets would never join with the others nor treat Germany as a single economic unit.

In June of 1948, representatives of the United States, France, Britain, Belgium, the Netherlands, and Luxemburg reached agreement at a meeting in London to hold elections for a German constituent assembly to meet in Bonn. The assembly convened there on September 21, 1948 and wrote a constitution that the military governors approved on May 12, 1949. On September 1, the new Federal Republic of Germany came into existence. Military government ended and the allied connection was maintained by high commissioners representing the former occupying powers. Konrad Adenauer, distinguished elder statesman, former mayor of Cologne, and long an anti-Nazi, became the new nation's first chancellor.

The end of the Berlin blockade eased the considerable tension that had built up between east and west since the harrowing events of the winter and spring of 1948. It did not, however, reverse or alter the decision by the United States to create a western military alliance capable of resisting or thwarting any Soviet designs on land not already under Russian control. What had crystallized that decision had been the very real war scare in the spring of 1948 following the Czech coup and the cutting off of Berlin from the west. At that time, General Clay had reported ominously from Berlin "A new tenseness in every Soviet individual with whom we have official relations . . . gives me a feeling that war may come with dramatic suddenness." And, in America there was the same feeling. Talk of the need for a western military alliance was heard on all sides. At a Senate hearing on foreign assistance in June of 1948 there was overwhelming agreement that a military pact with Europe was imperative. In the same month, an epoch-making resolution was introduced into the Senate by Arthur Vandenberg, Republican of Michigan, that the United States should associate itself "by constitutional process, with such regional and other collective arrangements as are based on continuous and effective self-help and mutual aid, and as affect its national security." It passed 64–4.

The North Atlantic Treaty

The way was now paved for American adherence to the Brussels Pact, a 50-year defensive alliance created in March of 1948 among Great Britain, France, Belgium, Luxemburg, and the Netherlands. At once, the Brussels states along with Canada, Norway, Iceland, Denmark, Portugal, and Italy were summoned to Washington for preliminary conversations. By September, the general character of a treaty was agreed upon. Negotiations began in December and continued into the winter and spring of 1949. They were completed in April and on April 4, the North Atlantic Treaty was signed. There was no question of its intent and purpose. It was designed to forestall a would-be aggressor by the common pledge in Article 5 that "an armed attack against one or more of them [the signatories] in Europe or North America shall be considered an attack against them all; . . ." An aggressor could not do what Hitler had done—

pick off certain nations one by one. He would have to contend at once with a grand coalition of nations. And that might be sufficient to give him pause. As President Truman noted upon signing the treaty, "If [this document] . . . had existed in 1914 and in 1939, supported by the nations who are represented today, I believe it would have prevented the acts of aggression which led to two world wars."

On April 12, 1949, the treaty was submitted to the Senate for its "advice and consent." There was no doubt of the outcome of the vote. Few questioned the desirability of a treaty. There were some senators who feared that the treaty did violence to the United Nations charter in that it substituted two hostile worlds for the one world envisaged by the world organization. They pointed, also, to the inconsistencies between the treaty and the charter. The charter permitted regional groupings among member states but some of the parties to the treaty were not UN members; nor could the treaty be said to be regional with signatories so widely scattered geographically. Then there were certain senators who were concerned that Article 3, which provided for the build-up of armaments ("maintain and develop their individual and collective capacity to resist armed attack"), would provoke Russia needlessly. Other legislators worried over the huge expenditures that would be incurred in furnishing military equipment to the allies in accordance with Article 3. Still others were concerned that Article 5 would plunge the United States automatically into war without a Congressional declaration. Three reservations, proposed by Republican senators Robert Taft, Arthur Watkins, and Kenneth Wherry designed chiefly to safeguard Congress's role, were beaten down. When the vote was taken on July 21, the approval was overwhelming: 82–13.

The North Atlantic Treaty along with the Marshall Plan constituted America's reply to the threat believed to be posed by the Soviet Union to the safety and security of western Europe and of the western hemisphere. Each served a different purpose. Marshall Plan money was designed to bolster the economic well-being of the continent, thereby rendering it immune to the blandishments of communism and forestalling revolution. The treaty was to serve to make the continent strong enough militarily to discourage an aggressor or to resist one foolhardy enough to attack. The significance of the treaty in the long perspective of American history must not be lost. It was the second military alliance ever made and the first in time of peace. So radical a departure from tradition may be explained in terms of the degree of danger felt by Americans but it must be viewed, as well, as the consequence of the realization that to *prevent* the conquest of the European continent was cheaper than to have to *liberate* it from an aggressor's domination. For Europeans, it was the fulfillment of a long dream. As the French foreign minister noted when the treaty negotiations were finished, "Today, we obtain what we sought between the two wars. The United States offers us both immediate military aid in the organization of our defense and a guarantee of assistance in case of conflict." Better late than never.

Drawing the Line for Freedom: The Truman Doctrine

Mark Willen

In the following article, Mark Willen paints a vivid picture of the events and people who shaped what became known as the Truman Doctrine. Willen explains that President Harry S. Truman gathered congressional leaders together one February morning in 1947, and Secretary of State George C. Marshall and his under secretary Dean Acheson described for the gathering the threat of Communist expansion in Europe and Asia, suggesting that the United States provide aid to Greece and Turkey so that these countries would not fall to communism. According to Willen, the gathering, profoundly affected by the remarks of these men, urged Truman to speak to Congress. Truman's speech, which drew a line between the democratic west and the Communist east, was met with enthusiastic support, and Congress overwhelmingly approved the bill, Willen writes, which set the stage for Marshall's plan for a European recovery that could withstand Soviet aggression. Willen is managing editor of *Congressional Quarterly Weekly Report*.

No reason was given for the White House summons, and the leaders in Congress who responded had no sense of impending crisis. "We hadn't a clue," Michigan

Excerpted from "Nation Draws a Line for Freedom," by Mark Willen, *Congressional Quarterly Weekly Report*, February 4, 1995. Reprinted by permission of *Congressional Quarterly Weekly Report* via the Copyright Clearance Center, Inc.

Sen. Arthur H. Vandenberg would later tell a colleague.

Flanked by Secretary of State George C. Marshall and Under Secretary Dean Acheson, President Harry S. Truman welcomed the congressional leaders to his executive office at 10 a.m. It was February 27, 1947, a chilly, damp, gray Thursday.

Protecting the World from Communism

As soon as everyone was seated, Truman set the scene. Britain, in desperate financial straits, had informed the United States that it could no longer provide support for Greece and Turkey. Both were in grave danger of falling to Communist insurgents—a fate the United States could not tolerate. The president told the members that he had decided on a major aid program and that he wanted their support in pushing it through Congress as quickly as possible. Truman was not asking for advice; he had already made up his mind.

Marshall came next. Although he had been secretary of state for only a month, Marshall's distinguished war record made him a hero, and he was revered by congressional leaders, who listened closely to him. With few dramatics and a plethora of detail, Marshall explained that British Ambassador Lord Inverchapel had told him personally February 24 that Britain's domestic woes would prevent it from providing further aid to Greece and Turkey. Without an infusion of aid from the United States, he said, the Greek economy would collapse, and the Greek government could not suppress the Communist-led guerrillas. A civil war would be likely to end with Greece as a Communist state under Soviet control. Then Turkey would almost surely fall as well.

"It is not alarmist to say that we are faced with the first crisis of a series which might extend Soviet domination to Europe, the Middle East and Asia," said Marshall. The choice for the United States was "acting with energy or losing by default."

The congressional leaders sat grim-faced. This was not what they wanted to hear. America was finally at peace, and Republicans had just won control of Congress with a mandate to address the nation's domestic problems.

Truman surveyed the room. The House delegation included Republican Speaker Joseph W. Martin Jr. of Massachusetts, Democratic Minority Leader Sam Rayburn of Texas, Foreign Affairs Chairman Charles A. Eaton of New Jersey, and New York's Sol Bloom, the ranking Democrat on Foreign Affairs. In addition to Vandenberg, the Senate delegation included Appropriations Chairman Styles Bridges of New Hampshire and Texas' Thomas T. Connally, the ranking Democrat on Foreign Relations. In an embarrassing oversight, no one had thought to invite Ohio Sen. Robert A. Taft, chairman of the Republican Policy Committee, a fact that Vandenberg brought to Truman's attention after the meeting.

Truman invited questions, and they came quickly, many tinged with skepticism. "Why do we have to pull British chestnuts out of the fire?" "How much is this going to cost ultimately?" "What are we letting ourselves in for?"

As Marshall responded, Acheson found himself growing increasingly agitated. He found the questions "rather trivial" and "adverse" and thought the answers took the discussion off track.

The Greek-Turkish challenge was close to Acheson's heart. In Marshall's State Department, Acheson had been working nonstop to formulate the U.S. response to the British decision. He couldn't understand why these congressmen did not recognize that the United States stood at Armageddon.

Although most accounts, including Truman's and Vandenberg's, credit Marshall with making a forceful and effective statement, Acheson was plainly disappointed. "My distinguished chief, most unusually and unhappily, flubbed his opening statement," Acheson wrote in his memoirs, "Present at the Creation."

"This was my crisis," Acheson continued. "For a week I had nurtured it. These congressmen had no conception of what challenged them; it was my task to bring it home."

Acheson leaned over to Marshall and asked in a stage

whisper: "Is this a private fight or can anyone get into it?" Truman gave Acheson the floor.

A Divided World

In the past 18 months, Acheson began, the position of the democracies of the world had seriously deteriorated. While the United States had been busy trying to save Central Europe from Soviet control, Moscow had been busy elsewhere and with greater success than generally realized.

The Soviet Union had laid down any number of bets, said Acheson, and if it won just one of them, it won them all. If it seized control of Turkey, then Greece and Iran would fall. If it controlled Greece, then Turkey and Iran would fall.

Acheson spoke for close to 15 minutes. Historian Robert J. Donovan reports that when he finished everyone in the room knew that not since ancient times had the world seen such a stark polarization. There were now only two world powers: the United States and the Soviet Union.

Vandenberg spoke first, saying he had been greatly impressed, even shaken, by what he had heard. It was clear that the situation went beyond the immediate question of Greece and Turkey.

Vandenberg told Truman that it was absolutely necessary that the request for aid be accompanied by an explanation to the American people of the entire grim situation just as it had been explained by Marshall and Acheson. "Mr. President," he declared, "if you will say that to the Congress and the country, I will support you, and I believe that most of its members will do the same."

Truman went around the room, inviting comments. Several members agreed with Vandenberg; no one spoke out in opposition to the aid request.

Truman agreed to Vandenberg's advice. As the conference broke up, Truman said, "Nobody knows where this will lead us."

Acheson moved quickly to steer newspaper coverage of the impending crisis to reflect the White House's perspective. And press accounts suggest he was largely successful.

But not all reaction was favorable. As word spread through Congress, many voiced concern. Florida's Democratic Sen. Claude Pepper said the whole matter should be turned over to the United Nations. Georgia's Democratic Sen. Richard B. Russell suggested that the United States might as well admit Britain as a state. "It would cost this country far less than the commitments now proposed as our obligations," he said. "The king could run for the Senate, as could Winston Churchill."

As preparations continued for Truman's address, the president began a long scheduled trip to Mexico, and Marshall departed for a six-week conference in Moscow. This again left the crisis in the lap of Acheson, who by all accounts enjoyed his finest hour. Acheson and Marshall had each other's complete trust—as well as Truman's—and many historians believe the combination of their skills made them the strongest one-two team ever to control the State Department.

Drafters of Truman's speech followed Vandenberg's advice and put the problem in the context of saving the world from the Soviet menace. The speech went through several drafts, with Truman aide Clark Clifford suggesting changes on Truman's behalf. At one point, the speech was cabled to Marshall in Paris. Marshall thought it far too strong.

"It seemed to Gen. Marshall and to me that there was a little too much flamboyant anti-communism in the speech," wrote Marshall's aide, Charles Bohlen, who was traveling with the secretary. Washington's reply to Marshall stated that "in the considered opinion of the executive branch, including the president, the Senate would not approve the doctrine without the emphasis on the Communist danger," according to Bohlen.

Truman met again with congressional leaders—including Taft this time—on March 10 and outlined his plan in detail. He would ask for $400 million in aid to Greece and Turkey, and he would make his speech to a joint session of Congress that would be broadcast on radio and television.

The President's Message

The speech was set for 1 p.m. March 12, but the House chamber was full by 12:30. Joseph M. Jones, a State Department official who recounted the crisis in his book, "The Fifteen Weeks," described the scene on the floor as chaotic. In addition to members, the Cabinet and invited guests, "dozens of ex-congressmen . . . loitered in conversation with old friends on the periphery of the chamber. Every clerk, secretary or functionary on Capitol Hill whose familiar face would get him past a guard at the door was also on the floor. One Democratic representative had planted himself, with his small daughter on his lap, in a seat on the center aisle."

Clifford accompanied the president on the drive to the Capitol. They went over the speech one last time, underlining sentences that needed emphasis. Then Truman spoke enthusiastically about the four-day Key West vacation he was to begin as soon as the speech was over.

At precisely 1 p.m. the doorkeeper announced the president, and everyone rose. Escorted by the traditional committee of senators and representatives and carrying his speech in a black folder under his arm, Truman strode down the aisle. He mounted the clerk's desk below the Speaker's rostrum, acknowledged the continuing ovation with a broad smile, opened his folder and began.

The speech lasted 18 minutes. Truman, whose style was normally flat and unimpressive, spoke with considerable authority, "tripping only occasionally, speaking with a newly acquired forcefulness," as *Time* magazine put it. Throughout the speech, members looked unusually grave, but with one notable exception, according to *Time*. Midway through the speech, Taft "took off his glasses, rubbed his face and yawned prodigiously."

The address was simple and direct. Truman described a desperate situation in Greece but quickly moved on to meet Vandenberg's demand for a broader explanation. In the process, he defined the Cold War that had already begun and set out what would come to be known as the Truman Doctrine of containment.

"At the present moment in world history, nearly every nation must choose between alternative ways of life. The choice is too often not a free one."

One way of life, Truman continued, was based on the will of the majority and was characterized by free elections, individual liberty and representative government. In the other, the will of a minority was imposed on the majority through terror and oppression, a controlled press and rigged elections. Then Truman made the case for U.S. aid. "I believe that it must be the policy of the United States to support free peoples who are resisting attempted subjugation by armed minorities or outside pressure. I believe that we must assist free peoples to work out their own destinies in their own way."

Growing Support for the Truman Doctrine

The speech was met by a standing ovation. Truman acknowledged it with a fleeting smile. He looked up to where his wife was sitting and bowed to her, and then made his way out of the chamber. He was driven directly to the airport so he could begin his short vacation.

Vandenberg met with reporters later that afternoon and expressed support: "The president's message faces facts, and so must Congress."

Vandenberg's role in the promulgation of the Truman Doctrine completed a process that turned him from isolationist to internationalist. By his own account, that transformation began with the Japanese attack on Pearl Harbor six years earlier. It can easily be argued that its culmination came at the White House meeting of Feb. 27, when he literally demanded that Truman expound his doctrine as the price for congressional support for Greek-Turkish aid.

The speech dominated the next day's newspapers. The *New York Times* ran a three-line banner headline and put the text of the address on the front page, along with stories about the speech and congressional reaction. The *Times* noted that there would be opposition but said congressional approval was assured. While some papers spoke out against U.S. involvement, most supported it.

Senate and House hearings began the next day. Concern focused on the breadth, scope, and cost of U.S. commitment. Specific objections were raised to the United States' bypassing the United Nations, which was still in its infancy and considered by many as a repository of hope for world peace.

The U.N. issue was quickly seized by Vandenberg, who had developed a method of playing both partisan politician and bipartisan statesman. His technique was to find a relatively minor objection to a particular administration policy and then insist on a negotiated compromise that would ensure support for the broader policy objective. In this case, Vandenberg added an amendment to the Greek-Turkish aid bill that had little real effect other than to make it seem as though proper respect had been paid to the United Nations. When the amendment was adopted, passage of the aid plan was assured.

The Senate passed the bill April 22 by 67–23; Republicans split 35–16 and Democrats, 32–7. The House followed two weeks later, voting 287–108, with Republicans split 127–94 and Democrats 160–13. (An American Labor Party member also voted no.) A short conference produced the final measure, which was cleared May 15 and which Truman signed May 22.

By then Marshall, Acheson and the rest of the foreign policy team were nearly ready with a broad recovery plan designed to do nothing less than rebuild Europe so it could withstand Soviet pressure. Marshall outlined the plan June 5. It was quickly welcomed in Europe, and from it grew the big four-year Marshall Plan for European recovery.

Clifford would later look back on these months of 1947 and describe them in momentous terms. "I think it's one of the proudest moments in American history," Clifford told Truman biographer David McCullough. "What happened during that period was that Harry Truman and the United States saved the free world."

Chronology

1940

April 9—German armies subdue Norway and Denmark.

June 13—President Roosevelt signs a $1.3 billion defense bill, and defense production helps pull the nation out of its economic depression.

June 22—France surrenders to Germany.

November 5—Roosevelt is reelected as president.

December 29—Roosevelt tells Americans in a fireside chat that the United States "must be the great arsenal of democracy."

Walt Disney releases the animated ballet, *Fantasia,* the first feature length film to use stereophonic sound.

1941

January 16—The War Department announces the formation of the 99th Pursuit Squadron, an African American unit that came to be known as the Tuskegee airmen.

March 11—Roosevelt signs the Lend-Lease Act, which provides aid to Britain.

July 17—Joe DiMaggio completes his fifty-six-game hit streak.

August 9–12—Roosevelt and Winston Churchill meet in Argentine Bay and create the Atlantic Charter; however, 74 percent of Americans still oppose entering the war.

August 12—Congress approves Roosevelt's request to extend the draft of young men into the military.

December 7—Pearl Harbor attack.

December 11—Guam, the first U.S. possession to be occupied, surrenders.

1942

February 19—Executive Order 9066 orders the internment of all Japanese Americans.

Spring—Rationing begins in the U.S. to preserve resources such as gas and food.

May 7–8—The Battle of the Coral Sea is the first naval action fought entirely with aircraft.

May 15—Women's Army Corp or WACs created.

June 4—Battle of Midway.

August 7–February 1943—Battle of Guadalcanal.

September 17—General Leslie Groves heads the Manhattan Project to construct an atomic weapon.

Warner Brothers releases *Casablanca*.

1943
January 14–24—Winston Churchill and Roosevelt meet in Casablanca, Morocco.

July 10–August 17—The Allies invade Sicily, and after land and air battles, the Germans begin to retreat on August 11.

July 26—The Italian dictator Mussolini falls from power.

Director Alfred Hitchcock releases *Shadow of a Doubt*.

1944
February 13–26—In Operation Argument, bombers drop 10,000 bomb tons to destroy Luftwaffe factories in central Germany.

June 5—The 101st Screaming Eagles parachute into Normandy prior to the amphibious landing on June 6th.

June 6—Often referred to as "The Longest Day" or D day, the invasion of Normandy begins.

June 22—Roosevelt signs the GI bill.

August 29—The 28th U.S. Infantry Division marches down the Champs Elysées in Paris and into combat.

November 6—Roosevelt wins a fourth term, defeating Thomas E. Dewey.

December 16–January 28, 1945—Battle of the Bulge.

1945
January 27—Auschwitz is liberated.

February 4–11—Churchill, Roosevelt, and Stalin meet in Yalta to make plans for the defeat of Germany, the policy for the division of postwar Europe, the formation of the United Nations, and the conditions of Russian involvement in the war against Japan.

April 1—Okinawa is taken when 458 ships land with 193,852 U.S. troops.

April 12—Franklin Delano Roosevelt dies in Warm Springs, Georgia, and Harry S. Truman assumes the presidency.

April 30—Hitler commits suicide.

May 8—Americans celebrate Germany's unconditional surrender on V-E Day.

July 17–August 2—Harry S. Truman, Josef Stalin, and Winston Churchill meet in Potsdam to demand Japanese surrender and the principles governing the treatment of Germany.

August 6—Little Boy, a twenty kiloton atomic bomb killed eighty thousand when dropped on Hiroshima.

August 9—Fat Man, a twenty-two kiloton atomic bomb killed seventy thousand when dropped on Nagasaki.

August 15—Emperor Hirohito surrenders—V-J Day.

Nuremberg Trials begin.

1946
April 25—The Paris Peace Conference begins, but the first conference of twenty-one nations ends in disagreement on May 16.

July 1—Operations Crossroads begins with atomic testing on Bikini Island.

August 1—The McMahon Act creates the Atomic Energy Commission.

Frank Capra's *It's a Wonderful Life* is released.

1947
February—The financial crisis at home forces the British to end aid to Greece and Turkey.

March 12—Congress grants $400 million in aid to Greece and Turkey to defend against communism.

June 5—The Marshall Plan involves the U.S. in European Recovery to protect Europe and America from the threat of Soviet aggression.

July 26—Congress passes the National Security Act creating the National Security Council and the National Security Agency to coordinate intelligence activities of the State and Defense departments with the Central Intelligence Agency (CIA).

Dr. Edwin H. Land introduces the Polaroid camera.

Tennessee Williams writes the play *A Streetcar Named Desire*.

1948

February—Communists gain control in Czechoslovakia.

April—Congress approves $5 billion of Marshall Plan aid to prevent Soviet expansion.

June 24—The Soviet Union blocks access to Berlin, Germany by road, rail, and river routes.

Summer—"The Ed Sullivan Show" begins.

November 2—Truman reelected.

The LP record arrives on a vinyl disk.

1949

April 4—The North Atlantic Treaty Organization (NATO) treaty is signed in Washington, D.C.

June—The U.S. begins to withdraw troops from Korea.

July 14—The U.S.S.R. explodes its first A-bomb.

October—For the first time all games of the World Series are broadcast on television.

December—Mao Zedong and Stalin sign a Sino-Soviet alliance.

Created at the Massachusetts Institute for Technology (MIT), "Whirlwind" becomes the first real-time computer.

RCA offers the first 45 rpm record.

For Further Reading

General Studies of the Decade

David Brinkley, "The '40s," *Newsweek*, January 1, 1994.

William Graebner, *The Age of Doubt: American Thought and Culture in the 1940s*. Boston: Twayne, 1998.

Lewis Lord and Jeannye Thornton, "1940 America," *U.S. News & World Report*, August 27, 1990.

Geoffrey Perrett, *Days of Sadness, Years of Triumph: The American People, 1939–1945*. New York: Coward, McCann and Geoghegan, 1973.

Arthur Schlessinger Jr., "Franklin Delano Roosevelt," *Time*, April 13, 1998.

Pearl Harbor and Japanese Internment

Roger Daniels, *Concentration Camps USA: Japanese America and World War II*. New York: Holt, Rinehart and Winston, 1972.

Otto Friedrich and Anne Hopkins, "Day of Infamy," *Time*, December 2, 1991.

Audrie Gardner and Anne Loftis, *The Great Betrayal: The Evacuation of the Japanese-Americans During World War II*. New York: MacMillan, 1969.

Arthur R. Lee, "Recollections [on the Japanese bombing of Pearl Harbor, Hawaii]," *American History*, December 1998. Available from Cowles Enthusiast Media, 6405 Flank Dr., Harrisburg, PA 17112.

William H. Rehnquist, "When the Laws Were Silent," *American Heritage*, October 1998. [Article on Japanese American Internment] Available from 60 Fifth Ave., New York, NY 10011.

World War II

Kenneth Auchincloss, "Americans Go to War," *Newsweek*, March 8, 1999.

Clay Blair Jr., *Silent Victory: The U.S. Submarine War Against Japan*. Philadelphia: Lippincott, 1975.

Albert Russell Buchanan, *The United States and World War II.* New York: Harper and Row, 1964.

John P. Cervone, "Remembering the Bataan Death March," *Military History*, December 1999. Available from PRIMEDIA Special Interest Publications, 741 Miller Dr. SE, D-2, Leesburg, VA 20175.

Charles E. Francis, *The Tuskegee Airmen: The Men Who Changed a Nation.* Boston: Branden, 1993.

Stanley Goldberg, "What Did Truman Know, and When Did He Know It?" *Bulletin of the Atomic Scientists*, May/June 1998. Available from 6042 South Kimbark, Chicago, IL 60637.

Hondon B. Hargrove, *Buffalo Soldiers in Italy: Black Americans in World War II.* Jefferson, NC: McFarland, 1985.

Waldo H. Heinrichs, *Threshold of War: Franklin D. Roosevelt and American Entry into World War II.* New York: Oxford University Press, 1988.

Leo Marks, *Between Silk and Cyanide: A Codemaker's War 1941–1945.* New York: Free Press, 1998.

Stephen L. McFarland, *To Command the Sky: The Battle for Air Superiority over Germany, 1942–1944.* Washington, DC: Smithsonian Institution Press, 1991.

Bruce W. Nelan, "1939–1948: War," *Time*, March 9, 1998.

R.A.C. Parker, *Struggle for Survival: The History of the Second World War.* New York: Oxford University Press, 1989.

Thomas Parrish, *The Ultra Americans: The U.S. Role in Breaking the Nazi Codes.* New York: Stein and Day, 1986.

Richard Rhodes, *The Making of the Atomic Bomb.* New York: Simon and Schuster, 1986.

Tom Seddon, *Atom Bomb.* New York: W.H. Freeman Company, 1995.

Doris Weatherford, *American Women and World War II.* New York: Facts On File, 1990.

Alan M. Winkler, *The Politics of Propaganda: The Office of War Information: 1942–1945.* New Haven, CT: Yale University Press, 1978.

The Home Front

Penny Colman, *Rosie the Riveter: Women Working on the Home Front in World War II*. New York: Crown, 1995.

Sherna Berger Gluck, *Rosie the Riveter Revisited: Women, the War, and Social Change*. Boston: Twayne, 1987.

Susan Hartmann, *Home Front and Beyond: American Women in the 1940s*. Boston: Twayne, 1982.

George Lipsitz, *Rainbow at Midnight: Labor and Culture in the 1940s*. Urbana: University of Illinois Press, 1994.

Michael Renov, *Hollywood's Wartime Women*. Ann Arbor, MI: UMI Research Press, 1988.

Popular Culture

Clayton R. Koppes and Gregory D. Black, *Hollywood Goes to War: How Politics, Profits, and Propaganda Shaped World War II Movies*. New York: Free Press, 1987.

Roger Manvell, *Films and the Second World War*. New York: Delta, 1974.

Jim Murray, *Legends of the 1930s and 1940s*. Broomall, PA: Chelsea House, 1995.

Thomas Schatz, *The Genius of the System: Hollywood Filmmaking in the Studio Era*. New York: Pantheon, 1988.

Gilbert Thomas, *Baseball at War*. New York: Franklin Watts, 1997.

Steven Watson, *The Birth of the Beat Generation: Visionaries, Rebels, and Hipsters, 1944–1960*. New York: Pantheon, 1995.

The Cold War

Madeleine K. Albright, "The Marshall Plan: Model for U.S. Leadership in the 21st Century," *U.S. Department of State Dispatch*, June 1997. Available from Superintendent of Documents, U.S. Government Printing Office, PO Box 371954, Pittsburgh, PA 15250-7954.

Phillip Knightly, *The Second Oldest Profession: Spies and Spying in the Twentieth Century*. New York: W.W. Norton, 1987.

Scott Parrish, "Soviet Reaction to the Marshall Plan: Opportunity or Threat?" *Problems of Post-Communism*, September/October 1995. Available from M.E. Sharpe, Inc., 80 Business Park Dr., Armonk, NY 10504.

Index

abolitionists, 104–105
Acheson, Dean G., 307, 315, 316–17, 318
Across the Pacific (movie), 235
Actors' Committee of the Hollywood
  Victory Committee for Stage, Screen, and
  Radio, 222
Adams, James Truslow, 40
Adenauer, Konrad, 310
advertising, 160–63
Aerial Nurse Corps, 222
African Americans, 20
  Jackie Robinson, 277
  World War II involvement, 22–23
    achievements and failures of, 127–29
    in combat, 123–24
    quantity of work by, 130–31
    questioning policies and training for,
      126–27
    reviews on, 124–26
    segregation of, 129–30
    sent overseas, 121–23
    as volunteers, 131–32
  see also jazz music
Agaki (ship), 66
Alaska, 194
Alexander, Sir Harold, 85
All-American Girls Professional Baseball
  League (AAGPBL), 271
  see also Girls of Summer
Allies
  advantages of, 81–83
  air bombings by, 84–85
  in Atlantic, 20–21
  defeating Germany, 90
  invasions by
    Italy and North Africa, 85–86
    Normandy, 26–27, 86–87
  propaganda by, 138
  see also England; Soviet Union; United
    States
America First movement, 16
Americana Quiz (TV show), 263
Americans
  on end of war, 92–93
  on Holocaust, 87–88
  as isolationists, 15
  on Jewish refugees, 89
  on postwar aid to Europe, 308
  preparing for war, 43–44
  pre-WWII income, 35
  pre-WWII money spending by, 42–43
  reaction to Pearl Harbor, 76–77
  on Roosevelt's death, 90
  supporting Japanese Americans, 196–97
  supporting WWII involvement, 16–17, 54
  unready for WWII, 48
  see also Japanese Americans; rations;
    United States
Anzio, 23, 113, 115–16
Arnold, H.H., 124, 125, 230
assembly centers, 200–203

  see also internment camps
Atlantic Charter, 20, 56
atom bomb, 91–92
  control over, 300–301
  development of, 141–42
  dropping on Japan, 27–28, 91–92,
    144–49
  Manhattan Project, 142–44
Atomic Energy Commission, 300
Augusta (ship), 55–56
Australia, 121
automobiles
  and gas rationing, 168–71
  prices, 36
  production, 48
  see also rubber shortage

Bancroft, Mary, 109–13
Barney Blake (TV show), 263
baseball. See Girls of Summer
BBC (British Broadcasting Corporation),
  137
bebop music, 292, 293
Berle, Milton, 267–68
Berlin, Irving, 39
Berlin blockade, 30, 309–11
Bidault, Georges, 307
Black Orchestra. See Schwarze Kapelle
Blum, John Morton, 152
Board of War Information, 154
Bogart, Humphrey, 25, 236
Bohlen, Charles, 318
Bowes, Edward, 259
Boys and Girls Together (play), 38
Breuer, William B., 23–24, 108
Broadway theater, 38
Buchanan, A. Russell, 120
Bulgaria, 309
Bulge, Battle of the, 27, 87
Byrnes, James F., 149, 236, 298, 299, 302

Cafe Society, 284–85
Cairo Declaration, 102
Camel Newsreel Theater (TV news show),
  264
Canada, 194
Capra, Frank, 26, 222
Carter, Boake, 37
Cassini, Oleg, 233
Castleman, Harry, 255
celebrities
  accused of communism, 251–52
  in armed forces, 226–28
  meeting at Hollywood Canteen, 232–34
  selling war bonds, 228–29
  war efforts by, 221
  see also Hollywood
Charade Quiz (TV show), 263
Charley's Aunt (play), 38
Chiang Kai-shek, 91, 102, 107
China, 17, 57, 90–91

Churchill, Winston, 81
  on Japanese surrender, 95, 101
  meeting with Roosevelt, 55–56
  on U.S. aiding England, 52, 53
  on U.S.-Soviet relations, 298–99
Civil Air Patrol, 222
Clifford, Clark, 318, 321
Coast Guard, U.S., 55
  SPARS, 23, 178
Cold War, 29–30, 298
Collin, Dottie, 279
comic strips, 159–60
Committee for the First Amendment, 287
Committee of European Economic
  Cooperation, 308
Committee to Defend America by Aiding
  the Allies, 57
communism
  in Hollywood, accusation of, 241–43
    assumed guilt of, 250–51
    destroyed creativity, 252–53
      eliminating Hollywood members,
      243–45
    and employment blacklist, 248–49
    testimony on, 245–48
  jazz musicians accused of, 283–87
  preventing spread of, in Greece and
    Turkey, 30, 303–304, 305, 315–17
Communist Information Bureau, 309
concentration camps, 28
  see also Holocaust
Condor (ship), 62–63
Connally, Thomas T., 316
Cooper, Gary, 246
Coral Sea, Battle of the, 21
Corn Is Green, The (play), 38
Coughlin, Father Charles, 16
Court of Current Issues (TV show), 263
Cowles, Gardner, Jr., 154, 155, 160–61
Cowling, William, 28
Crawford, Joan, 230
Crisis (magazine), 126, 128, 129–30
Czechoslovakia, 27, 309

Dancer, Faye, 278, 279
Darlan, Jean, 97
Darwell, Jane, 37
Davis, Benjamin Oliver, 122, 123, 124,
  125, 132
Davis, Bette, 26, 231
Davis, Elmer, 153, 154, 155
  conflicts with
    Office of Strategic Services, 156–57
    military, 155–56
  on reporting the truth, 158–59
Davis, Lavone "Pepper" Paire, 275, 276,
  279
de Gaulle, Charles, 87, 97
de Haviland, Olivia, 37
Dewitt, John, 19, 189–91
Dictionary of American History (Adams),
  40
Diggins, John Patrick, 15, 21, 24, 80
Disney, Walt, 37–38
Donald Duck, 222, 224
Donovan, William, 156–57

Doolittle, James H., 21, 83
Douglas Edwards and the News (TV news
  show), 264
Doyle, Charles H., 115–16
draft, military, 17, 44
Dulles, Allen W., 108–10

Early, Steve, 76
economy, 164
  emerging from depression, 48
  pre-WWII prosperity, 35–36, 41
  Roosevelt's role in recovering, 14–15
  see also rations
E-Day, 199–200
Edwards, Douglas, 264, 265
Einstein, Albert, 142, 146, 147
Eisen, Thelma "Tiby," 276
Eisenhower, Dwight D., 81, 97
  on African Americans in combat, 125,
  131
Eisenhower, Milton, 154, 206
Ellington, Duke, 286
Emergency Committee to Save the Jewish
  People of Europe, 88
Emergency Price Control Act, 164
employment
  African Americans in, 19–20
  after the war, 181–82
  New Deal legislation for, 15
  optimism in, 35
  women in, 25, 178–81
England
  aid to Greece and Turkey, 304, 315
  Atlantic Charter, 56
  lend-lease program for, 53–54
  U.S. aid to, 52–53
  U.S. alliance with, 54–55
  see also Allies
English, Maddy, 278
Erenberg, Lewis A., 281

Fagan, Myron C., 250–51
Fairbanks, Jerry, 258–59
FBI (Federal Bureau of Investigation), 186,
  188
Federal Republic of Germany, 310
films. See movies
Fincher, Jack, 270
Finland, 309
fireside chats, 135
Fonda, Henry, 37, 226–27
Ford, John, 222
Foreign Assistance Act, 308
Foreign Information Service (FIS), 136–37
For Whom the Bell Tolls (Hemingway),
  39–40
forties. See African Americans; economy;
  Hollywood; internment camps; music;
  propaganda; rations; television; women;
  World War II
Foxx, Jimmie, 276
France
  fall of, 50, 51, 52
  fortification in, 40
  liberation of, 27, 87
  Marshall Plan aid to, 309

Franck Report, 145
French, Edward F., 67–68
Friedrich, Otto, 226
Fuchs, Klaus, 144

Gable, Clark, 37, 222
    and Carole Lombard, 229, 230
    recruited in army, 230–31
Garland, Judy, 39
gas rations, 24, 168–71
    counterfeiting coupons, 171–72
    outcome of, 170–71
George Washington Slept Here (play), 38
Germany
    Berlin blockade in, 309–11
    bombings by/on, 22
    Japanese alliance with, 57
    naval forces, 82–83
    postwar, 297–98, 301–303
    Roosevelt's intentions toward, 99–100
    see also World War II
GI bill, 29
Gibson, Truman K., Jr., 126, 128–29
Gilford, Jack, 285
Girls of Summer, 270–71
    chaperoning, 276–77
    daring plays by, 278–79
    fans of, 276, 277–78
    games of, 271–73
    image of, 274–75
    skills of, 279–80
    start-up of, 273–74
Gisevius, Hans Bernd, 111–12
Gone with the Wind (movie), 37
Goodman, Benny, 286, 289
Goodson, Mark, 263
Grable, Betty, 13, 26, 232, 240
Grant, Cary, 37
Grant, Ulysses, 99
Grapes of Wrath, The (movie), 37
Great Britain. See England
Great Depression, the, 14, 48
Greece, 30, 303, 304, 305, 315–17
Greene, Melissa Fay, 114
Greer (ship), 56
Grimm, Charlie, 279
Groves, Leslie, 144
Guinzburg, Harold, 136, 162

Halsey, William F., 84
Hammerstein II, Oscar, 39
Hampton, Lionel, 286–87
Hanford, Washington, 142, 143
Harkness, Richard, 265
Harnett, Ann, 275–76
Hawaii, 19
    see also Pearl Harbor
Hayes, Helen, 38
Hemingway, Ernest, 39–40
Henderson, Leon, 164, 168, 169
Hepburn, Katharine, 37
Hershey, Lewis B., 44, 222
Hirohito, emperor of Japan, 104, 106, 149
Hiroshima, 92, 147–48
Hitchcock, Alfred, 237
Hitler, Adolf
    on Maginot line, 40
    plot to murder, 111, 112–13
    suicide, 27, 90
    see also Nazism
Hoff, Carl, 288–89
Holden, William, 226
Holliday, Billie, 288
Hollywood, 37–38
    accusations of propaganda in, 214–16
    anti-Communist attacks on, 241–43
        assumed guilt in, 250–51
            defending, 216–19
        destroyed creativity in, 252–53
        employment blacklist from, 245–47,
            248–49
        stars attacked in, 251–52
        testimonies for, 247–48
    changing film scripts, 234–36
    division within, 243–44
    government policies affecting, 222–25
    government suspicion of, 240–41
    pressure to discharge Communists in,
        244–45
    war efforts by people in, 221–23
    see also movies
Hollywood Canteen, 26, 231–32
Hollywood Screen Test (TV show), 262
Holocaust, 28, 87–88
    rescue mission for Jews, 88–90
Hoover, Herbert, 14
Hope, Bob, 26
Hopkins, Harry, 55, 73
Horne, Lena, 285
Hour Glass (TV show), 266
Houseman, John, 137
House Un-American Activities Committee
    (HUAC), 241, 242
    on Hollywood ten, 247–48
    interrogation by, 244–45
    jazz musicians testifying for, 284
Houston, Jeanne Wakatsuki, 192, 205
Howard, Leslie, 37
Howdy Doody (TV show), 260–61
Howe, Quincy, 265
How Green Was My Valley (Llewellyn), 40
Hull, Cordell, 59, 73–74
Hull, William Franklin Cordell, 64, 65
Humphrey, Hubert, 265
Hungary, 309
Huston, John, 26

Iceland, 43, 55
Ickes, Harold L., 48, 158
Interim Committee, 144–45
International Atomic Development
    Authority, 300
internment camps, 19, 194
    as dusty and desolate, 204
    high security, 208–209
    improvement from assembly centers, 205
    physical arrangement of, 205
    preparing to move to, 197–200
    supervision and control in, 206–207
    surrounded by barbed wire, 204–205
    transfer from assembly centers to,
        203–204

see also Japanese Americans
Interstate Commerce Commission
 accusations against Hollywood, 214–16
 demise of, 218–19
 testimony before, 216–18
Iran, 301
isolationism, 15
 on films as propaganda, 214–19
 opposing U.S. involvement, 56–57
 Roosevelt opposing, 51
Italy
 allied invasion of, 85–86
 capturing Mussolini, 90
 Marshall Plan aid to, 309

James, Harry, 46, 232
Japan
 air bombing of, 91
 alliance with Germany, 57, 80–81
 dropping atomic bomb on, 27–28, 91–92
  choosing targets for, 144–45
   impact of, 147–48
  warning or demonstrating for, 145
 invasion of Pacific, 17–18
 naval battle by, 83–84
 rejecting Potsdam Declaration, 145–47
 relations with U.S., 57–59
 responsibility for war, 106
 Roosevelt declaring war on, 68, 69
 Roosevelt's intentions toward, 100–101
 Soviet invasion of, 148
 surrender by, 149–50
 unconditional surrender by, 101–103
  debate on, 103–107
 see also Pearl Harbor
Japanese Americans
 in assembly centers, 200–203
 day of evacuation for, 199–200
 government rejection of, 189–90
 loyalty to America, 184–86
 media on, 188
 as model citizens, 196–97
 preparing for move, 197–98
 relocation
  as compulsory, 193–94
  proposal for, 190–92
  reaction to, by, 194–96
  voluntary, 192–93
 resistance and despair of, 200
 selling belongings, 198–99
 suspected as enemy aliens, 186–88
 threats against, 189
 see also internment camps
jazz music
 associated with drug use, 287–88
 as divided and vulnerable, 282–83
 musicians
  anti-Communist attacks on, 283–87
  drug use by, 288–89
  in headlines, 282
  outsider status of, 293–94
 see also swing music
Jeffers, William M., 157
Jews, 28
 and film propaganda, 215
 justifying property seizures of, 41

 rescue mission for refugee, 88–90
Johnny Belinda (play), 38
Johnston, Eric, 242, 244–45, 246
Josephson, Barney, 284
Josephson, Leon, 285
jukeboxes, 38–39
Jung, Carl Gustav, 110

Kaltenborn, H.V., 37, 265
Kamenshek, Dorothy, 279
kamikazes, 83
Kaminsky, Harold, 71–72
Kennan, George F., 304
Kern, Jerome, 39
Kikuchi, Charles, 184, 203, 206, 207
King, Ernest J., 155–56
Kinkaid, Thomas C., 84
Konoye, Prince Fimimaro, 17, 58
Korda, Alexander, 215
Kostclanetz, Andre, 39
Krupa, Gene, 288
Kurys, Sophie, 272–73, 274, 276–77

labor. *See* employment
Lamarr, Hedy, 26, 228
Lamour, Dorothy, 222, 228
Lawton, K.B., 240
Lee, Ulysses, 127, 130
legislation, New Deal, 15
Leigh, Vivien, 37
lend-lease program, 53–54
Levine, Alan J., 141
Lewis, Fulton, 37
Lewis, Jerry, 269
Lewis, William B., 161–62
Leyte Gulf, Battle of, 84
Liberia, 121
Life with Father (play), 38
Lindbergh, Charles A., 16, 56
Lingeman, Richard R., 163, 237
literature, 39–40
Llewellyn, Richard, 40
Lombard, Carole, 26, 222, 229
Long-Range Aid to Navigation (LORAN), 117
Los Alamos, New Mexico, 143
Louisiana Purchase (play), 38
Luce, Henry, 215

MacArthur, Douglas, 17, 83
 on using African American troops, 121
 working with women, 118, 119
Mack, Ted, 259, 260, 266
MacLeish, Archibald, 154–55
Maddox, Robert James, 94
Maginot line, 40
Male Animal, The (play), 38
Mangerich, Agnes, 116
Manhattan Project, 91, 142–44
Marine Corps Reserve, 43
Marshall, George C., 303
 and Pearl Harbor, 18, 67, 70
 and Truman Doctrine, 315, 318
Marshall Plan, 306–308, 312–13
Martin, Dean, 269
Martin, Joseph W., 316

Index

Mary Kay and Johnny (TV show), 263
Mayer, Louis B., 246
McFarland, Ernest, 216
McIntyre, Andrew, 230–31
media
  on Holocaust, 88
  on Japanese Americans, 188
  on Pearl Harbor, 76
  on Truman Doctrine, 320–21
  see also Office of War Information
    (OWI); Voice of America
Meet the Press (TV news show), 257
Mellett, Lowell, 223, 224
Mickey Mouse, 222
Midway, Battle of, 21
military
  African Americans in
    achievements and failures of, 127–29
    in combat, 123–24
    quantity of work by, 130–31
    question, 127–29
    questioning policies and training for,
      126–27
    reviews on, 124–26
    segregation of, 129–30
    sent overseas, 121–23
    as volunteers, 131–32
  building of, in peacetime, 43–44
  celebrities in, 226–28
    conflict with OWI, 155–56
  draft for, 17, 44
    for internment camps, 207
  number serving in, 177
  spending, 41
  U.S., pre-WWII, 46–47
  unready for war, 49
Miner, Worthington, 262, 269
Mitchell, Thomas, 37
Molotov, V.M., 299, 302
Montgomery, Robert, 226, 246
Montgomery, Sir Bernard L., 21, 27, 85
Morgan, Edward, 37
Morgenthau, Henry, Jr., 89, 100, 229
Mormon Church, 121
Morris, Carolyn, 272
Mostel, Zero, 285
Motion Picture Alliance for the
  Preservation of American Values (MPA),
  243, 251
movies, 37–38
  OWI on content in, 159–60
  prices, 36
  war, 13, 25–26, 213–14, 219–21, 238
  see also Hollywood
Munson, Curtis B., 185–86
Murphy, George, 71–72, 246
Murphy, Vincent R., 71–72
Murrow, Edward R., 37, 188, 265
music
  bebop, 292, 293
  critique of America through, 292–93
  hit songs, 39
  jukebox, 38–39
  live on television, 261–62
  see also jazz music; swing music
musicals, 38

Mussolini, Benito, 82, 90
My Sister Eileen (play), 38

Nagasaki, 92, 148–49
Nash, Gerald D., 50
National Coffee Association, 174–75
National Guard, 43
National Recovery Act (NRA), 15
NATO (North Atlantic Treaty
  Organization), 30, 311–13
Naval Reserve, 43
Nazism
  Americans witnessing, 16–17
  and movie industry, 216–17
  propaganda by, 138
  as threat to U.S. democracy, 61
  triumph of, 81
  and use of radio propaganda, 136
New Deal, 15, 283–84
News and Views (TV news show), 264
News from Washington (TV news show),
  264
Nimitz, Charles W., 21, 83
Nomura, Kichisaburo, 64, 65, 70, 73–74
Normandy invasion, 26–27, 86–87
North Africa, 85–86, 96–97
Nugent, Frank S., 219, 225
nurses, 113, 115–17
Nye, Gerald, 214–16, 240–41

Oak Ridge, Tennessee, 142, 143
O'Day, Anita, 288–89
Office of Price Administration (OPA), 24,
  164, 170
Office of Price Administration and Civilian
  Supply, 164
Office of Strategic Services (OSS), 82, 109,
  156–57
Office of War Information (OWI), 152–53
  on advertising, 160–62
  on comic strips, 159–60
  conflicts with military, 155–56
  conflicts within, 154–55
  on content of movies, 159–60
  organization of, 153–54
  on reporting the truth, 158–59
  on rubber shortage, 157
  war effort of film industry, 223–24
O'Hara, John, 40
One Hundred Days, 15
Operation Overload, 26, 86
Operation Torch, 85
Opportunity (magazine), 122–23
Original Amateur Hour, The (TV show),
  259
Osborne, Mary, 117–18
Overseas Branch of the Office of War
  Information (OWI), 136–37

Pal Joey (play), 38
Pal Joey (O'Hara), 40
Panama Canal, 17, 58
Panama Hattie (play), 38
Pan American Airways, 40–41
Paris, 87, 299
  songs on, 39

see also France
Patton, George S., 21, 27, 85
Pearl Harbor, 18, 59–61, 183
 aftermath of, 74–76
 army not suspecting, 70–71
 arrests of Japanese Americans following,
  186
 bombing, 71–72
 Japan's message to Washington before,
  64–66
 Japanese force for, 66–67
 reaction from Americans, 76–77
 spotting submarines prior to, 62–64
 U.S. government's reaction to, 72–74,
  77–78
 U.S. warning armed forces before, 67–70
Peattie, Donald Culross, 170
Peppas, June, 278
Pepper, Claude, 318
Philadelphia Story, The (movie), 37
Phillips, Cabell, 62
pilots, women as, 114
Pinocchio (movie), 37, 38
Pipp, Wally, 279
Podrazik, Walter J., 255
Poland, 298
Police Reporter (TV show), 263
Potsdam Conference, 29, 91, 296–98
Potsdam Declaration, 27, 145–47
Power, Tyrone, 26, 226
Presidential Timber (TV show), 264
Pringle, Henry F., 162
Prohibition, 42
propaganda
 films as, 214–16
 Nazi use of, 136
 radio
  American use of, 136–37
  changing style of, 137–38
  development of, 134–36
  myths and symbols in, 138–39
Public Prosecutor (TV show), 258–59
Purple Hearts, 116

radio, 36–37
 politics on, 264
 programs transformed to television, 259
 propaganda
  American use of, 136–37
  changing style of, 137–38
  development of, 134–36
  myths and symbols in, 138–39
  Nazi use of, 136
  reflecting America in war, 139–40
 vs. television, 263–64
Randolph, A. Philip, 20
Rankin, John, 189, 241
Rappaport, Armin, 296
rations, 24, 164
 bicycle, 172
 clothing, 172–73
 coffee, 174–75
 counterfeiting books for, 171–72
 gasoline, 168–72
 and hoarding, 175–76
 and Hollywood, 236–38

 rubber, 165–68
 shoe, 172
 silk stockings, 47
 sugar, 173–74
Rayburn, Sam, 316
Reagan, Ronald, 227–28, 238, 246
retentionists, 103–104
riots, 20
Robertson, Paul, 206, 208
Robinson, Jackie, 277
Rogers, Donald I., 34
Rogers, Edith, 23
Romania, 309
Rommel, Erwin, 85, 86
Roosevelt, Eleanor, 46, 89
Roosevelt, Franklin D., 81
 on Darlan deal, 97
 death of, 90
 declaring war on Japan, 18–19, 60, 68,
  69
 Einstein's letter to, 146, 147
 fireside chats by, 135
 on gas shortage, 168–69
 intentions toward
  Germany, 99–100
  Japan, 100–101
 on Japanese American relocation, 191–92
 lend-lease program by, 53–54
 meeting with Churchill, 55–56
 on naval aid to England, 52–53
 reaction to Pearl Harbor bombing, 73,
  77–78
 role in recovering economy, 14–15
 on Soviet Union, 107
 third presidential election, 45–46
 on unconditional surrender, 95, 96,
  98–99, 104
 on WWII involvement, 16–17, 51
  opposition to, 56–57
  preparing Americans for, 43–44
Roosevelt, Theodore, 98
Rosie the Riveter, 13, 180
Royal Navy, 55
Ruark, Robert, 284
rubber shortage, 24, 165–66
 Roosevelt on, 167–68
 solution for, 166–67
 telling American public about, 157

Saroyan, William, 40
Schlesinger, Arthur J., Jr., 162
Schroeder, Dorothy, 279
Schwarze Kapelle, 111, 112–13
Screen Writers Guild, 244
SeaBees, 43
Selective Service and Training Act, 43–44
Sells, Ken, 273, 274
Separate Rooms (play), 38
Sherwood, Robert E., 38, 136, 154
Short, Walter C., 59, 70
Shulman, Holly Cowan, 133
Sigman, Blanche F., 116–17
Silver Stars, 116
Simon, George, 286, 288, 289
Sinatra, Frank, 46, 283–84
Sklar, Robert, 26, 239

Index

Smith, Buffalo Bob, 260
Social Security Act, 15
South America, 52
Soviet Union
  attack on Japan, 148
  and Berlin blockade, 309–11
  containment of power, 304
  and Darlan deal, 97–98
  influence on Japanese surrender, 106–107
  jazz broadcast in, 285–86
  joining in war against Japan, 101
  lend-lease aid to, 56
  postwar relations with U.S., 93, 296–98
  rift with U.S., 29–30, 298–300
    and Marshall Plan, 306–309
    over atomic weapons control, 300
    over Germany, 301–303
    and Truman Doctrine, 303–306
  see also Allies; communism
Spaatz, Carl, 124
spies
  for atom bomb, 144
  women as, 109–13
Spink, J.G. Taylor, 277
sports
  on television, 257–58
  see also Girls of Summer
Stalin, Joseph
  on atom bomb, 148
  on Iran, 301
  relations with Truman, 296–97
  see also Soviet Union
Stark, Harold R., 67, 70, 73
Stassen, Harold, 264–65
steel scrap, 41
Stein, Jules, 231–32
Stewart, James, 26, 37, 222, 226
Stimson, Henry L.
  on atom bomb, 144–45
  on African Americans in military, 121, 126, 127
  on Japanese Americans, 191
  and military draft, 44
  on Nazi propaganda, 136
  on Office of War Information, 156–57
  and Pearl Harbor, 65
Stoll, Jane "Jeep," 274
Stop the Music (radio show), 263
strikes, mine workers, 158
Sullivan, Ed, 268–69
swing music
  appeal to youth, 290–91
  collapse of, 292–93
  expressing individual freedom, 289–90
  vision of pluralism in, 291–92

Taft, Robert A., 316, 319
Taylor, Maxwell D., 131
Taylor, Robert, 246
television
  birth of network, 255–56
  for children, 260–61
  live music on, 261–62
  local vs. network, 258–59
  new programs on, 256–58
  nominating conventions on, 265–66

and politics, 264–65
  vs. radio, 263–64
  rating, 259–60
  theater on, 262–63
  vaudeville on, 266–69
Teller, Edward, 145
Tesseine, Dolly Pearson, 278
Texaco Star Theater, The (TV show), 267
theater, 38
There Shall Be No Night (play), 38
Thomas, J. Parnell, 245, 248
Thomas, Lowell, 37
Tierney, Gene, 232–34
Toast of the Town (TV show), 268–69
Tojo, Hideki, 17, 59
Tonight on Broadway (TV show), 262
Tono, Jack, 184, 195, 196
Toscanini, Arturo, 261
transportation. *See* automobile
Trezza, Betty "Moe," 276
Tripartite Agreement, 57
Truman, Harry S., 90
  on aid to Europe, 308
  on Japan's unconditional surrender, 102–103
  on North Atlantic Treaty, 312
  relations with Stalin, 296–97, 299
  television speech by, 265–66
  on using atom bomb, 27, 91–92
Truman Doctrine, 30, 303–306
  discussions leading to, 315–17
  reaction to, 317–18
  support for, 320–21
  Truman's speech on, 318–20
Turkey, 30, 303, 304, 305, 315–17
Turner, Lana, 228
Turrou, Leon G., 220–21
Tuskegee airmen, 23
Twelfth Night (play), 38

Uchida, Yoshiko, 186, 189, 198, 201
Ulanov, Barry, 285, 286
United Mine Workers' strike, 158
United Nations, 300–301
United Nations Relief and Rehabilitation Association, 307
United States
  air bombing of Japan, 91
  Army Nurse Corps, 23, 113, 115
  dropping atomic bomb on Japan, 27–29, 91–92
    choosing targets, 144–45
    impact of, 147–48
    warning or demonstration for, 145
  on Japan's Pacific invasion, 17–18
  on postwar Berlin, 309–311
  postwar relations with Soviet Union, 28–29, 31–32
  pre-WWII
    defense plants, 46–47
    money spending, 42–43
    prosperity, 35–36
  relations with Japan, 57–59
  rescue mission for Jews by, 89–90
  rift with Soviet Union, 29–30, 298–300
  and Marshall Plan, 306–309

over atomic weapons control, 300–301
over Germany, 301–303
and Truman Doctrine, 303–306
shortages in, 47–48
see also Allies; Americans; Pearl Harbor;
Voice of America; World War II
University of Chicago, 142

Vandenberg, Arthur H., 305, 311, 314–15,
316, 320, 321
on peace treaties, 299–300
Truman Doctrine and, 314–15, 316, 317,
320, 321
Vichy government, 97
Victory (magazine), 161
Voice of America, 133–34
changing style of, 137–38
development of, 136–37
as factual, 139
myths used in, 138–39
reflecting America in war, 139–40
Volunteer Army Canteen Service, 222
Von Stauffenberg, Klaus Philip Maria,
112–13

WACs (Women's Army Corps), 23, 117,
118–19, 178
Walker, Dixie, 277
Wallace, Henry, 306
war bonds, 228–29
Ward (ship), 63–64, 71
Warner, Harry M., 217–18
Warner, Jack, 236, 246
War Production Board (WPB), 166, 224
Warren, Earl, 189
WASPs (Women Airforce Service Pilots),
114
WAVES (Women Accepted for Volunteer
Emergency Service), 23, 117, 178
White, William Allen, 52, 57
Willen, Mark, 314
Willkie, Wendell, 17
defending Hollywood, 216–17
presidential election, 45–46
on U.S. aid to England, 52
Winchell, Walter, 265
Winter, Joanne, 272, 279
Wise, Christy, 177
Wise, Nancy Baker, 177
Wolfe, Thomas, 40
Woll, Allen L., 213
women
helping in armed services, 117–18, 178
labor by, 25
after the war, 181–82
benefits, 179, 181
motives, 178–79
for war effort, 178
in music, 291
as nurses, 113, 115–17

as service pilots, 114
and silk stocking shortage for, 47
as spies, 109–13
WWII involvement, 23–24
see also Girls of Summer
Women's Ambulance Defense Corps, 222
Works Projects Administration (WPA), 15
World Series, 257
World's Fair, 46
World War I, 43
World War II
advantages of Allies in, 81–83
African Americans in, 22–23
air bombing of Japan, 84–85, 91
in Atlantic, 20–21
celebration of ending, 92–93
films preparing for, 213–14
Germany following, 297–98
new technology in, 22
Normandy invasion, 26–27, 86–87
North Africa and Italy, 85–86
in the Pacific, 21, 83–84
post-, 28–29, 31–32
shaping the forties, 13
shortages from, 163–64
see also rations
spreading in Europe, 40–41
U.S. involvement in, 16–17, 18–19
aid traded for military bases, 52–53
Darlan deal, 97–98
declaring war on Japan, 68, 69
naval, 56
from neutrality to alliance, 54–55
opposition to, 56–57
in Pacific, 21, 83–84
preparing Americans for, 43–44
Roosevelt's appeal for, 51
uncommitted to, 41–42
unready for, 48–49
unconditional surrender in, 95–96,
98–99, 101–105
women's role in, 23–24, 113, 115–18
see also atom bomb; Holocaust; military;
Pearl Harbor; propaganda; Voice of
America
Wrigley, Philip, 273–74, 280
Wyman, Jane, 228

Yalta Far Eastern agreement, 106–107
Yamamoto, Isoroku, 83–84
Yancey, Diane, 183
You Can't Go Home Again (Wolfe), 40
youth, and music, 290–91

Zanuck, Darryl F., 26, 215, 218, 219, 222,
227
Zhdanov, Andrei, 308–309
Ziegler, Alma "Ziggy," 278–79
zippers, 47